The Complete Executor's Guidebook

A Step-by-Step Guide for Executors and Personal Representatives

Benjamin H. Berkley
Attorney at Law

SPHINX® PUBLISHING
AN IMPRINT OF SOURCEBOOKS, INC.®
NAPERVILLE, ILLINOIS
www.SphinxLegal.com

First Edition: 2007

Published by: Sphinx® Publishing, An Imprint of Sourcebooks, Inc.®

Naperville Office
P.O. Box 4410
Naperville, Illinois 60567-4410
630-961-3900
Fax: 630-961-2168
www.sourcebooks.com
www.SphinxLegal.com

This publication is designed to provide accurate and authoritative information in regard to the subject matter covered. It is sold with the understanding that the publisher is not engaged in rendering legal, accounting, or other professional service. If legal advice or other expert assistance is required, the services of a competent professional person should be sought.

From a Declaration of Principles Jointly Adopted by a Committee of the American Bar Association and a Committee of Publishers and Associations

This product is not a substitute for legal advice.

Disclaimer required by Texas statutes.

Library of Congress Cataloging-in-Publication Data

Berkley, Benjamin.
  The complete executor's guidebook / by Benjamin H. Berkley.
    p. cm.
  ISBN-13: 978-1-57248-604-1 (pbk. : alk. paper)
  ISBN-10: 1-57248-604-X (pbk. : alk. paper)
  1. Estate planning--United States--Popular works. I. Title.

KF750.Z9B47177 2007
346.7305'2--dc22
                              2007008706

Printed and bound in the United States of America.
SB — 10 9 8 7 6 5 4 3 2 1

To Rabbi Haim Asa.
You have made the world a better place to live.

To my client Harriet DeForde.
Your life was worth living!

And to my lovely wife Phyllis,
who everyday proclaims that a lifetime's value
need not be measured by material wealth.

TABLE OF CONTENTS

Preface xiii

Introduction xv

Frequently Asked Questions...xix

Part One: Preplanning and Transition

Chapter 1: Plain English Definitions..3
Wills and Probate
Trusts

Chapter 2: Making Sure the Shoe Fits 7
Accepting or Declining the Appointment
Anticipating Demands of the Heirs
Stepping Up in a Time of Need
Think About it
Resigning After Accepting the Appointment

Chapter 3: Preplanning: A Conversation with Your Loved One 17
The Testator's Last Wishes for Funeral and Final Interment
Storage of the Documents
The Consequences of Items being Kept in a Safe-Deposit Box

The Reluctant Testator
Potential Future Issues that could Affect the Estate

Chapter 4: When Death is Imminent..25
Providing Assistance in Making Legal Decisions
Petition for Conservatorship
Alternative Housing Options
Hospice Care

Chapter 5: At the Time of Passing: Your First Steps.........................33
Making Funeral Arrangements
Managing the Estranged Spouse
Funeral Expenses
If Death Occurs at Home
Anatomical Gifts
Autopsies
Placement of Children with the Guardian
Taking Care of Pets
If the Decedent Lived Alone
Help Someone Else and Recycle

Chapter 6: At the Time of Passing: Managing the Survivors 49
Providing Emotional Support
Managing Sibling Rivalry
Show Me the Money: Managing the Greedy and Impatient Heirs
Managing the Heirs' Expectations
Managing the "Entitlement Disease" Factor
A Few More Words about the Grubby, Greedy Heirs
Dealing with Estranged Heirs
Do Not Take Sides
Be the Peacekeeper to Your Family
Confront Resentment Head-on
Respect the Grieving Process and Religious Customs

Chapter 7: At the Time of Passing: Notification and Getting Organized 61
Locating the Will and Other Estate Planning Documents
Reading of the Will
Notification
Obtaining Death Certificates
Solving Immediate Problems

Part Two: Estate Administration

**Chapter 8: Locating, Organizing, Itemizing, and Categorizing the
Assets and Liabilities of an Estate** 75
Locating the Assets of an Estate
Examine the Contents of a Safe-Deposit Box
Discovery of Embarrassing Assets
Discovering Stocks and Bonds
Review Correspondence from Attorneys and Other Professionals
Wrongful Death Claims
Review Past Tax Returns
Review Correspondence from Real Estate and Title Insurance Companies
Itemizing the Assets
Categorizing the Assets and Liabilities
When a Safe-Deposit Box is Jointly Owned

Chapter 9: Navigating the Sea of Probate 91
Understanding the Need for a Formal Probate
Getting Started: Initiating a Probate Action
Probate Time Line
Step One: Filing the Petition for Probate
The Role of an Attorney
Where to File the Petition
Ancillary Probate
Step Two: Producing the Original Will
Step Three: Giving Notice
Step Four: The Initial Probate Hearing

Proving the Validity of the Will
Handwritten Wills
If the Maker of the Will was Physically Unable to Sign His or Her Name
When There are Two or More Wills
Whether You Should be Appointed
The Requirements of a Surety Bond
Prior to the Hearing
Will Contests

Chapter 10: Formal Probate: The Next Steps...111
Acknowledgment of Responsibilities
Duties and Liabilities of Personal Representative
Overview of the Responsibilities of a Representative
Bank Accounts
Form SS-4
Inventorying the Estate
Formal Notification to Creditors
Collecting Debts Owed to the Estate
Filing the Accounting and Closing the Estate
Distributing Assets to Beneficiaries

Chapter 11: When There is No Will 129
Understanding the Need for Intestate Succession
Untangling the Legalese into English
Determining Who the Children Are
Other Heirs at Law

Chapter 12: Interpreting and Enforcing the Language of the Will 137
Interpreting Who Receives Specific Gifts
Interpreting Conditional Gifts
Interpreting When a Child is No Longer a Minor
Interpreting Who is the Child of the Decedent
Interpreting Gifts for Pets
Interpreting Assets Left to a Group
When a Will Makes Illegal Provisions

When the Maker of the Will Tries to Control from the Grave
When a Will's Provisions are Illogical
When a Will Leaves Property that No Longer Exists
When the Will Leaves Non-Probate Assets
When a Will Leaves Property to a Former Spouse
When a Will Excludes a Spouse's Legal Rights
When the Will Leaves Property to a Testamentary Trust
When the Will Leaves Property to a Pourover Trust

Chapter 13: When a Formal Probate is Not Required 149
Transfer of Assets by Affidavit
Sample Affidavit for Collection of Personal Property
Sample Affidavit of Domicile
Summary or Informal Probate

Chapter 14: Managing the Assets and Liabilities of an Estate 155
Managing Assets that Diminish in Value
Managing Real Estate
Evicting a Tenant
Managing Personal Property
Managing Investments
Managing an Ongoing Business
Managing Debts of the Estate
Creditor Claims

Chapter 15: Obtaining Benefits for the Estate 171
Life Insurance and Annuities
Mortgage Insurance
Widow's Social Security Benefits
Widow's Social Security Disability Benefits
Employment Retirement Plan Benefits
Bank Account Benefits that are Payable on Death
Savings Bond Benefits
Redeeming Traveler's Checks
Redeeming Unused Airplane Tickets and Prepaid Travel

Chapter 16: Personal and Estate Taxes 179
Federal and State Personal Tax Returns
Federal and State Estate Tax Returns
Gift Tax Returns

Chapter 17: Your Right to Compensation 185
Compensation for Administering an Estate
When there are No Available Assets to Pay Compensation
Waiving Compensation
Petitioning for Extraordinary Fees
Importance of Keeping Accurate Records

Chapter 18: Your Role as an Advisor 191
Payable on Death Bank Accounts
Retirement Accounts
Transfer on Death Registration of Securities
Transfer on Death Registration for Vehicles
Joint Tenancy
Revocable Living Trusts
Gifts
Life Insurance
Creating and Revising Wills and Other Documents for
    Surviving Spouses
Sample Affidavit—Death of Joint Tenant
*Sample Affidavit—Surviving Spouse Succeeding to Title to
    Community Property*
Revising the Named Guardian
Continued Emotional Support
Daily Living Assistance

Chapter 19: Revocable Trusts and Trust Management 201
Translating Trust Terminology into English
A/B Bypass Trusts
The Role of the Trustee
When the Trust Names Cotrustees

Declining Your Appointment as Trustee
Comparison of Trustee and Executor
Step-by-Step Guideline for Trustees
Investing the Assets of the Trust
Compensation for Managing a Trust
Seeking Professional Advice

Chapter 20: Do I Need an Attorney? 215
Attorney Fees
Preparing for Your Appointment
Do's and Don'ts for Your First Meeting with the Attorney
Finding a Probate Attorney

Chapter 21: Words of Thanks..221

Glossary 223

Appendix A: Representative's Checklist 227

Appendix B: Notification 229

Appendix C: State-by-State Summary of Probate Laws 231

Appendix D: Unclaimed Property 255

Appendix E: Sample Forms..263

Appendix F: Blank Forms 275

Appendix G: Resources 299

Index 301

About the Author..309

PREFACE

When I first set out to write this book, what immediately came to mind were the many stories told by my clients about their experiences in representing an estate. Some were humorous, while others were quite sad. Almost all of my clients had very little, if any, previous experience in managing an estate for a loved one. All too often, they were thrust into a situation with little, if any, warning.

As an estate planning attorney, I give advice on the legal process, answer questions, and provide guidance as issues arise. However, until a few years ago, I had personally never served as a representative of an estate for a loved one and therefore could not speak from personal experience. All that changed when my uncle Milton passed away. Though I was already assisting him in making his health care decisions, arranging for in-home care, and managing his financial affairs, I had no idea of the emotional issues I would face upon his passing. I was not fully prepared.

My uncle's estate took over two years to close. What I learned from that experience, along with my client's experiences, helped shape *The Complete Executor's Guidebook*.

Accepting that a loved one is no longer here is devastating. To then confront the decisions and arrangements that must be addressed can be emotionally exhausting. However, if you have been chosen by a loved one or appointed by the court to be the representative of an estate, it is your responsibility to navigate the emotional and legal issues that must be addressed after the loved one's passing. Sometimes this task seems overwhelming, but though you are grieving, you must appear strong.

The Complete Executor's Guidebook was written to guide you through this very difficult period in your life. It provides all the information needed to effectively administer both probate and trust assets. For estates that must be probated, it explains the probate process in an easy-to-understand format, supplying all the essential information that you will need to successfully administer the estate. If you have been named as the successor trustee of a trust, this book explains the language of the trust so that you can manage and distribute the assets of it.

The Complete Executor's Guidebook provides a logical step-by-step approach to handling an estate. In most cases, estate management does proceed smoothly. However, if it becomes too difficult to navigate solo through the sea of probate, this book provides referral and resource information so that you can effectively perform your role.

If issues are still too complex, such as negotiating the sale of a business or defending a will contest, *The Complete Executor's Guidebook* advises you to seek a consultation with an attorney who specializes in probate law and estate management. Even if you do seek representation, this book will assist you in understanding the legal process, and ultimately save the estate money in legal fees. This book is not a substitute for legal representation.

Finally, *The Complete Executor's Guidebook* is a reference book. Depending on the size of the estate and your role in managing the estate, some of the material may not be relevant. Accordingly, the book does not have to be read cover to cover.

—Ben Berkley

INTRODUCTION

The Complete Executor's Guidebook is an instructional guide for anyone administering and managing an estate. Regardless of whether the decedent left a will or a trust, or died without making any estate planning decisions, this book provides step-by-step instructions, checklists, and resource information. If it is determined that the estate must go through court procedures, the book provides a simple-to-follow explanation for navigating through the probate process. In addition, it discusses the many nonlegal and personal issues you must address when representing the survivors of an estate.

The Complete Executor's Guidebook also helps you avoid what could become very costly mistakes for the estate, as well as minimize or eliminate your personal exposure as the representative of the estate. From preplanning discussions with your loved one, to your role at the time of death, and concluding with the closing of the estate, the book will provide both legal and emotional support at a time when it is needed the most. Finally, it provides a discussion of the ways of avoiding probate.

The frequently asked questions section starting on page xix acts as a brief introduction to immediate issues. After these, the book is divided into two parts.

PART ONE: PREPLANNING AND TRANSITION

Chapter 1 provides an overview of estate administration and translates the often misunderstood legal terminology into everyday language.

Chapter 2 explains what is expected of you as the representative of the estate so that you can decide if you wish to accept your appointment.

If you have been informed, prior to someone's passing, that you have been appointed as the representative of that person's estate, Chapter 3 discusses conversations you should have with your loved one so that you will be better prepared to assume your role upon his or her passing.

If death is imminent, you may be called upon to make legal decisions on behalf of your loved one. Chapter 4 discusses powers of attorney, alternative living arrangements, and hospice care.

Chapter 5 discusses the most immediate issues that must be addressed at the time of passing, including funeral arrangements and the placement of children.

Chapter 6 discusses managing the immediate needs of the survivors at the time of passing, as well as how it is important for you to remain focused on your role and not allow others' personal agendas to interfere with your responsibilities.

Chapter 7 discusses who must be notified upon the deceased's passing and the steps you must take in preparation for commencing a probate.

PART TWO: ESTATE ADMINISTRATION

Chapter 8 discusses locating the will and other estate planning documents, as well as organizing, itemizing, and categorizing the assets of an estate.

Chapter 9 takes you step by step through the formal probate process and concludes with your court appointment as representative of the estate. It also discusses will contests.

Chapter 10 discusses all the steps required in completing a formal probate, including filing reports with the court, notifying creditors, and distributing assets.

If a person leaves an estate but does not leave a will, you may wonder how his or her property is divided. Chapter 11 discusses the laws of intestate succession.

Even if there is a will, it may be subject to interpretation or may be unenforceable. These matters are discussed in Chapter 12.

Chapter 13 discusses when a formal probate is not required and how the assets can be transferred by affidavit or an informal probate process.

Chapter 14 provides a complete discussion of the management of both the assets and liabilities of an estate, including when assets need to be sold and invested. Also, it discusses which bills must be paid even though the estate has not closed.

The loss of a loved one can create an immediate financial hardship for the survivors. Chapter 15 discusses obtaining benefits for the estate.

Chapter 16 discusses the decedent's personal tax liability as well as whether the estate will owe federal and estate taxes.

Chapter 17 discusses your legal rights to receive compensation from the estate for performing your role as the representative of the estate.

Chapter 18 provides a discussion of your role as an advisor to the estate's survivors, who may seek your recommendations for avoiding probate. In addition, it provides information for revising the survivor's estate planning documents as a result of the loss of the decedent.

Chapter 19 provides an overview of revocable living trusts and how to administer a trust after the trustor's passing.

Chapter 20 discusses the role of an attorney in representing an estate. It discusses when an attorney may be necessary. It also provides practical information to assist you in finding the right attorney.

Chapter 21 is my favorite chapter. Though very brief, it makes sense of the reason why books on estate administration are ever written. It provides information for saying thanks to your loved one.

Following Chapter 21 is a glossary of the most commonly used legal terms.

Appendices A–G include reference material, worksheets, questionnaires, and sample forms.

FREQUENTLY ASKED QUESTIONS

The following are some of the most common questions asked by representatives. Use this as a quick guide to the most pressing issues about administering an estate, and then refer to later chapters for a more in-depth discussion of each issue.

When does the representative read the will?
As soon as possible, you should find and carefully read the original will. However, this does not have to be done formally in the presence of the heirs.

Can I refuse to act as the representative?
Yes. You are under no obligation to act as a representative. You can refuse the position when the testator first asks you, or if you agree to act as the representative, you may still change your mind at the time of the decedent's death.

If I start my duties as representative can I change my mind later?
Yes, but only by formal resignation. Once you begin to carry out the duties of a representative, you cannot just walk away. By law, your intervention in the estate makes you responsible. If you wish to back out after you have been appointed by the court, you must formally resign your position. To do this, you must submit your resignation in writing to the probate court.

Can I be held responsible for mistakes I make while acting as a representative?
It depends on the circumstances. You must act for the estate as if it were your own property. A representative who is reasonably prudent in carrying out his or her duties will probably not be held responsible if things go wrong. However, if

the representative is careless, he or she can be held responsible for the losses suffered by the estate. For example, if you make frivolous investments or unauthorized expenditures on behalf of the estate, you may be liable. You might have to repay losses personally.

Can I get help if administering the estate becomes complicated? May I hire a professional?

Yes. It is important that you handle the estate properly, because you may be held responsible for your mistakes. When you are in doubt about what to do, it is wise to consult a professional. Reasonable fees charged for professional services would be paid by the estate.

When might I need the help of a lawyer?

A lawyer may be able to help a representative by:
- providing opinions about the interpretation of the will;
- offering advice on your duties as representative;
- drafting deeds and other instruments of re-conveyance;
- applying for probate of the will where necessary;
- defending the estate against will contests;
- addressing federal and tax issues;
- negotiating the sale of businesses and other assets of the estate;
- preparing and obtaining receipts from beneficiaries upon their receipt of distribution; and,
- arranging for the registration of assets in the name of the representative on behalf of the estate.

Will I be paid for my services as representative?

The representative has the right to be paid for his or her services. Depending on your state law, your fee is either based on a percentage value of the estate or by what is reasonable for the services you performed. The representative also has the right to be reimbursed for all reasonable expenses made while administering the estate. Often, family members will agree to administer an estate without taking a fee.

What expenses can be paid directly from the assets of the estate?

Maintaining the assets of the estate may include the payment of insurance and taxes. Accordingly, any expense that is related to maintaining or operating an asset of the estate is an expense of the estate and may be paid directly from the assets of the estate.

What expenses of the estate are reimbursable to the representative?

Reimbursable expenses are those that you must pay out-of-pocket and file for reimbursement later, as opposed to expenses that you pay directly from the estate (see previous question). All court-related expenses—including filing fees, publication fees, and premiums for bonding the estate—are reimbursable expenses to the representative. Accordingly, upon court approval, the representative may be reimbursed for such expenses. In addition, other expenses incurred by the representative, such as funeral-related costs and transportation of minors of the decedent, are reimbursable.

When do my duties as representative end?

The representative's duties end as soon as the estate is completely settled. This normally means when all the debts of the estate have been paid, including income tax, and the testator's property has been distributed according to the will.

Is there a deadline for closing the estate?

No. It all depends on the complexity of the estate. In most cases, one year is considered a reasonable period of time. The longer the representative does take, the more likely it is that the beneficiaries will complain. The beneficiaries may apply to the probate court for an order compelling the representative to carry out his or her duties on a timely basis.

Can the beneficiaries have me dismissed as representative?

Yes. Any interested party who has reason to believe that a representative has acted improperly in the administration of an estate may start a legal action to have the representative removed by making an application to the probate court. He or she must show that the representative committed a fraud or acted in an unreasonable manner that has resulted in a loss to the estate. In other words, an interested party cannot request that you be dismissed simply because he or she does not like one of your decisions.

Do I have to submit accounts to the probate court?

Sometimes. In the administration of simple estates, the beneficiaries often sign a release. This relieves the representative from his or her duty to account to the beneficiaries for the administration of the estate. However, any beneficiary who has not signed such a release or who has done so without knowing what he or she signed may apply to the court to require the representative to account to the court for his or her administration of the estate.

What is the purpose of probate?

Probate is the court procedure by which a will is proved to be valid or invalid. Creditors of the estate have the opportunity to file claims against the estate and receive payment of those claims. After the administration fees and creditor claims are paid, the assets of the estate are distributed to the beneficiaries.

What is a will contest?

A will contest is a legal action that challenges the validity of a will and/or the terms of the will. A will may be invalid if it was the result of forgery, undue influence, inadequate execution, or other issues. A later will may invalidate an earlier version. If the will is held invalid, the probate court may invalidate all provisions or only the challenged portion. If the entire will is held invalid, generally the proceeds are distributed under the laws of intestate succession. Questions on the validity of a will must be filed in probate court within a certain number of days after receiving notice of the death or a petition to admit the will to probate.

What type of assets are typically non-probate assets?

Non-probate assets can be transferred without approval by the probate court. Some examples of non-probate assets are proceeds from life insurance policies, an IRA account, a 401(k) account, or any other tax-deferred retirement plan account with a named beneficiary.

What role does the representative play in the probate process?

The representative is responsible for initiating the probate proceeding, collecting and inventorying assets, collecting debts owed to the estate, distributing assets to the estate, and closing the estate. The representative is entitled to compensation for time and expenses spent during the process.

Where does a probate have to be filed?

The laws of the state in which the deceased was a permanent resident or domiciliary governs where the probate is filed. In addition, if the decedent owned real property in another state, you may need to file what is known as an ancillary probate proceeding in that state so that the property can be transferred.

What happens if a person dies without a will?

If a person dies without a will (known as dying intestate), the probate court appoints a personal representative, frequently called an administrator, to receive all claims against the estate, pay creditors, and distribute all remaining property in accordance with the laws of the state. The major difference between dying testate and dying intestate is that without a valid will an intestate estate is distributed to beneficiaries in accordance with the distribution plan established by state law, whereas a testate estate is distributed in accordance with the instructions provided by the decedent in his or her will.

How much does a probate cost?

The cost of probate is set by state law and may include appraisal costs, executor's fees, court costs, costs for a type of insurance policy known as a surety bond, plus legal and accounting fees. Probate can easily cost 3%–7% of the total estate value or more. Further, if there is a will contest, the overall cost can escalate greatly.

What happens if the will cannot be found?

The will may be missing because the deceased intentionally revoked it, in which case, depending on state law, an earlier will or the state's rules on interstate succession would determine who gets the deceased's estate.

Alternatively, the will may be missing because it can be proven the will was stored in a bank vault that was destroyed in an explosion and fire. In that case the probate court may accept a photocopy of the will (or the lawyer's draft or computer file), together with evidence that the deceased duly signed the original.

How are creditors paid?

As part of the probate process, creditors are notified of the death. Creditors must file a claim for the amounts due within a fixed period of time to either the personal representative, or in some states, the court. If the claim is approved by the executor, the bill is paid out of the estate. If the claim is rejected, creditors must sue for payment.

If there are insufficient funds to pay debts, states have statutes of one kind or another establishing who gets paid first. Executors most likely will commence selling property to pay off approved creditor claims. Any claims remaining are prorated.

How long does a probate take?

The duration varies with the size and complexity of the estate, the difficulty in locating the beneficiaries, who would take under the will (if there is one), and state law. If there is a will contest, or anyone objects to any actions of the personal representative, things can really drag out. Some matters have taken decades to resolve.

How are taxes paid?

For federal tax purposes, it may be necessary to complete and file an income tax return, a fiduciary income tax return, a gift tax return, and/or an estate tax return, depending on the decedent's income, the size of the estate, and the income of the estate.

For state purposes, the representative must file the appropriate state income tax return (assuming the decedent was required to do so while living) and any state income tax returns during the probate period, plus possible estate tax, inheritance tax, and gift tax returns. (In many states, gift, estate, and inheritance taxes have been eliminated for most small and medium-sized estates.) The requirements for filing and payment vary widely from state-to-state.

Other taxes require the attention of the personal representative in the probate process, such as local real estate and personal property taxes, business taxes, and any special state taxes.

The representative should also be alert to the possibility of issues arising from tax years prior to the decedent's death.

Does all property have to go through probate?

No. Depending on the size of the estate, most states also allow a limited amount of several types of property to pass to certain beneficiaries free of probate, or through a simplified probate procedure.

Real and personal property owned by the decedent as a joint tenant passes to the surviving co-owners without going through probate.

Other types of benefits, such as a life insurance policy or annuity payable directly to a named beneficiary, bypass probate. Money from IRAs, Keoghs, and 401(k) accounts transfer automatically to the persons named as beneficiaries. Bank accounts that are set up as payable on death (POD) or "in trust for" account with a named beneficiary also pass to that beneficiary without probate.

If a living trust holds legal title to some of the decedent's property, that also passes to the beneficiaries without probate.

PART ONE:
PREPLANNING AND TRANSITION

CHAPTER 1:
PLAIN ENGLISH DEFINITIONS

Every profession has its own terminology, and the legal field is no exception. Perhaps that is why the phrase *in layman's terms* was born, so that the non-attorney could understand the legal process.

Wills and estates probably contain the most misunderstood and misinterpreted words and phrases of all areas of the law. Add in all the forms that must be completed and the deadlines that the courts impose, and it is an understatement to say that estate administration can be confusing.

To illustrate the confusion, think about this. The person chosen or named in a will to manage the estate is commonly referred to as the "representative of the estate" or "personal representative." However, depending on in which state the documents were prepared, the word "representative" is often used interchangeably with the terms "executor" if referring to a male or "executrix" if referring to a female. Furthermore, if a person passed away without leaving a will, the person appointed by the court to manage the estate is often known as the "administrator," though he or she has the same responsibilities as an executor. This chapter translates the often misunderstood legal terminology into everyday language so you can at least start to make sense of your new role.

WILLS AND PROBATE

For simplification, this book refers to the maker of the will as the *testator*, and if that person has passed away, then he or she is called the *decedent*. The term *representative* refers to the person chosen to carry out the terms of a will. This also applies to identify the person appointed by the court to administer the estate if there is no will.

As the representative, your duties may include:
• placing underage children with a guardian who is named in the will;
• paying the last expenses of the decedent, such as medical bills;
• making funeral arrangements;
• probating the estate;
• maintaining and investing the assets of the estate; and,
• distributing to the beneficiaries the assets of the estate.

These duties are more specifically discussed in Chapter 10.

TRUSTS

It is becoming a very common practice for a person to leave his or her assets in a trust rather than a will. This is being done more often, since property that passes through a trust avoids the costs and delays often associated with probate. The document is commonly known as an *inter vivos trust* or *living trust*, as it is made during one's lifetime. During that person's lifetime, it is common for the person who makes the trust (the *trustor*) to also be the person who manages it as the *trustee*. Since a person cannot always maintain those duties, in is also common to designate a *successor trustee* to step in and manage the assets of the trust as if the trustor were still alive. You may be standing in the role of the successor trustee, who now must do all the things outlined in the trust that the original trustee did. You will now be carrying out the terms of the trust.

As the new trustee, your duties typically include distribution of the assets as set out in the trust document. In addition, if there are underage children, the language of the trust may require that the trustee invest the assets for the children until the children reach a stated age. Until that time, the trustee would make disbursements to the guardian of the minor child for *necessities of life*.

Pourover Will

A *pourover will* is a will that is made in conjunction with a revocable trust. However, pourover wills are usually limited to appointing a guardian of children, specifying wishes for a funeral and final interment, and naming individuals or charities who are to receive specific gifts. All of the remaining assets, however, are distributed to the revocable trust. For this reason, it is called a pourover will, as all of the remaining assets "pour over" into the trust.

> **PRACTICAL POINT.** Often, the maker of a will and trust names the same person to be both the representative and successor trustee. However, the trustor may choose a different person to be his or her successor if he or she has concerns for the representative's ability to carry out the financial responsibilities required of a trustee.

BRIAN'S STORY

My clients Charles and Shirley had one adult child, Brian. Brian, who had a love affair with the race track and was always betting on the long shot that never came in, had filed bankruptcy. Charles and Shirley, who had an estate valued at over $2 million, feared that if Brian received all of his money upon their deaths, it would be gone in a very short period of time. They decided to appoint Brian as their representative, limiting his role to carrying out their wishes for burial, but in their trust, they appointed Shirley's brother, Sid, to be the successor trustee. Upon his parents' passing, Brian received monthly installments on his inheritance for a set period of time.

LEGALLY SPEAKING

Prior to the death of the decedent, he or she may have appointed you as his or her power of attorney to carry out financial decisions. Upon his or her death, those powers terminate. Therefore, you can no longer legally endorse his or her name on checks or transact any business on behalf of the decedent until you receive court appointment to act. If you continue to use such powers, you may be subjecting yourself to civil penalties. Refer to Chapter 9 for a complete discussion of the process to be formally appointed as the representative of the estate.

Chapter 2:
Making Sure the Shoe Fits

During my initial meeting with a client to discuss his or her estate planning needs, I ask:

Who would you like to be in charge of your estate?

In most cases, the client is well prepared for this question, but occasionally a client responds that he or she is having difficulty making this choice. I then rephrase the question:

When you close your eyes at night and put your head on your pillow, who would you feel most comfortable with being in charge when you are no longer here?

After consideration, the choice usually becomes very clear. The selection of a representative is often made based upon how one is perceived to be able to handle both emotional and legal issues.

Although no one wants to think about the inevitable, everyone wants to be confident in their decision that whoever takes their place is the right person to carry out their wishes as if they were still here. Accepting that someone is no longer here is daunting. To be able to pick up the pieces and carry out your loved one's wishes requires that you remain focused on the task at hand and not allow emotions to get in the way of the decisions that need to be made. When you accept the position of representative, you step into the shoes of the decedent, and you need to make sure the shoe fits.

ACCEPTING OR DECLINING THE APPOINTMENT

Most people accept the appointment as a representative without questioning what will be asked of them. Perhaps this is because people feel that it would be an insult to their loved ones to not accept. However, accepting the appointment is not for everyone. Whether you have been appointed as a representative, successor trustee, or both, your responsibility is to carry out the wishes of the testator for the estate. In legal terms, you are known as a *fiduciary*, as you have been placed into a position of trust. Before you make your decision, consider the following questions.

Will you have travel or time constrictions that could interfere with managing the estate, especially if you live in a different state from your loved one?
If your work requires you to travel or if you live out of state, you must balance your work commitment with the time required to manage the estate. The size of the estate and whether the assets are to be invested or distributed immediately will help you decide whether you can make the time commitment.

Are you able to adhere to strict timetables?
By accepting your appointment, you are agreeing to comply with the probate court's requirements. That is, you must follow and adhere to the court rules of probate. Specifically, there are timetables in which specific documents must be filed with the court. While courts sometimes show some leniency to non-attorneys the first time they do not have all the paperwork in on time, a judge's patience runs very thin after subsequent failures to comply. In a worst case scenario, you can be held in contempt of court for failing to follow a court order. As a result, the court can impose fines and penalties against you, which cannot be paid from the assets of the estate. In addition, your misconduct can result in your removal as the executor the estate.

STEVE'S STORY

I was contacted by Steve, who was representing an estate without an attorney. He needed representation, as he was recently sanctioned by the court. Apparently, he had failed to file the final accounting of all of the assets and liabilities after the court had given him three chances to produce the paperwork. After the third hearing, the judge had grown tired of Steve's excuses and decided he needed to send a message to Steve. As the probate process was nearing its conclusion, I agreed to step in. However, when I appeared in court, the judge advised me that Steve had already been removed as representative. Steve had forgotten to tell me that at the last hearing he had lashed out at the judge and then sent the court a very insulting email, which prompted the court to order Steve to attend anger management classes.

Are you a good communicator?

Whether you are a good communicator really means whether you will be available to answer questions that the heirs may have. Also, when managing a trust, the trustee is expected, and in some states required, to provide written status reports to the beneficiaries of the trust.

Are you organized and do you have some knowledge of the decedent's affairs?

You do not have to excel in finances to handle this responsibility, as most probates simply require that accounts be transferred into the name of the estate and then distributed to the heirs. Plus, you can always employ professionals, such as attorneys and accountants, if you have questions or run into trouble. Any expenses incurred by consulting or retaining professionals are expenses chargeable to the estate and not owed by you personally. Still, you should evaluate your level of skill in handling financial matters and keeping good and detailed records, and then determine whether the estate would be best served by a stranger appointed by the court.

ERNIE'S STORY

Gordon owned several apartment buildings and was fortunate to ride the real estate boom, often buying and selling properties and earning impressive profits. After his death, his son Ernie was reluctant to serve as representative. Ernie told me that he had no knowledge of the real estate business. I introduced him to a property manager who managed many buildings for other investors, and a management contract was negotiated, allowing Ernie to feel confident to serve as representative.

Are you in poor health?

If you are experiencing health issues, your well-being is your priority. Therefore, do not feel you are insulting the estate or the deceased by turning down the appointment.

Will your acceptance result in a rivalry with another family member that you will find impossible to resolve? Do you foresee any conflicts with other heirs?

Whether your appointment will spark family rivalry is an unknown and you may not have any insight that there is going to be a problem until after you have accepted the appointment. It is human nature for a sibling, for example, to feel slighted when his younger brother was chosen by his father over him to manage the estate. Unfortunately, sisters-in-law and brothers-in-law only compound the problem when they tell their spouse who was not chosen to watch out, because the chosen representative might be up to something.

Can you manage your emotions at this particular time?

As the representative, you may find yourself having to balance the emotional concerns and demands of the heirs with your need to remain focused on the job at hand. Likewise, as you have lost a loved one, you may have unresolved emotional issues that could blur your ability to be effective as a representative. If you cannot separate your emotional issues from the responsibilities of the representative, you should decline the appointment.

Is the estate involved in ongoing litigation?

If the decedent was pursuing or defending a lawsuit or was involved in legal matters that are ongoing, you should consult with the attorney who was representing the decedent to determine your time commitment. This is because, as the representative, you step into the shoes of the decedent and will be required to defend or pursue all legal proceedings that were pending at the time of the decedent's passing.

Further, for as long as the estate is open, you are also at risk of being named, in your capacity as representative, as a defendant in a lawsuit.

LARRY'S STORY

Larry's dad passed away, naming him as the successor trustee. The major asset of the estate was a pest control business that Larry's brother and dad had operated for fifteen years. However, in the one year his brother took over running the business, he ran the business into the ground. Specifically, he did not pay the company's creditors and taxes that were owed. Even worse, claims were made against the company's insurance for shoddy work. These claims eventually turned into lawsuits in which Larry, as trustee, was named as a defendant. Needless to say, this was not what he signed up for when he became trustee.

In many ways an estate is like a business, and if you are in charge of the estate, you are the one pursuing (or being pursued for) any court actions for or against the estate.

Are you easily intimidated?

Though the imminent passing of a loved one may bring families closer together as they enter the grieving period, money (or an unequal division of it) can quickly erase family bonding that may have immediately taken place. Further, ill feelings that existed in the past between family members are further aggravated when a family member questions the selection of the representative.

MICHAEL'S STORY

Michael was the youngest of three sons. His two brothers lived out of state and Michael resided with his wife and family close to his parents. He was the more sensitive, caring son. For that reason, his parents chose him to be their representative. Upon the parents' passing, the two older brothers immediately voiced their resentment to Michael's appointment. He was not as financially successful as his two brothers, and they quickly reminded him of a past business failure of his. Michael was easily intimidated and decided it was not worth the aggravation to act as representative.

Do you understand the financial liability to the estate you may be placing yourself in?

The first thing you should know is that you could be held personally liable to the estate. For this to occur, it must be proven that you negligently or intentionally mismanaged the estate, which resulted in a loss of value to the estate. This burden is placed on you because your acceptance of the appointment is an acknowledgment by you that you will protect the assets of the estate to the best of your ability. If a court were to decide that you intentionally or negligently mismanaged an estate, you could be ordered to reimburse the estate for those actions of yours that resulted in a financial loss to the estate. This repayment is known as *restitution*.

JERRY'S STORY

Jerry loved playing poker online. However, when his own financial resources were exhausted, he transferred $5,000 from an estate account into his own checking account. His losses grew larger and eventually the $5,000 was gone. Guilt-ridden, he confessed his act to his brother, who promptly called an attorney. Jerry was removed by the court as representative and was ordered to pay back the $5,000.

LEGALLY SPEAKING

A *surety bond* is an insurance policy purchased by the estate to insure the estate for any losses due to embezzlement, fraud, or negligence by the representative. If a loss occurred, the insurance company would reimburse the estate for the loss. Surety bonds are often required by the court and are more fully discussed in Chapter 9.

ANTICIPATING DEMANDS OF THE HEIRS

In representing an estate, especially when there are several heirs, you will need to be able to anticipate that demands may be placed on you from different parties, and you will need to respond accordingly. Unfortunately, estate administration often brings out the worst in people's personalities. Accordingly, be prepared to answer questions like:

- Why is it taking so long?
- What is the next step we need to take?
- When can we disburse the assets? I need the money.
- The will said nothing about mom's piano. Can I have it?
- How much are you getting paid?
- Are you going to waive your fee?

It is advisable that you keep the beneficiaries informed at all times as to what you are doing. Even an explanation of the court process will help avoid future questions, as most people are not aware of how probate works and often assume it is simply a matter of filing a lot of papers. Even when there is little to report, providing some communication is better than allowing a period of time to pass without any information being provided.

Remember that you have been chosen by the decedent because he or she believed you would be the best person to do this important role. You must earn the confidence of the beneficiaries. Keeping an open line of communication will help reduce any concerns they may have about your ability to do the job.

STEPPING UP IN A TIME OF NEED

Since not every person prepares a will or a trust, many families have to deal with an estate for which no one has been named representative. You may be the person that your family often turns to in times of trouble. Perhaps you are the oldest, or wisest, or most experienced. As such, you may be the person the family seeks to administer an estate when no one was appointed in a will or trust. If this happens, congratulate yourself. It is an honor and not a burden. Unless your time constraints will seriously interfere with your ability to serve, you should welcome the appointment.

THINK ABOUT IT

Whether you are appointed in a will or trust, or whether your family looks to you to fill the role of representative, give it some careful and serious thought. Although a person's prior approval is not required for that person to be named as a representative of an estate, if named, that person has no legal duty or responsibility to accept the appointment. However, before you decline, consider the following.

- You have been chosen because your loved one believed you were the person most qualified to serve on his or her behalf.
- If you decline, the estate's interest may not be competently represented by someone else.
- You are entitled to compensation for your work efforts.
- The actual time that you will be involved in administering the estate may not be overwhelming.
- Your family needs you.

Many consider it an honor to fill this role. True, it has its drawbacks and comes at a time of grief, but the benefit to your family can be one of the best steps you can take in working through this difficult time.

RESIGNING AFTER ACCEPTING THE APPOINTMENT

Once an appointment is accepted, you may still choose to resign at a later date. However, the procedure for resigning differs depending on whether you are a representative of an estate and a probate action has been commenced, or if the estate is being managed pursuant to the terms of a trust.

If a probate has been filed and the court has approved your petition for appointment as the representative, a hearing is required to consider your request to resign and to appoint your replacement. If there is a will, the court will look to the alternative representative named in the will to replace you. If no one else has expressed an interest in being appointed, the court will appoint the *public guardian* to administer the estate.

> **PRACTICAL POINT.** Before you resign, consider the fact that in many states, the day-to-day activities of public guardians are not regulated. This has resulted in cases of abuse wherein assets of an estate were used by the public guardian for personal use. In California, an investigation by the *Los Angeles Times* exposing the practices of unscrupulous public guardians has now resulted in a requirement that all public guardians be recertified every three years. However, most states do not have such programs in place.

Resigning Appointment As Successor Trustee

If your appointment was as a result of being named as a successor trustee in a trust and you now wish to resign, a properly drafted trust will include a section that names an alternate successor trustee. In such a case, no court approval is required. Instead, the alternate trustee assumes the management of the trust. Refer to Chapter 19 for the process of declining as successor trustee.

CHAPTER 3:

PREPLANNING: A CONVERSATION WITH YOUR LOVED ONE

Estate planning is not just about how an estate is divided upon someone's passing. There are various other practical issues that must be addressed, and it is helpful if you have a conversation with your loved one about these issues. After a loved one dies, you will have many questions for which the answers may not be readily available, including the following.

- Who do I need to notify about the passing?
- Should there be a funeral or a memorial service?
- When asked, should I tell people to send flowers or make a donation to a charity?
- Did the decedent prepare a will or living trust? If so, where are the documents?
- Did the decedent own a life insurance policy? Did he or she have a pension, retirement account, or annuity? Where are the documents being kept?
- Did the decedent have bank accounts?
- Did he or she have a safe-deposit box?
- Did he or she own stocks, bonds, or money in mutual funds? If so, where are the records?
- Did he or she own real estate? Where are the deeds?

Most people carry this information around in their heads. While many make extensive plans for vacations and special events, planning for the inevitable is rarely a high priority. As a result, when someone passes away, stocks, bonds, bank accounts, real estate, and insurance policy benefits may go unclaimed by their intended heirs, resulting in these assets being turned over to the state. Not surprisingly, this happens quite often; each year, millions of dollars go into state treasuries because the rightful property owners could not be found. However, losses like these can be avoided with a little bit of planning, sorting, and organizing. As you discuss the following issues with the testator, store the information in a safe place—one that you will have immediate access to upon the testator's passing.

THE TESTATOR'S LAST WISHES FOR FUNERAL AND FINAL INTERMENT

At the appropriate time after learning that you have been named as a representative, you should have a conversation with the testator. Your conversation should begin with asking what his or her *last wishes* are regarding funeral, final interment, and organ donation. Needless to say, such conversations are difficult to begin. However, many people report a feeling of relief knowing what their loved ones want, and they feel much more confident in accepting the role of representative knowing that they are doing what their loved ones wanted.

> **PRACTICAL POINT.** When discussing funeral arrangements or other highly emotional issues, you may want to ask someone who is somewhat removed from the immediate family to start the discussion if you anticipate that having this talk may be difficult for you or your loved one.

SEAN'S STORY

My neighbor Sean was dying at home on hospice care. He was divorced and had two daughters. His daughters advised me that Sean had not made any arrangements for final interment. They also had no idea what his wishes were and could not approach the subject with him. My wife, who was very close with Sean, volunteered to have a talk with him. The sisters were surprised to learn he wished to be buried back East where his brother was interred, thinking all along that he wanted to be buried in California. They were also very relieved knowing that upon his passing, they would be carrying out his last wishes.

On a more personal level, discuss with the testator if he or she has any articles of personal property that represent his or her family or any stories that he or she would like to pass down for generations to come. You may also suggest that he or she write a *legacy will*, in which a personal message to designated members of the family can be read after his or her passing.

STORAGE OF THE DOCUMENTS

Your conversation should also include questions concerning where your loved one is keeping his or her estate planning and other important documents. Your questions may include the following.

- Where are wills, living trusts, deeds, and other important documents being stored?
- Where are the insurance policies?
- Where are the pensions and retirement account records?
- Where does the testator bank?
- Where are the investment account records?
- Are there any stock and bond certificates that need to be found?
- Is there a home safe, and if so, what items are in it?
- Is there a safe-deposit box, where is the key, and what are the contents of the box?
- Are there items of family history, including photographs and other family heirlooms, that need to be safely stored?

PRACTICAL POINT. Your questioning should never appear overly aggressive, which might make it seem that you are trying to take control of the estate now. It should be impressed upon the testator that it is in the best interest of the estate that, in the event of his or her passing, the personal and legal affairs are in order. You should emphasize that you are doing this for the testator's estate and heirs, not for yourself.

THE CONSEQUENCES OF ITEMS BEING KEPT IN A SAFE-DEPOSIT BOX

The last place you hope to have to look for estate planning documents is in a safe-deposit box. In most states, if you are not a signatory on the box, it cannot be opened without court permission upon the decedent's passing. Accordingly, in assisting your loved one, recommend that estate planning documents be kept at home in some secure place and that you are aware of that location. This way, in the event of a death, you will be able to have immediate access.

TIM'S STORY

Tim did not trust banks but reluctantly, on his son's advice, opened a safe-deposit box. In the box he placed his house deed, title to his car, birth certificate, military records, life insurance policies, and his will and trust. Even though he had named his son as his representative in his will, Tim only put his name on the box. It took his son sixty days to get court permission to open the box after Tim's death. Upon reading the will, he was horrified to discover that Tim had made prearrangements for cremation. He had already buried his father.

PRACTICAL POINT. For matters of privacy and other reasons, your loved one may not want you to have a copy of his or her estate planning documents. Therefore, you should not insist but only suggest. You should respect his or her decision, but be aware of potential problems and work to resolve issues that would develop immediately at his or her passing, such as funeral arrangements.

THE RELUCTANT TESTATOR

Even if the testator wants you to be the representative of his or her estate, he or she may be reluctant to provide any information to you, especially information concerning assets and finances. Many people will openly state something to the effect of the following.

I don't want the kids to know how much money I have or where I keep it.
I have everything in a folder. They'll find it when they need it.
They're going to inherit a lot of money. Let them work for it.

Accordingly, in the nicest of ways, you should impress upon the testator that his or her cooperation today makes your later role much simpler. It should be emphasized that it is his or her survivors who must continue after he or she is gone. By providing the necessary information, the testator will make the transition for his or her surviving loved ones less stressful.

POTENTIAL FUTURE ISSUES THAT COULD AFFECT THE ESTATE

In your conversation with the testator, you should include questions about whether there exist possible future issues that could concern the estate.

Are there lawsuits or claims pending against the testator?

It is a common misconception that after you are gone, your estate is no longer liable for your debts. In some situations this may be correct, such as for credit card debt, which is discussed in Chapter 13. However, if you are party to an action for a claim for money, your estate may be liable to the person bringing the action.

JOE'S STORY

Joe's estate was valued at over $500,000. Prior to his death, he was a defendant in a franchise lawsuit in which he was sued for failing to pay monthly franchise fees. The franchisor was seeking $95,000. So as to protect the assets of the estate, we negotiated on behalf of the estate a settlement for $55,000. By settling now, the estate avoided a possible judgment for a larger amount, as well as attorney fees to defend the action. As the representative, you may be able to jump-start negotiations on behalf of the estate if you are alerted of potential claims that could ultimately reduce the value of the estate.

Are there any claims pending by the testator?

If the testator has a claim against another party for money owing to him or her, or is pursuing an action for a breach of contract, such actions will survive his or her passing and any money awarded will become an asset of the estate.

LEGALLY SPEAKING

If the testator was injured in an automobile accident, or sustained some type of injury that does not result in death, most courts have held that such claims may not be continued after the person has passed away. However, if the testator passes away and the injuries were the primary cause of death, the estate may have a claim against the negligent party for a *wrongful death action*. This claim is more fully discussed in Chapter 8.

Does the testator anticipate any family rivalry?

No matter how close you may think you are with your brothers and sisters, family rivalries tend to surface after a loved one's passing. The testator may be aware of potential issues that, with advance knowledge, may help you in administering the estate.

DWAYNE AND ERMA'S STORY

Dwayne and Erma had two daughters. They were disappointed with their eldest. She had been married several times, could never hold a job, was irresponsible with finances, and rarely called her parents. Though they were leaving their estate in trust to both girls equally, they wanted their youngest daughter to be in charge of the estate and provide a monthly allowance to the oldest. I told them they needed to discuss this with the youngest to prepare her for any anticipated problems, but they failed to do so.

Erma died in 2002. Dwayne passed away two years later. A few months after his death, the youngest daughter contacted me. Her sister was making all kinds of threats, wanting all of her money now. The executor was not prepared for her role, was getting physically ill from dealing with her sister's constant abuse, and wanted out. If her parents had told her of their intentions out of fairness to her, other arrangements could have been made.

Has the testator already made any loans or gifts to family members who are named in the will?

Often, testators give money to their children. The children assume it is a gift, only to learn upon their parents' passing that it was an advance against their inheritance. Disgruntled children then contest the will on the grounds that they should inherit more than the will states, because the pervious gift was separate from their inheritance. By having notice that a beneficiary may contest the will, you will be better prepared to address these issues when they arise. Chapter 8 provides a complete discussion of will contests.

How specific is the will regarding the dividing of personal property?

The will should be specific as to who is to receive items of personal property, such as jewelry or items of sentimental value. Too often, a testator makes a promise to someone that the heir will receive a particular item upon the testator's passing. However, the will is silent as to that promise. This then leads to confusion as to who is the intended recipient of a gift, causing heirs to squabble over who is to receive what. Accordingly, with the testator's permission, you should review the will with him or her, so that you understand what specific items should be directed to whom.

After you have obtained the information, organize this information in a way that will help you handle the testator's affairs after his or her death. You can structure the information any way you like, but make sure it will be in a format that will be easy for you to access at the appropriate time. What is most important is that you create a clear, easily accessible system that will make your job easier. When you have everything in order, be sure that the information is stored in a safe place. You might consider keeping everything in a fireproof metal box, file cabinet, or home safe.

Form 4, found in Appendix F, is an asset and debt organizer. Form 5 is a record locator. You may wish to use these forms with the testator. Upon completion, the forms should be kept together with the testator's will and other estate planning documents.

My book, *My Wishes*, (Sourcebooks, 2006) includes an extensive discussion of preplanning issues, including funeral arrangements and the organization of records.

CHAPTER 4:

WHEN DEATH IS IMMINENT

When a docter tells someone to get his or her affairs in order, that ominous phrase can only be interpreted to mean that the patient needs to address his or her legal and personal issues, as time may not be on his or her side. Your loved one may ask you, as the representative and as the person most trusted, to assist in making some of these difficult decisions. Remember, during this time, it is especially important that you remain focused on your responsibilities and not allow emotional feelings to cloud your decisions.

PROVIDING ASSISTANCE IN MAKING LEGAL DECISIONS

If your loved one may soon no longer be capable of making decisions for him- or herself, you should closely examine any documents that he or she has signed, in order to determine the scope of your role both before and after your loved one's passing. If estate planning documents have not been created, you should suggest to your loved one that documents be prepared so that a plan is in place in the event of his or her incapacity and eventual passing. A discussion of proper drafting of wills and trusts is beyond the scope of this book, but the following documents are recommended.

Advance Power of Attorney for Health Care

A *power of attorney for health care* appoints someone to make health care decisions if the maker of the document were to become disabled.

Once you have been appointed power of attorney for health care, you can communicate directly with your loved one's health care providers and make decisions that are in his or her best interest. This may include determining the type of treatment to be provided, or withholding certain treatments.

PRACTICAL POINT. Without a health care power of attorney, unless you are the spouse, a medical provider does not have to discuss medical issues with you concerning your loved one.

Power of Attorney for Financial Decisions

Similar to the power of attorney for health care, the *financial power of attorney* appoints you to make everyday decisions concerning your loved one's finances. This can include routine matters such as paying bills and making deposits. The powers can also include major decisions such as signing your name on a deed on behalf of your loved one for the sale of real property. In some states it is also referred to as a *durable power of attorney*.

Advance Directive to Physician

An *advance directive to physician*, also known as a *living will*, expresses a person's wishes for—or refusal of—medical treatment. Whether the medical condition was the result of a terminal illness or injury, an advance directive guides those providing medical care. Likewise, it removes the burden of making agonizing decisions from the person's family and allows the person's wishes to be respected.

Appendix F includes sample Powers of Attorney for Health Care and Financial Decisions, as well as a Directive to Physician, with complete step-by-step instructions.

Organ Donation

Organ donations are legally referred to as *anatomical gifts*. All fifty states have laws regarding organ donation, and the federal government has passed the *Uniform Anatomical Gift Act,* which allows a person to donate organs and tissues to be used for transplantation, therapy, research, and medical education.

If your loved one has expressed to you his or her desire to be an organ donor, he or she has several options. He or she can carry a donor card, which is available from Donate Life America (formerly the Coalition on Donation) at **www.share yourlife.org** or by calling 800-782-4920. In addition, some states provide check boxes to elect organ donation on a driver's license application or renewal form.

PETITION FOR CONSERVATORSHIP

If your loved one is no longer capable of making decisions and estate planning documents have not been prepared, unless you are the spouse or an adult child of the deceased, you cannot make health or financial decisions without written authority from the loved one or the court.

If your loved one is too ill to sign a document, or if your loved one were to sign but be unaware of what he or she were signing, you will need to obtain court approval before you can act. This process is known as a *petition for conservatorship*, as you are petitioning the court to be appointed the conservator of someone's estate for financial and/or health decisions.

Note that conservatorships are expensive. In addition to filing fees, there are medical examination fees. Courts require that the proposed conservatee's medical records be reviewed by a medical professional appointed by the court. Fees vary from state to state, and the total amount also varies depending on the time involved for the medical examiner to complete his or her work. For example, if the examiner is only reviewing medical records, most states approve examiner fees at between $500 and $1,000. However, if he or she is required to testify in court for a contested matter, most examiners bill their time based on an hourly rate. Although these expenses are reimbursable to you from the assets of the estate, you will have to initially advance the fees.

ALTERNATIVE HOUSING OPTIONS

As the representative, you may be asked to assist in making alternative living arrangements for your loved one. Alternative arrangements, such as assisted living residences, provide care and comfort for your loved one when living alone becomes too difficult or a physical disability makes attending to daily needs a challenge. In addition to having your loved one live with you, there are many housing options that may be available.

Housing options generally fall into six categories, based on the level of services required. They include the following options.

Independent Living Retirement Communities

Independent living retirement communities are complexes for seniors who are able to live on their own, but want the convenience of a comprehensive service package. Meals, housekeeping, activities, transportation, and security are provided to active older adults.

Assisted Living Facilities

In addition to the services provided in independent living retirement communities, *assisted living facilities* provide personal care assistance to residents. This means that residents receive assistance in managing their medications as well as a helping hand with bathing, grooming, and dressing. Assisted living facilities come in all shapes and sizes. Settings can range from three or more older people in a homelike setting, to dozens of residents in an institutional environment.

Nursing Homes

For individuals already disabled to the point of requiring daily nursing care as well as other support services, *nursing homes* provide comprehensive care services in a single setting. While most older persons and their families see nursing home care only as a last resort, this kind of care may in fact be the best setting for disabled persons requiring multiple types of services.

Board and Care

Board and care facilities are private residences converted to accommodate up to six residents. These residences are typically owned and managed by persons with nursing backgrounds.

Group Homes

Group homes provide independent, private living in a house shared by several senior citizens who split the cost of rent, housekeeping services, utilities, and meals.

Adult Foster Care

Adult foster care involves a family caring for a dependent person in their home. Meals, housekeeping, and help with dressing, eating, bathing, and other personal care are provided.

Even when relocation for your loved one has become apparent to you as the best option, your loved one may avoid the discussion. This could be because he or she does not want to give up his or her sense of independence, or because he or she feels any relocation could cause a further burden on you. Due to this, you may need to initiate the conversation.

ANDREW AND PHIL'S STORY

Phil's father, Andrew, was in declining health. When Andrew appeared in my office, it was very apparent that he required assistance for daily activities. Phil had called me in advance of the appointment and asked if I could approach the subject of relocation with Andrew, as he felt uncomfortable suggesting it to his dad. Andrew was a very proud man, had served in WWII, and never wanted to be looked upon as weak. I was happy to assist, and to my surprise, Andrew was very open to the discussion. Sometimes it just takes a little prodding.

HOSPICE CARE

The most difficult end-of-life decision to make is acknowledging that there is no longer any chance of living. When all medical options have been exhausted, part of planning for the inevitable includes choosing professional care that will help your loved one during this time. If your loved one is terminally ill, his or her medical provider may recommend hospice care. As his or her representative, you will be required to help select hospice options that are in your loved one's best interests. The following is an overview of hospice.

Defining Hospice

Considered to be the model for quality, compassionate care for people facing a life-limiting illness or injury, *hospice care* involves a team-oriented approach. It provides expert medical care, pain management, and emotional and spiritual support expressly tailored to the patient's needs and wishes. At the center of hospice care is the belief that each of us has the right to die pain-free and with dignity, and that our families will receive the necessary support to allow us to do so.

Hospice focuses on caring, not curing, and in most cases, care is provided in the patient's home. Hospice care may also be provided in hospice centers, hospitals, and nursing homes and other long-term care facilities. Hospice care is a philosophy of care that accepts dying as a natural part of life. When death is inevitable, hospice seeks neither to hasten nor postpone it.

How Hospice Care Works

Members of the hospice staff make regular visits to assess the patient and provide additional care or other services. Hospice staff is on-call twenty-four hours a day, seven days a week. The hospice team develops a care plan that meets each patient's individual needs for pain management and symptom control. The team usually consists of:

- the patient's personal physician;
- hospice physician (or medical director);
- nurses;

- home health aides;
- social workers;
- clergy or other counselors;
- trained volunteers; and,
- speech, physical, and occupational therapists, if needed.

Hospice Services

Among its major responsibilities, the hospice team:
- manages the patient's pain and symptoms;
- assists the patient with the emotional, psychosocial, and spiritual aspects of dying;
- provides needed drugs, medical supplies, and equipment;
- coaches the family on how to care for the patient;
- delivers special services like speech and physical therapy when needed;
- makes short-term inpatient care available when pain or symptoms become too difficult to manage at home; and,
- provides bereavement care and counseling to surviving family and friends.

Qualifying for Hospice Care

Hospice services are available to patients of any age, religion, race, or illness. Hospice care is covered under Medicare, Medicaid, most private insurance plans, HMOs, and other managed care organizations.

Hospice care is for any person who has a life-threatening or terminal illness. To be eligible, your loved one's doctor must provide a statement that his or her patient's life expectancy is six months or less if the illness runs its normal course. Patients with both cancer and non-cancer illnesses are eligible to receive hospice care.

It is a common belief that a person must have a physical disease or disorder to be diagnosed as terminal. Up until 2004, that was the requirement to qualify for hospice care. However, Medicare expanded the definition of eligibility requirements to now include the diagnosis of *failure to thrive*. In such cases, the patient has mentally given up the will to live and stops eating.

Affording Hospice Care

Eighty percent of people who use hospice care are over the age of 65, and are entitled to the services offered by their *Medicare hospice benefit*. This benefit covers virtually all aspects of hospice care with little out-of-pocket expense to the patient or family. As a result, the financial burdens usually associated with caring for a terminally ill patient are virtually nonexistent. In addition, most private health plans and Medicaid in forty-five states and the District of Columbia cover hospice services.

PRACTICAL POINT. If your loved one is under age 65, has qualified for Social Security Disability, and has a terminal illness, he or she is also receiving Medicare and therefore qualifies for hospice through the Medicare hospice benefits.

CHAPTER 5:

AT THE TIME OF PASSING: YOUR FIRST STEPS

As previously mentioned, as representative you may wear many hats. At the time of passing, your role will be dependent upon your relationship with the decedent. Of immediate concern is making arrangements for the funeral, placing children with the guardian, and arranging for the safe caring of pets.

Appendix A is a representative's checklist of the most common issues that must be addressed upon the decedent's passing.

MAKING FUNERAL ARRANGEMENTS

If you are an immediate family member, you may be called upon to make funeral arrangements. Although this is a very emotional time for you and your loved ones, you must proceed cautiously and not allow your decisions to be influenced by others.

If the decedent left specific written instructions for his or her funeral and final interment, or had discussed his or her wishes with the family, it would be highly inappropriate to disregard his or her wishes. This is not to say that this does not often occur. For example, I had a client who, though raised Catholic, never practiced his religion as an adult. Even though he made his wishes known to his family that he only wanted to be cremated, his wife had him buried in a Catholic cemetery. This is wrong.

Review the Will

Quite often a will contains a provision for final interment, and though the decedent may have never expressed his or her wishes to you or anyone else, reviewing the will prior to completing funeral arrangements could help you avoid making a decision for the decedent's final resting that may be in complete contradiction to his or her wishes. Further, the testator may have made pre-need arrangements with a funeral home that you may not be aware of. Read the will for any requests before completing funeral arrangements.

LAURIE'S STORY

Laurie's mom and dad were divorced several years ago. When her mom died, she had her cremated. When Laurie's dad recently passed away, she likewise had him cremated. A few days later, when she read his will, she discovered that he had wanted to be buried in a veterans' cemetery. She felt terrible and was beyond remorse. I asked if she kept her dad's ashes, thinking that these could at least be interred at the cemetery, but they had already been scattered at sea.

The following is a guideline for making funeral arrangements in the event that the decedent had not expressed his or her wishes or made any pre-need arrangements.

Funeral Services and Goods

Most decisions about purchasing funeral goods and services are made when people are grieving and under time constraints. The funeral industry has been accused of taking advantage of people during their time of grief by selling goods and services that may not be needed. As a result, the *Federal Trade Commission* (FTC) has developed a trade regulation rule concerning funeral industry practices. It is called the *Funeral Rule*, and its purpose is to enable consumers to easily obtain information about funeral arrangements.

In general, the Funeral Rule makes it easier for you to select only those goods and services you want or need and to pay for only those you select. When you inquire about funeral arrangements, the funeral home will give you a written price list of the goods and services available. When arranging a funeral, you can purchase individual items or buy an entire package of goods and services. If you want to purchase a casket, the funeral provider will supply a list that describes all the available selections and their prices.

Costs

A traditional funeral generally includes the following costs:
- moving the body to the funeral home;
- using the funeral home facilities;
- embalming, providing cosmetology and restoration, and dressing the body;
- purchasing the coffin;
- using the hearse;
- arranging for pallbearers; and,
- providing a guest register and acknowledgment cards.

A funeral also includes professional service fees, a burial and transit permit, newspaper death notices, and fees for completion and filing of the death certificate.

All of the above goods and services are generally included in a package-priced traditional funeral. The following costs are usually additional, depending on the type of service selected:
- clergy's honorarium;
- music;
- limousines;
- flowers;
- burial clothes;
- cremation service charges;
- urn;
- marker or monument;
- crypt;
- cemetery charges for opening and closing the grave;
- burial plot;

- cemetery perpetual care charges; and,
- burial vault or grave liner.

The following are commonly asked questions of funeral home directors. Remember, do not be intimidated. You have the right to be informed and should not hesitate to ask questions.

- Can I have your general price list, casket price list, and outer burial container price list?
- Is your funeral home independently owned and operated, or is it part of a funeral home chain?
- What is your basic service fee?
- What is your fee for *immediate burial?* (Immediate burial is burial without embalming, and no service or viewing.)
- Does this fee include the transfer of the remains to the funeral home?
- Do you use a hearse for the transfer of the body, or a station wagon or van?
- Do you use a contract service to do the pickup or do you, the director, do the pickup?
- In the case that I choose arrangements that require embalming, is the embalming done by you, or is it done by an outside contract embalmer?
- Do you charge a fee for the refrigeration of remains that are not embalmed?
- What is your fee for washing and disinfecting?
- Do you charge a casketing fee? If so, how much?
- Does this fee include body preparation and makeup? If not, what is your fee?
- In the case that I choose an immediate burial, do you charge an extra fee for transporting the remains to the cemetery?
- What is the charge to open the grave at the cemetery? Is a burial container necessary at that cemetery, and if so, what is the cost of a basic cement liner?

Caskets and Outer Burial Containers

A *casket* is the single most expensive item in a traditional funeral and can cost between $500 and $1,000, with funeral homes traditionally marking up the price by as much as 300%. Under the federal Funeral Rule, a funeral home cannot charge extra if you provide your own casket from an outside source. Note that no casket is required for direct cremation, immediate burial, or donation of the body to science.

In addition, most cemeteries require the use of a grave liner or vault. These outer burial containers surround the casket in the grave to prevent the ground from sinking, as settling occurs over time. In some locations, both funeral homes and cemeteries sell vaults and liners.

Embalming

The federal Funeral Rule requires funeral providers to give consumers information about *embalming* that can help them decide whether to purchase this service. Under the Rule, a funeral provider must disclose:
• in writing that, except in certain special cases, embalming is not required by law;
• in writing that you usually have the right to choose cremation or immediate burial if you do not want embalming;
• in writing that certain funeral arrangements, such as a funeral with a viewing, may make embalming a practical necessity and, thus, a required purchase; and,
• that the embalming process is not reversible.

As ridiculous as this last disclosure may sound, there was a case in which a family requested embalming for their loved one and then had a change of heart. When the funeral home advised the family that the embalming process had taken place and that there was nothing that could be done to reverse it, the family sued. They lost the case, but the funeral industry, in an effort to protect itself from further suits, has now made this part of their disclosures.

Cremation

Generally less expensive than a traditional funeral, the costs of *cremation* may include the cremation itself, transportation of the body and cremated remains, an urn or other container for the ashes, burial in a niche in a *columbarium* (a special building designed to hold cremation urns) or in a burial plot, a memorialization plaque, and scattering of the ashes (unless done personally).

> **PRACTICAL POINT.** State and local laws should be checked before disposing of ashes, as states and localities have regulations restricting the process of scattering cremated remains over land or water.

Cemeteries

Funeral arrangements are only part of the expense if you choose burial in a cemetery or entombment in a mausoleum. Cemetery costs generally include:

- a burial plot or mausoleum crypt;
- opening and closing the grave (which can be more expensive on weekends);
- a vault or a less expensive grave liner (although not required by law, one may be required by individual cemeteries to prevent subsequent collapse of the grave); and,
- a memorial (marker, monument, or plaque).

The location of the plot and the use of materials for markers or stones have a direct affect on the cost.

> **PRACTICAL POINT.** Most cemeteries require that a plot be paid for in full before it is used.

Veteran Funerals

If the decedent was a veteran, the U.S. Department of Veterans Affairs provides for a small burial allowance for burial in a private cemetery. In addition, all veterans can receive a burial flag and burial in a national cemetery at no charge. For the location of the closest national cemetery, call 800-555-1212 and ask for the Veterans Affairs office for your region.

Gravesites in Department of Veterans Affairs (VA) national cemeteries cannot be reserved in advance; however, reservations made prior to 1962 will be honored.

If burial will be in a private cemetery and you desire a government headstone or marker, you must complete VA Form 40-1330 (Application for Standard Government Headstone or Marker for Installation in a Private or State Veteran's Cemetery).

MANAGING THE ESTRANGED SPOUSE

If the decedent is survived by a spouse from whom he or she is separated or estranged, state laws vary as to whether the spouse can make funeral arrangements. Some states hold that unless a divorce proceeding has been filed, the spouse is the proper person to be in charge. Other states look to the intent of the partics. That is, if the decedent and his or her spouse have been living separate and apart for a *considerable* period of time, and have not held themselves out as husband and wife, case law would not favor the surviving spouse. As the representative, it is best for you to play the role of the peacekeeper in such situations and try to accommodate everyone's interests.

GILBERT'S STORY

Gilbert died, leaving behind his son from his first marriage and his second wife, from whom he was separated. The son had not spoken to his father in years but learned that his dad had died from his cousin. Despite protests from the family, the second wife informed the family that she was making the funeral arrangements. At the graveside service, the second wife threatened to call security when the son showed up. Fortunately, the representative was able to intercede and the funeral proceeded, though the stepson and stepmother kept their distance from one another.

FUNERAL EXPENSES

Even though you may not be actively involved in making the funeral and final interment decisions, you will be responsible, as the representative of the estate, for paying the funeral costs and other related expenses. All states have adopted case law that says that the estate is responsible for all *reasonable* expenses, even if the arrangements are made by someone who is not the representative. Likewise, if a non-representative has incurred out-of-pocket expenses, he or she is entitled to be reimbursed for those expenses from the assets of the estate.

DAVID'S STORY

David was the grandchild of Cyrus and was named his grandfather's representative. David's mom had passed away and the estate was left to him and his aunt Betty. Betty took it upon herself to arrange the funeral, which included a very elaborate catered reception afterwards. Cyrus did not have many friends, whereas Betty spent her days having expensive lunches with her friends. David believed Betty saw his grandfather's death as another opportunity for Betty to throw a big bash. When she presented him with the tab for over $5,000, he refused. She then sued the estate. The court sided with David, agreeing that the expenses were not reasonable.

IF DEATH OCCURS AT HOME

If a person passes away in a hospital or some other nursing care facility, the attending physician is available to sign the death certificate so that the body can be moved to a funeral home. However, if death occurs in a residence, state laws require that a death certificate be signed by the decedent's physician or the county medical examiner. Until the certificate is signed, you cannot make any arrangements to have the body moved.

ANATOMICAL GIFTS

If the decedent left a properly executed living will designating all or parts of his or her body for organ donation, under the *Uniform Anatomical Gift Act*, which has been recognized by all states, the wishes of the decedent must be honored by his or her survivors. Even if the survivors do not want to donate the decedent's organs, a properly executed living will directing as much must be obeyed. Also, the decedent may have carried a donor card, sometimes found on the reverse side of a driver's license, authorizing the gifting of his or her organs.

If the decedent did not leave any written instructions for organ donation, the surviving family members may still make an election to donate some or all of the decdent's organs. You should therefore inquire with the immediate family members as to their wishes. Time is of the essence in this situation.

AUTOPSIES

In the event that the immediate cause of death cannot be determined, an autopsy may be required. This could delay funeral arrangements, as well as deny the decedent's wishes to be an organ donor. Also, even though the family may want to move forward with the grieving process, it is your role to explain why the autopsy is necessary. Families may take comfort in knowing that what is learned from the autopsy could in some way benefit someone else. In addition, the results of an autopsy may provide information to family members that may be relevant to their own health and well-being.

> **PRACTICAL POINT.** A state's right to perform an autopsy is sometimes challenged by an individual's religious beliefs. For example, by Jewish tradition, an autopsy cannot be performed, as it desecrates the body. Therefore, unless death was the result of a violent act and a crime investigation is pending, states will often yield to the family's objections based on religion.

PLACEMENT OF CHILDREN WITH THE GUARDIAN

When there are minor children, a properly drafted will includes a provision naming a guardian of the children upon the testator's passing. If death is imminent, such arrangements may already be in place. However, when death is sudden, your role as representative may include arranging for the placement of the children with the guardian named in the will.

As you can imagine, this can be a terribly emotional task to perform. However, in the best interests of the children, it is important that placement occur as soon as possible. If the person named resides out of state, this creates logistical problems that need to be addressed immediately, as the last thing you would want to happen is for the children to be placed under the care of the state in a protective service facility.

GIL'S STORY

Victor and his wife Renée died in a car accident, leaving two minor children. Their will named Renée's sister, Barbara, as guardian. It also named their friend, Gil, as executor. Barbara resided in Florida and was on a cruise with her husband when the accident occurred. When Gil could not reach Barbara, he called the state's protective service agency, which placed the children in a foster home, where they remained for ten days until Barbara was contacted.

If the Guardian Declines

If the named guardian refuses, most wills include the name of an alternate guardian to assume custody. However, if you cannot immediately place the child, it is your responsibility to contact every heir and any friends to arrange a temporary placement of the minor. Again, the alternative of protective custody with a state agency is not in the best interests of the children.

JORDAN'S STORY

One of my saddest cases involved a single mother who died of cancer. She was raising her teenage daughter, Jordan. Her will named her sister as guardian, and even though death was expected, when she died the sister declined the guardianship. The only other living relative was the grandmother, who was too old and frail to raise her granddaughter.

As the attorney for the estate, I advised the grandmother to call all of her daughter's friends and coworkers to inquire if anyone wanted to raise Jordan. Fortunately, a friend at work who had been trying to adopt was thrilled to get the call. We immediately filed a petition for her and her husband to be the temporary guardians of Jordan. There is a happy ending, as a year later they filed a petition for her adoption. However, it is so hard to imagine what went through Jordan's mind those first few weeks after she lost her mother and then had to confront the fact that no one wanted her.

Divorced or Separated Parents

When parents divorce and one parent is awarded physical custody, it is always assumed that upon the sudden passing of that parent, the children will thereafter reside with the surviving parent. However, the will of the decedent may name someone other than the noncustodial parent to raise the children.

LEGALLY SPEAKING

The legal process where a nonparent assumes the legal responsibility for raising a child is known as *guardianship*.

It is ultimately up to a court to decide who will be awarded guardianship of a child. Even if there is a surviving parent, if the decedent has named someone else, the named person can petition the court to be the guardian. The court, of course, will consider the age of the child, where the child will reside, and the overall best interests of the child. The court may also look at the relationship that the noncustodial parent had with the child after the parties ended their relationship. Likewise, they will also look to the intent of the decedent in choosing someone other than the noncustodial parent to raise the children.

BRIANNES'S STORY

Sherri and Dennis had a very bitter divorce. Sherri was awarded full custody of Brianne, who was then 11 years old, and Dennis had alternate weekends for visitation. However, in the two years since their divorce, he exercised his right to visitation only six times. When Sherri became ill, she made it very clear to everyone in her family as well as Dennis's parents that she could not see Dennis raising Brianne. In her will, she named her sister, Ellen, as guardian. When Dennis got the call that Sherri had passed away, he called his mother to come with him to pick up Brianne. My associate was contacted by Ellen and she filed a petition for guardianship of Brianne. After a much-contested hearing, the court decided that it was in the best interest of Brianne that she should be raised by Ellen. Dennis was again awarded visitation, but in the year that followed, he only saw his daughter a handful of times. In hindsight, the court made the right decision.

If There is No Will

If a parent dies without a will, the state does not automatically step in to assume custody of a child. As representative, you should arrange for immediate placement of the child in your home or the home of a relative or friend. Only as a last resort should the state be contacted.

LEGALLY SPEAKING

Any expenses that result from the placement of the child are expenses that may be charged against the assets of the estate and are reimbursable to the person who advanced the expenses. For example, if the decedent resided in California but the children will now be raised by the decedent's sister in New York, it is reasonable for the estate to pay for transportation to relocate the child to New York.

TAKING CARE OF PETS

In *My Wishes* (Sourcebooks, 2006), I discuss that as part of estate planning, you should have a conversation with the person whom you have asked to take care of your pet when you are no longer here. Sometimes, however, that conversation never takes place. When death occurs suddenly with no arrangements in place, disposition of animals becomes a priority.

When there is a will or trust that specifically mentions the disposition of an animal, it is your responsibility to care for the pet until the pet is placed with the person named in the trust or will document.

If the decedent died without leaving a will, or any instructions for care of the pet, you should take whatever steps are reasonable and necessary for securing the safety and future care of the animal.

ANGELA'S STORY

Several years ago, I read a story about a lady who had over thirty-five cats. Angela died in her sleep. When her neighbor reported to the police that there was a foul smell coming from Angela's apartment, they investigated, only to find her body as well as thirty-five hungry animals. It turns out that she had a will naming her son, who lived out of state, as the representative. Further investigation showed that her son had visited his mother the day she died. Aware that his mother was ill, he chose to do nothing. He was later charged with cruelty to animals.

IF THE DECEDENT LIVED ALONE

If the decedent lived alone, you will want to secure his or her residence. This includes making sure all doors are locked and windows are closed. If appropriate, you should consider changing the locks.

In addition, turn off any equipment, such as fans, that are running so as to avoid any electrical problems. Move the thermostat to the "off" position. You will also want to discard any perishable food items.

If the decedent was taking prescription medication, you should remove all such medication immediately. Finally, if the decedent was renting home health care equipment, such as a hospital bed or wheelchair, notify the provider immediately so that arrangements can be made for the equipment to be picked up.

HELP SOMEONE ELSE AND RECYCLE

Home health aids and other articles can often be recycled, and there are many organizations that would welcome your generosity. For example, the American Cancer Society has a program to recycle wigs from cancer patients who have lost their hair as a result of radiation and chemotherapy. The wigs will be cleaned, restyled, and made available for someone else.

There are also programs that will recycle crutches, walkers, wheelchairs, eyeglasses, hearing aids, and even some types of pacemakers. Simply contact the local chapter of your favorite charity for more information.

Please see Appendix A, which is a representative's checklist to be used at the time of passing.

CHAPTER 6:

AT THE TIME OF PASSING: MANAGING THE SURVIVORS

Regardless of whether the decedent's passing was expected or sudden, you must be available to step into his or her shoes immediately. There are no rehearsals or tryouts. This is the real thing and your loved ones will be evaluating your performance from the minute you take the stage. Your first few days will most likely involve managing the survivors and addressing their personal concerns. You may need to provide emotional support, manage sibling rivalry, manage greedy heirs, manage the heirs' expectations, deal with estranged heirs, avoid taking sides in familial disputes, confront resentment head-on, be the peacekeeper to your family, and respect the grieving process.

PROVIDING EMOTIONAL SUPPORT

Though your role as the representative of the estate may not occur until you have been officially appointed by the court, as discussed in Chapter 8, you may be called upon to provide emotional support to the survivors, who are likely overwhelmed by their loss. Therefore, it is advisable that you are always available to any family member who may seek your assistance. Be available to listen and console them, and to direct them toward counseling or support groups if necessary.

When You May Need Emotional Support

As the representative, you will be looked to for guidance—but what if you need emotional support? We all have emotions and react differently to different situations. Remember that though it may not be your nature to shed a tear in public, it is all right to do so. Your community may offer support organizations that can help you through this difficult time. In addition, if your loved one was receiving benefits through a hospice program, hospice does have support services available for survivors.

JOE'S STORY

Joe was the youngest of five children. While his brothers and sisters moved away, Joe stayed close to home, raising his family within a block of his parents' house. His mother passed away first and his father died within the next year. Joe was named as the representative and seemed to handle his responsibilities very well. However, one day, when he was in my office reviewing the expenses of the estate, he suddenly paused. I saw his eyes well up and I offered him a box of tissues. He began to sob and tears poured from eyes. He told me that this was the first time he had cried. He had been holding back his feelings but could not any longer. I reassured him that it was perfectly okay to cry, that he was not made of steel and needed to express his emotions.

The Continuing Role of Hospice

Hospice provides care for the dying, but it also provides emotional support for the survivors, both before and after the loved one's death. If the decedent was under hospice care, the hospice worker assigned to the case will make contact with a family member within days after the death to offer information about the grieving process. This may include books to read as well as resources where one can receive counseling. It is your ethical responsibility to pass this information on to your family members. Whether they decide to act on the information is their decision and you should not prejudge anyone.

MANAGING SIBLING RIVALRY

If you have brothers or sisters, growing up you may have heard them grumble that one or both of your parents liked you best. Typically this was said out of jealousy. Perhaps you always got to sit in the front seat when Dad drove or your toys were better than theirs.

As adults we know better than to be jealous of our brothers and sisters, but feelings of jealousy may still persist if one child believes he or she was unfairly passed over for his or her sibling when he or she was not chosen to be the representative.

As a result, while you are trying to effectively manage the estate, you may be confronted with requests and demands from your siblings—even petty ones are intended to upset you. In managing sibling rivalry, it is best to confront the issue as soon as it becomes apparent. Do not allow ill feelings to linger, as they will only create further divisions amongst family members in the future. It is most important that you remain objective and not allow emotions to effect your judgment. Most important, when making any decisions, you must always consider what is in the best interest of the estate and not what may be most advantageous to one particular beneficiary.

DIONDRE'S STORY

I was contacted by the youngest of three sons. Diondre's father had passed away and named him as representative. He said his two older brothers felt it was an insult that his dad appointed him and that they wanted to challenge the appointment. I explained that unless they could prove he was not competent, it would be a futile effort to pursue. They told Diondre that they would try to dig up some dirt on him. I suggested a meeting in my office with all three brothers, which was successful. The older brothers only needed an open forum to air their differences, which were quickly resolved. Everyone shook hands and the estate went forward.

SHOW ME THE MONEY: MANAGING THE GREEDY AND IMPATIENT HEIRS

Chapter 10 discusses when certain assets may be distributed to their intended heirs without having to wait for the probate process to be concluded.

However, beneficiaries who are aware that they will be receiving a distribution from an estate often grow impatient. They may not be tolerant of the court process and may call you to ask for their money now.

As the representative, you are obliged to comply with the law. Therefore, you should not make any early disbursements to any beneficiary if it would in any way affect preserving the assets of the estate.

MITCHELL'S STORY

Mitchell's estate had a value of over $600,000 consisting mostly of bank accounts and insurance policies. The estate was left to three brothers in equal shares. The oldest son was named the representative and the youngest brother wanted his one-third share immediately to invest in a franchise. He claimed it was a golden opportunity and that if he did not act quickly, he would lose out. During consultation, I learned that Mitchell had not filed tax returns for over three years and the IRS was threatening to place a lien on his home.

I advised Mitchell that he should not disburse the $200,000 to his brother until it was determined whether the estate had any tax liability or owed money to creditors. Despite his brother's relentless demands and his sister-in-law's insistence that they would never talk to him again, Mitchell's first responsibility was to the estate.

MANAGING THE HEIRS' EXPECTATIONS

The taste of money often brings out the worst qualities in people. Families who have been estranged for years are suddenly talking—because there is that big payday coming soon. As the representative, you are in the sometimes uncomfortable position of holding the keys to the safe.

The best advice is to maintain communication with all of the beneficiaries. Whether you write status letters or make phone calls, keep them informed. You know that they know they are expecting to receive their share of the estate.

However, so long as you maintain an open line of communication, you will send an important message that you are in charge. In contrast, failing to communicate in a timely manner could raise questions about your abilities to manage. Even worse, an impatient beneficiary could challenge your authority and seek to have you removed, and regardless of whether the court rules in your favor, the estate could be liable for paying additional attorney fees.

GRAHAM'S STORY

A colleague of mine was contacted by Graham. His mom had passed away, leaving an estate valued at over two million dollars. Graham said that it had been six months since his sister's appointment as representative, and although she had an attorney, no one was talking to Graham. Unfortunately, many attorneys, upon hearing this, will jump to file a motion with the court to intervene, especially when they know the estate is large and they can be awarded attorney fees for their work. My colleague instead elected to write a stern but diplomatic letter to the attorney for the estate, outlining Graham's concerns. Within a few days the attorney called my colleague and advised that the decedent had been involved in a lawsuit before her passing, and that was what was holding up the estate's closing. Had Graham been made aware of this, he would not have assumed that he was being left out.

MANAGING THE "ENTITLEMENT DISEASE" FACTOR

Some heirs believe that they are entitled to certain things regardless of whether such bequests are stated in the will or not. I refer to this condition as a disease because there are no symptoms during the decedent's lifetime and it first surfaces after he or she passes away. For example, the heir may tell you that "Mom promised me the piano" or "Dad said that if he died, I would get his car."

These requests often turn to demands, as the message the heir is really sending is that "even if the written document doesn't say it, I deserve it anyway." As discussed in managing an heir's expectations, your only responsibility is to the estate. Until you have completed inventorying and valuing the assets of the estate, as well as evaluating whether the estate owes debts or taxes, you cannot arbitrarily begin making distributions of personal property. Instead, you must explain to all of the heirs that everyone will be treated fairly and any heir's expressions of wanting something specific from the estate will be considered, but only after you have completed evaluating the financial situation of the estate. Often, however, you may have to repeat this message several times.

A FEW MORE WORDS ABOUT THE GRUBBY, GREEDY HEIRS

When I was in law school, one of the required courses was wills and trusts. It was in this class that I heard for the first time the phrase "grubby, greedy heirs." This is certainly not a nice way to be referring to persons who may be your family, but all too often, the passing of a loved one brings out the worst in personalities. As the representative, your ability to manage may be severely tested by family members who have their own agenda. However, your role is to represent the estate and not any individual heir. Accordingly, when talking with your family, consider the following.

Respond with Logic, Not Emotion

As the representative, you may have the discretionary power to interpret the testator's intentions when a provision in a will or trust appears vague. To illustrate, when a will says that the estate will pay for the college education of a grandchild, you would be correct in concluding that *education* was not meant to include tuition for beauty school instead of college.

DONNA'S STORY

My client left his estate to his three grandchildren. Donna had received numerous advances against her inheritance during my client's lifetime. Upon his death, Donna approached the executor and asked for a $50,000 advance to cover the start-up costs of a masseuse business. She had had a poor track record of paying back other family loans. After she failed to provide the executor with a business plan for how the money would be spent, the executor rightfully denied her request.

PRACTICAL POINT. In most cases, the beneficiaries will accept your interpretations of will provisions. However, if a beneficiary protests, you should seek representation immediately. If you proceed with your interpretation, and it is later found to be incorrect, you could be removed as representative. In addition, if the estate was to incur a loss in value as a result of your decision, you could be held personally liable for reimbursement to the estate for the loss in value.

Question the Source of Communication

As discussed in Chapter 2, a representative must be a good communicator. That is, he or she needs to keep an open dialogue with all of the heirs in order to reduce the number of questions they might have. However, the other side of open communication is that heirs may try to contact you to provide information or details in an attempt to influence your decision concerning distribution.

Rose's Story

In her will, Rose left all of her jewelry to her four granddaughters, without specifying which item was to go to each. Her unmarried son Charles was named as representative. He received a call from his sister Laurie, who was lobbying for her daughter, Dianna, to get the antique gold, ruby, and diamond ring. Laurie claimed that Rose had told her that she wanted Dianna to have it when she was gone. The ring was valued at three times what the other items of jewelry were valued at. Laurie and her husband had recently filed bankruptcy, and Charles feared that Laurie would sell the ring and not give it to Dianna. Since Dianna was 16 years old, he elected to hold the ring and give it to her on her 18th birthday.

DEALING WITH ESTRANGED HEIRS

Often a will is drafted many, many years prior to one's passing, and then is not updated to reflect changes that may have occurred. One of the changes may be that a family member has become estranged from the maker of the will. No matter how serious the reason that led to the estrangement, if the terms of the will were not changed, that heir is still entitled to receive his or her inheritance, despite any protests from other family members.

RICK AND VINCENT'S STORY

Vincent made his will over ten years prior to his death. He left his estate to his three children. His oldest son, Rick, became involved with drugs and ended up in jail. Prior to his last arrest, he forged a check from his father's account to pay for his drug habit. Vincent did not prosecute but swore he was cutting his son off. He announced this to his other two children but never changed his will. The children who were named as co-representatives refused to distribute to Rick his share of the estate. Rick hired an attorney, who successfully challenged their position.

DO NOT TAKE SIDES

As the representative, you must be fair and not biased, and you should not side with any one party, even an heir you are particularly close to. Different heirs will have different opinions and reasons why theirs is the most compelling case, but never forget that your duty is first to the estate. You must follow the dictates of the will to the best of your ability.

As the representative, you now may become the surrogate for the decedent. However, even if a relative was always coaxing the decedent for personal financial favors, it would be wrong for you to follow in the decedent's footsteps. Further, heirs may try to influence you by explaining their misfortunes in hopes of getting favoritism when the estate is distributed. No matter how concerned or sympathetic you may feel towards one heir, it is wrong to play favorites. As the representative, you must maintain your objectivity. If you do not, your actions can come back to haunt you if ever an heir decides to challenge your ability to represent the estate. Note also that the court will not tolerate anything less than equal treatment towards all of the beneficiaries of the estate.

EMILY'S STORY

Emily was a single mom who lived with her father, Gordon, in his home. He was frail and she provided for his everyday needs. He came to my office to make a will, leaving his estate to Emily and excluding his older daughter Janet. He told me that Janet never visited him, and that her husband had done very well and she did not need his money. Upon Gordon's passing, Janet offered her home to welcome guests after the funeral. However, when she later found out that she was left out of her dad's will, she promptly asked Emily to pay for the deli rolls, mayonnaise, and plastic plates and forks that she had used after the funeral. When Emily did not, Janet sued her in small claims court and then retained an attorney to challenge the will. I was called to testify and the judge accepted my testimony that Gordon was competent and not acting under anyone's influence when he made his will. Janet also lost in small claims, as the judge found her demand outrageous.

BE THE PEACEKEEPER TO YOUR FAMILY

If at all possible, you should make every effort to bring family members together. The reason why John has not talked to his sister in ten years or why Bill has always felt resentment for his brother's wife does not really matter now. This is the time to bury the hatchet and come together as a family as you enter the grieving period. You should make every effort to be the peacemaker. That way, the mourning for a loved one is shared by all and not individually. This is not the time for survivors to be alone.

ANNETTE'S STORY

Annette's dad died. She and her sister had not spoken to each other for many years. Standing at the grave was very difficult for both of them. Other than a few cordial exchanges, they maintained their silence towards each other. Rather than return to her dad's house after the service where the other sister had invited friends to gather, Annette chose to go to a restaurant with her husband and son to grieve alone. Six months later, Annette's sister was killed in a traffic accident. Annette missed the one opportunity to make peace with her sister.

CONFRONT RESENTMENT HEAD-ON

In the first few days after a loved one's passing, you may feel alienated, as a family member may be upset that you were chosen over him or her. It is human nature for a sibling to feel hurt or slighted if a parent chose you to execute his or her estate over your sibling. If you sense resentment, it is best to try to resolve any ill feelings now. Your goal is to have the support and cooperation of all of the beneficiaries.

JERRY'S STORY

Jerry was the youngest of three brothers. He lived near his father, while the two older brothers lived out of state. Though all of the boys were close with their dad, Jerry was the most involved because he lived in such close proximity to their dad, and though Jerry had not achieved the financial success of his two older brothers, his dad chose him to be the representative. When their father died, the eldest, Robert, became incensed that Jerry was chosen over him. Soon after the funeral, Robert contacted an attorney to have Jerry removed as the representative. At my urging, I advised Jerry to have a heart-to-heart talk with his brother. Fortunately, their talk was successful and they resolved their differences. In addition to repairing a potential family rift, by avoiding unnecessary court proceedings, this talk saved the estate from having to pay additional attorney fees.

RESPECT THE GRIEVING PROCESS AND RELIGIOUS CUSTOMS

Whether it is finding solace in a favorite book of poems or exchanging stories with friends, everyone has their own way of grieving. Still, despite the personal nature of grief, you may be looked upon to set the tone for the grieving process. Likewise, there may be certain family members who choose to mourn in a manner you may not approve or believe in. I remember returning to a friend's home after the funeral for her dad. Though southern California can be especially warm, my wife and I thought it was most inappropriate when several family members jumped into the pool and the whole event turned into a wild, drinking pool party. Regardless, this is the time to respect and not question. Such behavior, no matter how distasteful or inappropriate it may be, should have no effect on your management of the estate. Further, although you may be ultimately charged with paying the expenses of the estate, it may not be proper for you to *nickel and dime* or question a family member's behavior or wishes.

JOEL'S STORY

Joshua was of the Jewish faith. Joel, the nephew who was named representative, was not a practicing Jew. In Jewish custom, a family mourns the loss of a loved one for seven days by sitting shiva. In simplest terms, *shiva* means that friends and family are invited to visit the home of where the family is mourning each night. Although some guests bring something sweet to the home of a mourner or arrange to have a meal delivered, it is not unusual to have a home filled with guests at dinner time expecting something to eat. Joel, when presented with the bills for food and other related expenses from his sister, who was religious, refused to pay, saying they were not necessary. In handling the estate for Joshua, I advised Joel that he should respect his sister's wishes.

CHAPTER 7:

AT THE TIME OF PASSING: NOTIFICATION AND GETTING ORGANIZED

Chapter 6 discusses your role in managing the personal issues of the survivors that must be addressed upon a loved one's passing. Next, you must turn your attention to the organizational and legal issues that present themselves at the time of passing. Having an organized plan in place will enable you to carry out your responsibilities more efficiently.

LOCATING THE WILL AND OTHER ESTATE PLANNING DOCUMENTS

In prioritizing your responsibilities, locating the will and any other estate planning documents and securing them in a safe place should be at the top of your list.

Wills are frequently kept in safe-deposit boxes at banks, at home in a locked box, or somewhere in the home where valuable papers might be maintained. It is extremely unlikely that the attorney who prepared the will kept the original. If the will is not at the residence, ask family members and friends if the decedent had a safe-deposit box. Chapter 8 discusses how to gain access to a safe-deposit box.

LEGALLY SPEAKING

If a probate is required, the courts require that the original will—not a copy—be produced. Refer to Chapter 9, which discusses what to do if the original will cannot be found.

READING OF THE WILL

Those who remember the Perry Mason show will recall Perry summoning to his office the family of his late client. The client mysteriously disappeared two years ago and is now legally presumed dead. As Perry takes his seat behind his oversized wooden desk, the camera pans to the widow, who pulls a tissue from her purse to wipe her tears. Also in the room is the playboy son, who is estranged from his mother. He has never worked and the most lifting he has ever done is picking up his golf clubs. The son appears nervous as he fears he may have been cut out of his father's fortunes. The father's secretary is also there, seated next to her boyfriend, who is half her age. She is rumored to have had an affair with the father. The camera catches the widow and the secretary exchanging evil glances.

As Perry begins the *reading of the will*, all the faces of the attendees turn stoic as they await the verdict. Will the widow continue to enjoy society luncheons or will she have to cancel her country club membership? Will the son go from riches to rags and have to look for a job? Will the secretary reap a windfall and then relocate to the south of France, where she cannot be extradited for the murder of the father?

Well, that's television, but in the real world, rarely is there a formal reading of the will. In fact, in my twenty-nine years of practice, I have never been called to assist in a reading of a will.

Instead, it is common practice for the testator to have shared a copy of his or her will with his or her chosen representative. Or, upon locating the will, the representative reviews the will in private in preparation for beginning his or her role as the representative of the estate. Family members, who believe there is an estate, generally assume that they will be notified of the will's contents in a reasonable period of time. Therefore, gathering together in suspense as the will's contents are revealed is generally limited to television and the movies.

PRACTICAL POINT. After you have read the will's contents, it is perfectly permissible for you to contact the heirs simply to advise them that they have been named and that they will be receiving further information from you in a reasonable period of time. This way you will be maintaining an open line of communication, which is most important to effectively perform your role as the representative. If a formal probate will be required, it will be necessary for you to follow the requirement of giving formal notice to the heirs, as discussed further in Chapter 9.

NOTIFICATION

You have now stepped into the shoes of the decedent and must take whatever action is necessary to secure the decedent's assets. This includes providing notification to all interested parties.

Notification to the Post Office of a Change of Address

Unless you or someone you designate will be able to receive mail at the last address of the decedent on a regular basis, it is important that you notify the post office of the decedent's passing. Otherwise, mail will continue to be delivered to that address. You can obtain a change of address form at any post office or online at **www.usps.gov**. The form requires that you provide proof of death by supplying a copy of the death certificate.

PRACTICAL POINT. Once the post office learns of the decedent's passing, perhaps by the postman reporting that the mail is not being removed from the mail box, mail will be held at the local post office for only fifteen days. Thereafter, it will be returned to the sender and marked as "undeliverable." Therefore, it is very important that you file a change of address at the earliest possible time and have the mail forwarded to you.

ISAAC AND REUBEN'S STORY

Isaac lived alone. He had given his house key to a neighbor so she could feed his cat, take in the newspaper, and collect his mail. Isaac died suddenly while on vacation. Sixty days passed from the time of his death before Isaac's brother, Reuben, contacted the neighbor to pick up the mail. In the mail was a claim form that Isaac had to complete, as he was part of a class action law suit against a securities company. Reuben waited another sixty days to complete the form, which was later rejected because it was filed late. As a result, Isaac's estate did not share in the class action settlement, at a loss to the estate of $3,000.

Notifying the Social Security Administration

If the decedent was receiving either Social Security Disability or retirement benefits, upon his or her passing the Social Security Administration (SSA) must be notified so that future checks can be discontinued. Their toll-free phone number is 800-772-1213. Be prepared to provide the decedent's Social Security number.

In addition, if the SSA issued a monthly check prior to the decedent's passing and before they were notified of his or her death, the check may have to be returned. Whether the check has to be returned depends upon the date that the decedent passed away and when the check was received. To illustrate, if the decedent died on September 10th, and the check is received on September 3rd, it does not have to be returned, as the check represents Social Security benefits for the month of August. However, if the decedent died on September 20th, and the check was received on October 3rd, it must be returned, as the check represents benefits for the month that the decedent passed away.

If benefits were automatically deposited into the decedent's checking account, you will also need to notify the banking institution so that it can withdraw the deposit and return the benefits to the SSA.

> **PRACTICAL POINT.** If you receive any checks that must be returned, you can deliver the check to any Social Security office. To locate the nearest office, call 800-772-1213 or check online at **www.ssa.gov**.

If the decedent was receiving Social Security benefits, his or her spouse may be entitled to continue receiving those benefits. For a complete discussion of both Social Security retirement and Social Security Disability benefits, please refer to Chapter 15.

Notifying Employers and Governmental Providers of Benefits

In addition to the Social Security Administration, you should notify the Department of Veterans Affairs (for any deceased veteran), other governmental agencies, employers, and anyone else who may have been sending monthly checks to the decedent so they can discontinue the payments. Likewise, there may be death benefits available from Social Security, the Department of Veterans Affairs, or the decedent's last employer that will be processed only after notice is given. If monthly benefits were being paid via direct deposit to a bank account, notify the bank of the death so that any amounts paid in error after the death can be returned. Please refer to Chapter 16, which discusses obtaining death benefits for the estate.

Notifying Utility Companies and Recurring Service Providers

Unless you or someone else will be remaining in the decedent's residence, utility companies should be notified as soon as possible so that service is discontinued. This would include phone, electric, gas, water, cable, satellite, Internet, and cell phone services. Also advise the utility companies of the address where any refund or the closing bill should be sent.

In addition, you should also do the following.

- Cancel newspaper and magazine subscriptions and health club and other memberships, and inquire if the decedent is entitled to a refund for any unused period.
- Notify the decedent's life insurance company so that the company can contact the designated beneficiaries and begin to process insurance benefits.
- Send letters to all credit card companies and other creditors of the decedent, notifying them of a possible delay in payment of amounts owed the creditors because of the death. Also request verification and evidence of the nature and amount owed.
- Cancel any automatic charges that are placed on credit cards, such as Internet service providers and health clubs.
- If the decedent executed a power of attorney during his or her lifetime naming an agent to handle his or her financial affairs, notify the agent under the power of attorney of the decedent's passing.

LEGALLY SPEAKING

One of the most common misconceptions about the law concerns powers of attorney. Though a power of attorney confers powers on someone to act for another, those powers terminate at the time of death. Unless the person receiving the powers is named as the representative (executor) or trustee, his or her power to act terminates. If he or she is not named, but wants to continue representing the estate, he or she must petition the court to be appointed as the representative. His or her appointment is not automatic.

To simplify the notification process, please refer to Appendix B, which is a checklist of the most common parties to be notified at the time of a loved one's passing.

If the Decedent Owned Real Estate

It is very important that you do not cancel insurance that insures any real estate owned by the decedent and is part of his estate until that property is sold or title is transferred. This is because if someone was injured while on the property, or there was fire damage, you as the representative would be personally liable for not taking proper precautions to protect the asset.

ROBERTA'S STORY

Roberta's father passed away. He lived alone and Roberta lived out of state. Roberta decided to sell the home, and put it on the market. Over a July 4th weekend, some kids in a neighboring home lit off some fireworks. One landed on the roof of the house and set it on fire. Roberta had not renewed the insurance policy. Her father's heirs sued her personally for the costs to repair the home.

Notifying Landlords

If the decedent was renting, his or landlord should be notified in writing of his or her passing. The estate could be liable for unpaid rent. Therefore, it is important to locate the rental agreement. If the decedent had a month-to-month arrangement, the estate probably has to provide thirty days' written notice of termination. If there was a lease, the estate could be responsible for rent for the remaining months owing on the lease. However, landlords in all states have a duty to mitigate the losses. This means that the landlord must make every effort to rent the property as soon as possible. Therefore, the estate may only owe for the months that the property was vacant. To research your state law or code online, visit **www.findlaw.com/casecode/#statelaw**. You will find the site to be very simple to navigate.

PRACTICAL POINT. If the decedent was renting and living alone, arrange to have his or her personal property moved as soon as is feasible. In addition, remove all perishable items as soon as possible.

The requirement to notify beneficiaries and heirs at law of a possible probate administration is discussed in Chapter 9.

OBTAINING DEATH CERTIFICATES

If a probate is required, a *death certificate* must be attached to the probate petition. Regardless, if you are acting as the representative of an estate, any institution that holds assets of the decedent will require that you provide a death certificate prior to the release of assets.

A death certificate can be obtained in person, by mail, or by fax. You can write to the office of birth and death records in the county where the decedent last resided. In addition, many counties have websites to obtain such records. The quickest way of finding out if a website is available is to do a search for the decedent's county and state and the phrase "death certificates." To illustrate, to find the site for Clark County, Nevada, in your toolbar search window, enter "Clark County and Nevada and death certificates."

If the assets of the estate include financial accounts, life insurance policies, and other monetary assets, you will need to provide the account holders with *certified* copies of the death certificate, as a photocopy is not acceptable. It is advisable to order at least twelve certified copies, though you can always request more. The cost to obtain a death certificate varies from state to state, but the average is $10 to $12 per copy.

LEGALLY SPEAKING

Because a death certificate includes the decedent's Social Security number, many states have restricted the ordering of death certificates to persons who are immediately related to the decedent. Accordingly, you may have to establish your relationship to the decedent to obtain a certificate.

PRACTICAL POINT. As part of the services they offer, funeral homes will obtain certified copies of the death certificate upon your request.

SOLVING IMMEDIATE PROBLEMS

As a result of the loss of a loved one, there are interruptions of daily life that are immediately felt by the survivors. The fact that in six months Aunt Shirley will receive a check from the estate is great for her, but that does not solve the more pressing issues, such as the following.

How is Mom supposed to pay for the mortgage on her home now that Dad has passed away and there is no other income?

How long will it take for the life insurance company to send the check?

Dad had health insurance through his work that covered Mom and Dad. Now that he has passed away, will Mom still be covered for health insurance?

Often, when a parent dies, the surviving spouse will turn to their child to assume many of the roles that the passing parent had performed. This may include paying monthly bills, keeping up the maintenance of the home, and generally stepping into the shoes of the parent. However, unless you were very familiar with the operations of the home, you will need to obtain information so that you can restore normalcy of life as quickly as possible for your loved ones.

The following checklist contains questions you should ask of various people and institutions in order to solve immediate issues.

Of the Decedent's Employer:

___ Is there any unpaid salary owing?

___ Was the decedent entitled to any bonuses or compensation for unused sick time or vacation pay?

___ Did the decedent have life insurance through his or her employment?

___ Did the decedent have a retirement plan or pension?

___ Are there any death benefits through the decedent's employer?

___ Does the company offer any funeral or burial assistance?

___ Are health insurance benefits transferable to surviving family members?

___ Are the surviving family members entitled to receive the same health coverage and preferred group premium benefits?

Of Insurance Carriers:

___ Is the estate owed a refund for any unused health insurance premiums that were paid?

___ Is the health insurance policy transferable to the surviving family members?

___ How long will it take to process the life insurance death benefits? What documentation will you require?

___ Did the decedent borrow against the insurance policy and is there now a loan owing?

___ If the insurance policy cannot be located, what is the procedure for claiming death benefits against a lost policy?

___ Have the premiums been paid up to date on the vehicles/home insurance?

___ If I cancel the insurance, am I entitled to a refund?

Of Banks, Credit Card Companies, and Other Creditors:

____ What is the current balance on the account?

____ What is the procedure to cancel the credit card?

____ Did the decedent have disability insurance that will pay the balance on the credit card?

____ Did the decedent have mortgage insurance that will pay the balance on the home loan?

____ Is there a co-signor named on the account or anyone else who has guaranteed the account?

Of Investment Advisors:

____ Did the decedent have any open orders to purchase stocks, mutual funds, municipal bonds, or any other types of securities?

____ What are the balances of his or her accounts?

Of Accountants and Other Tax Professionals:

____ Did the decedent owe money for any prior tax year or was he or she entitled to a refund?

____ Are there any tax issues that must be addressed immediately?

Because of the increased problem of identify theft and privacy issues, most institutions will not provide this information by phone and will request that you submit your question in writing. The letter on page 72 is a sample letter than can easily be adopted for any of the above questions.

Isabel Jones
22773 Marilyn Drive
Laguna Niguel, CA 92677

The Troy Company
748 Mission Blvd
Fullerton, CA 92835

Re: The estate of Randall Jones
Account #: 9781-4531-7852

To Whom It May Concern:

I represent the estate of Randall Jones. Mr. Jones passed away on February 27, 2007. I am related to the decedent, as he was my father.

For identification purposes, the decedent's Social Security number was 909-12-1256 and his date of birth was March 18, 1924. Enclosed for your review is a certified copy of the death certificate.

At this time, it is necessary to determine the following:
What is the current balance on the account?
Is there a co-signor named on the account or anyone else who has guaranteed the account?

Accordingly, please be so kind as to provide the information as soon as possible.

Very truly yours,

PART TWO:
ESTATE ADMINISTRATION

CHAPTER 8:

LOCATING, ORGANIZING, ITEMIZING, AND CATEGORIZING THE ASSETS AND LIABILITIES OF AN ESTATE

When a client contacts my office seeking representation, I tell him or her to bring as much information available about the estate's assets. However, when he or she appears for the appointment, instead of carrying boxes and files, he is empty-handed and often proclaims, "I cannot find anything. Dad had his own system for recordkeeping. I don't know where to begin," or "All I could find was Mom's checkbook but not the bank statements. Bills are coming in that need to be paid but the bank won't tell me what the balance in the account is."

Since planning for the inevitable is not something we want to think about, let alone actually plan for, often the decedent has left little in the way of organized records. Perhaps it is because many of us prefer to maintain a sense of privacy when it comes to our financial situation. However, as a result of no planning, locating the assets and determining the liabilities of an estate is sometimes the most time consuming task for the representative.

Regardless of whether the assets of the estate are subject to a formal probate, as discussed in Chapter 9, or may be transferred by affidavit or summary probate, which is discussed in Chapter 13, your role includes making a thorough search to locate all of the assets of the estate.

PRACTICAL POINT. You can be held personally liable for any additional taxes and penalties that are due on assets that are discovered after the estate has been distributed.

LOCATING THE ASSETS OF AN ESTATE

The most common assets found in an estate are:

• Social Security and other government benefits;

• pension, annuity, and insurance benefits;

• real estate;

• motor vehicles;

• savings accounts;

• life insurance and annuities;

• retirement accounts, including 401(k)s and individual retirement accounts;

• credit union accounts;

• brokerage accounts; and,

• stocks and bonds.

How do you begin a search to locate assets? Assuming you know little or nothing about the decedent's estate, the following is an *asset map* that may lead to the discovery of assets and liabilities of the estate.

Examine Checkbooks, Bank Statements, and Cancelled Checks

Locating checkbooks, bank statements and cancelled checks is an excellent place to start, as these documents may identify assets as well as the sources of income that the assets may produce.

To illustrate, a checking account statement reveals that every month the decedent received an automatic deposit for the same amount. Upon closer examination, the statement includes the name of an annuity company with an account number. By calling the company, you can obtain the value of the annuity. In the same conversation, you find out that the annuity company issues a 1099 tax reporting statement at the end of each year that reports the total amount of income that the decedent received for the past twelve months. Had you not examined the checking account statement, you may have never discovered this asset.

Examining cancelled checks and checking account statements may also lead to the discovery of other assets. For example, a checking account statement may show an annual charge for a safe-deposit box rental. Upon opening the box, you may discover that the decedent was storing jewelry and other valuable assets. Also, cancelled checks may reveal checks recently written to a real estate broker for a deposit to purchase a rental property.

Search the Residence

Your investigation should include making a thorough search of the residence, including looking under mattresses and behind books. This may sound like an overwhelming task, but there are many people who still do not trust banks to keep their savings.

SUE'S STORY

Sue's mother told my client that she kept her most valuable pieces of jewelry in an empty Maxwell House coffee can on the second shelf of the refrigerator. The older woman feared that, if she died, her two daughter-in-laws would take inventory of her jewelry before her daughter could arrive from out of state. This was her way of protecting her jewelry. Sure enough, when Sue arrived, she was greeted with such questions as, "Didn't Mom have a string of pearls? I know I have seen her wear them."

Search Online for Unclaimed Property

All fifty states have websites with links to *unclaimed property*—that is, property that has been forwarded to the state after there has been no activity on an account. The account holder, whether it is a bank or other financial institution, must turn the asset over to the state. This can occur whether the owner of the account is alive or has passed away. If the asset is still not claimed after a set period of time, the asset *escheats*, or becomes the property of the state, and the lawful owner can no longer make a claim for it. The most common types of assets that are turned over to state governments include:

- bank accounts that have remained dormant for as little as five years;
- refund checks for which the issuing company could not locate the recipient;
- insurance premium refunds due to overpayments for which the recipient cannot be found; and,
- jewelry and other items of personal property that have been left in safe-deposit boxes where the owner failed to pay the annual rental fees to maintain the box and the bank turned over the contents of the box to the state.

As the representative, you can search for unclaimed property by simply entering the decedent's name and Social Security number on the state's website. A state-by-state list of state addresses and websites is provided in Appendix D.

If an asset is listed, the site will describe the asset as well as its value. In addition, the site will provide specific instructions for how you, as the representative, can claim the asset on behalf of the estate. In most cases, you will need to complete a form and provide a certified copy of the death certificate along with some documentation that establishes your legal authority to represent the estate. This may require producing letters of administration. For a complete discussion of letters of administration, please see Chapter 9.

> **PRACTICAL POINT.** There are many companies that will perform searches for you and charge, as their fee, a percentage of the value of the asset that is discovered. I strongly discourage using these services, since the Internet has made the search so simple that it makes no sense to give up a fee for something you can easily do yourself.

Review Online Bank and Brokerage Statements

Because of the convenience of online banking, many consumers have opted to receive their monthly statements online rather than in the mail. As a result, information that you may need is stored on the decedent's computer or only available by accessing the banking institution's website. Unless you have the decedent's password and screen name, this information will not be readily available.

Banking institutions, however, are generally sensitive to the need to have access to information about a decedent and will often issue new passwords, provided that you can satisfy their legal requirements of proving your relationship to the decedent. In most instances, this will require producing a certified copy of the death certificate along with written authority authorizing you to act on behalf of the estate. See Chapter 9 for a more complete discussion.

Obtain Current Bank Statements

You may locate a bank statement only to find it is not current, or that the account is closed. To obtain accurate information, you will need to contact the bank or other financial institution and provide them with documentation establishing your legal authority. If a probate has been commenced, the bank will require court documentation. If a probate will not be required, the financial institution will usually require an affidavit stating that a probate will not be filed. The following sample letter can be used when a probate action has not been filed. Though you do not have to use to exact language, what is important is that the financial institution is aware that a probate is not pending.

ABC Bank
100 South Laguna Road
Fullerton, CA 92835

Re: Estate of Joan Lynch
Social Security Number: 550-00-0000

Attn: Accounts

To Whom It May Concern:

Please be advised that I represent the estate of Joan Lynch, who passed away on May 31, 2007. Enclosed please find a certified copy of the death certificate.

It is my understanding that Ms. Lynch may have had a savings account with your bank, account # 444-33-22222.

At this time, there is no probate pending, as the total value of the assets is less than $100,000 and therefore exempt from the requirements of probate under California Probate Code Section 13100. Therefore, it is my intention to transfer the assets without the need for court approval.

Accordingly, please provide me with a current statement balance as of the date of this letter. In the alternative, if the account has been closed, please verify the date that the account was closed, as well as the closing balance.

Very truly yours,

The filing of a probate may not be required if all of the assets were held in trust and if the value of the assets is less than what is prescribed by state law. (See Appendix C for a state-by-state summary of probate requirements.) Regardless, bank statements should be obtained as soon as possible, as the name on the account will immediately indicate how the account was held—that is, in the name of the decedent alone or in the name of his or her trust. Further, if a probate is necessary, the probate petition requires that the assets are listed. By having the bank statements, the representative will be able to itemize the assets and their respective values—though this can always be amended.

If a probate is required, the court will need to be presented with court documentation of the probate, including a copy of the court order appointing you as the administrator.

Review the Decedent's Mail

A review of the decedent's mail is another great source for locating assets and liabilities of the estate. As mail will continued to be generated until the sender is notified of a death, mail will reveal the names of creditors that the decedent owed money to, as well as sources for income such as pensions, annuities, and dividends. If the estate is responsible for paying creditors as discussed in Chapter 14, the decedent's mail will identify the names of potential creditors. For a complete discussion of providing notice to creditors, please see Chapter 10.

PRACTICAL POINT. As discussed in Chapter 6, you should apply for a change of address for the decedent's mail, since you do not want mail to accumulate, especially if you are out of town and it is impractical for you to retrieve mail on a regular basis. The United States Postal Service will require you to complete a change of address form, which establishes your legal authority to receive mail on behalf of the decedent. This form is available at any post office, as well as online at **www.usps.gov**. It is recommended that you review the decedent's mail for at least six months.

EXAMINE THE CONTENTS OF A SAFE-DEPOSIT BOX

The opening of a safe-deposit box can be dramatic or disappointing, as was Geraldo Rivera's televised opening of Al Capone's vault. However, there is always some mystique as to what will be found behind the closed doors.

RICARDO'S STORY

Ricardo was one of the early pioneers of Las Vegas. When he died, I arranged to have his safe-deposit box drilled open, since the representative could not find the key. As we waited in anticipation, we wondered whether there would be stacks of money or bars of gold. As the lid to the box was lifted, the bank employee gingerly removed a faded manila envelope. However, instead of greenbacks inside, she removed three romance novels and nothing else. Bupkes. Zilch. Nada. Ricardo must have been laughing from wherever he was.

If the decedent had previously arranged to have you sign a signature card so that you had access to the safe-deposit box, you can examine the box without having to provide any legal authority to the bank. However, if you have learned that a safe-deposit box exists but your name is not authorized, state laws vary as to whether or not you may gain access.

In some states, if you have the key to the box and can prove your relationship to the decedent, a box may be opened for the limited purpose of retrieving a will and inventorying the contents of the box. However, the box's contents cannot be removed. This is to ensure that all contents are accounted for so as to prevent an estate from failing to declare an asset's value and avoid having to pay taxes.

If You Do Not Have the Key to the Box

What happens if you discover a safe-deposit box but cannot locate the key? This situation is much more common than you might imagine. Opening a safe-deposit box requires two keys—the one that was given to the owner of the box by the bank and the one used by the bank. The box will not open unless both keys are inserted. The only way of opening the box if the key is missing is to drill open the lock.

Provided you can establish your legal authority to gain access to the box, all banks have procedures to drill open the lock. To do so, you will need to make an appointment with the bank, which will arrange for a locksmith to meet you and the bank representative at a designated time. The bank will charge you for the cost of drilling out the lock and will typically add on an administrative fee.

PRACTICAL POINT. Never assume that a safe-deposit box does not exist simply because bank statements do not reveal a box rental charge. Many banks offer free boxes to their customers if they maintain a certain balance. Accordingly, you should inquire with all banks where the decedent had accounts to determine if a box exists.

> ### LEGALLY SPEAKING
>
> **In most states, whether you hold the key is irrelevant. If you are not a signor on the safe-deposit box, the only way that you can gain access is with court authority. This includes producing the death certificate along with letters of authority, which are issued by the court. For a more complete discussion, see Chapter 10.**

DISCOVERY OF EMBARRASSING ASSETS

In *My Wishes*, (Sourcebooks, 2006) I advise readers never to leave anything that can be discovered after their passing that could be later perceived as embarrassing. If you have worked hard during your lifetime to protect your reputation, it would be unfortunate to have it tarnished by an heir uncovering something that brings into question your character after you are gone.

As the representative, you may face a moral dilemma in deciding how to manage a discovery that challenges the character of the deceased. As there is no textbook on handling such a situation, I often tell my clients to decide on the side that protects rather than embarrasses. As the decedent is no longer here to defend him- or herself, you are now his or her spokesperson and you should strive to protect his or her reputation. Further, unless the discovery involved a criminal activity, you should protect the decedent's secret. If, however, you use a discovery to commit a crime, you could face criminal liability.

If your investigation of assets reveals criminal activity, you have a legal obligation to report the criminal act to the appropriate parties. If you do not, your inaction can be viewed as condoning the act, which could lead to criminal charges being filed against you.

EARL'S STORY

Earl's son was killed in a traffic accident. His only major asset was a home. He did not have a will. Earl's son always bragged to his father that he had a green thumb and that his crop was bountiful. Upon inspection, Earl realized why. His son was growing marijuana. He promptly called the police, and they confiscated the crop.

DISCOVERING STOCKS AND BONDS

If the decedent had stocks or bonds that were invested with a stock brokerage company, the monthly brokerage statement would provide a list of the account's assets and their values. In addition, a review of the decedent's tax returns would include any interest or dividend income that has been reported from the brokerage company.

> **PRACTICAL POINT.** The decedent may have purchased stocks and bonds and maintained possession of the actual certificates rather than keeping them on deposit with a brokerage firm. Upon discovering these assets, you should place the original documents in a safe place and make copies of the certificates, which should be kept separate from their originals.

Determining the Value of Stock Certificates

Even though you have located stock and bond certificates, that does not mean that the company that issued the certificates is still in business. The company may have filed bankruptcy and the certificates are now worthless. However, before you assume that those 5,000 shares of Atlas Mining are destined for the dumpster, there are many ways you can quickly check online to determine if the company still exists. One popular option is **http://finance.yahoo.com**. You can either enter the stock or bond symbol or look up the company name.

RAVI'S STORY

When Ravi's uncle passed away, he discovered a box that contained at least fifty stock certificates for companies he had never heard of, along with some famous ones that terminated their life in bankruptcy court. In the pile was Pan Am stock. Being an e-bay junkie, Ravi did a search and found that Pan Am certificates were a collectors' item. He promptly listed them for sale, and with the proceeds he and his wife enjoyed a fine evening of dining at their favorite restaurant.

REVIEW CORRESPONDENCE FROM ATTORNEYS AND OTHER PROFESSIONALS

A review of correspondence may reveal a potential claim that would otherwise go undiscovered. For example, the decedent may have been involved in an accident or may have been considering pursuing a claim for money owing to him or her. It is your responsibility to investigate whether this asset is worth pursuing.

WRONGFUL DEATH CLAIMS

A *wrongful death claim* exists when the cause of the decedent's death was not due to an illness but instead an injury caused by some other party. In such a case, the estate may be entitled to pursue a claim against the party. To illustrate, suppose that the decedent was killed in a car accident caused by a negligent driver who is liable. You would then pursue a wrongful death action against the insurance carrier of the negligent driver.

In all matters where there exists a potential claim, it is your responsibility as the representative to make an initial evaluation. It is also strongly advisable that you consult with a personal injury attorney who specializes in wrongful death actions.

CARLOS'S STORY

Pedro's father, Carlos, went to his doctor for abdominal pain. He was otherwise in good health. His doctor scheduled a colonoscopy. During the procedure, the probe pierced the small intestine. Within days, Carlos was fighting a high fever. He returned to the hospital, where it was discovered that he had a large abscess caused by the initial procedure. Despite several rounds of antibiotic therapy, he never fully recovered, always complaining of abdominal discomfort. Nine months later, Carlos died. The initial cause of death was listed as a heart attack, but Pedro successfully brought a lawsuit against the hospital and doctor for medical malpractice, linking Carlos's death to the negligence of the physician.

LEGALLY SPEAKING

As in all causes of actions that are a result of injuries, state laws impose very strict time limits in which a lawsuit must be filed or the case cannot be pursued. In some states, if a death was caused as result of a governmental entity, the statute of limitations is only six months after the death occurred.

REVIEW PAST TAX RETURNS

Tax returns filed for previous years may reveal sources of income that are assets of the estate. For example, if the decedent had written a book, composed music, or created any work that was published, the estate may be entitled to royalties. However, payments are typically not paid monthly and bank account records may not provide any information. Further, if the material was published many years ago, there is also the possibility that royalties or copyrights have not been paid on a regular basis. Accordingly, you should closely examine past tax returns, which would list what is classified as *miscellaneous income*, to discover the sources of any copyright and royalty payments.

REVIEW CORRESPONDENCE FROM REAL ESTATE AND TITLE INSURANCE COMPANIES

If the decedent sold a piece of property close in time to his or her passing, there may not have been any payments made yet. There are also situations in which the terms of the loan call for only one payment, known as a *balloon payment*, that is made some time in the future.

Discovering such assets could be tricky if there has not been any past evidence of payment. Therefore, your search should focus on any correspondence with real estate and title companies that may have been involved in preparing the deeds and mortgage. You should also closely examine bank account deposit records to look for any larger deposits that seem out of the ordinary.

ITEMIZING THE ASSETS

After all of the assets have been collected, they need to be itemized. At this point, all this means is that you need to make an accurate record of all of the assets and liabilities. It is not necessary at this time to assign value.

Grouping Assets

As already stated, the task of locating assets can be very time-consuming. However, when locating and listing assets, there are some shortcuts you can take when grouping assets. Specifically, no one expects you to count every book on the shelf or every dinner plate in the dining room cabinet. Instead, you can list the items of personal property as "dishes" and "books." However, if there are items of personal property, such as artwork or collections, that you believe have value as they appear to be more than ordinary household items, they must be individually listed.

ROB'S STORY

Rob called me to say he was at his dad's house and had found a collection of Nazi memorabilia. Specifically, there were badges, knives, medals, and hats all bearing the Nazi symbol. He assumed his father, who served in WWII, brought them back from Europe and kept them all these years. Because some people collect this questionable form of memorabilia, I advised Rob to put them on the inventory list.

CATEGORIZING THE ASSETS AND LIABILITIES

Now that you have completed your search and have taken inventory of the assets, the next step is to categorize the assets. That is, you must determine whether the asset was solely owned by the decedent, whether the asset was owned by the decedent jointly with someone else, or whether the asset was the property of the decedent's trust. Only the assets and liabilities of the decedent may be subject to a probate action. That is, assets that are jointly held or are in a trust are not subject to probate. Assets that must be probated are known as *probateable assets* and are fully discussed in Chapter 9.

LEGALLY SPEAKING

Assets that are in the names of both the decedent and the decedent's spouse become the property of the surviving spouse. These assets are known as *joint tenancy assets*, as they *inure* (or pass) to the benefit of the surviving joint tenant. Such assets should be separated from the assets of the estate.

WHEN A SAFE-DEPOSIT BOX IS JOINTLY OWNED

If two or more names are on a safe-deposit box, it would seem logical to presume that the contents are also jointly owned. In a husband and wife situation, upon the passing of one spouse, the contents would become the property of the surviving spouse.

However, it would be wrong to automatically accept this presumption. Property acquired before marriage and property acquired by way of inheritance is deemed separate property, and such assets should not be categorized until you have some sufficient proof as to the history of how the asset was acquired. For example, an autographed baseball signed by Mickey Mantle that a husband owned before his marriage would probably become part of the estate, as it was not joint property.

PRACTICAL POINT. Most courts apply the rule that, with the exception of women's jewelry, which is presumed to have been the property of a deceased female, any evidence that would suggest that the property is not jointly owned will be considered by the court.

CHAPTER 9:
NAVIGATING THE SEA OF PROBATE

Not all estates are subject to a long, drawn-out probate process. For example, if the decedent left a few items of personal property of little value, your role may be limited to distributing the property to the intended heirs named in the will.

However, as probate laws vary from state to state, whether some type of probate is required is determined by the value of the estate. To illustrate, in the state of Washington, a formal probate is not required if the estate is valued at less than $60,000. In California, the estate must be over $100,000 to trigger a formal probate.

In some states, if the estate's value is less that what the decedent's state of residence requires for a formal, court-supervised probate, the assets may be transferred by an affidavit signed by you attesting under oath as to the estate's value.

In other states, however, the courts may impose what is known as a *summary probate*, in which court filings are required but the process is abbreviated because the estate is valued under a certain amount.

To add to the confusion, even when the value exceeds what the state has established for requiring a formal probate, if the asset is of a certain type, probate may not be necessary. In California, for example, a mobile home, regardless of its value, may be transferred to the intended beneficiaries if it is owned free and clear. Upon the owner's passing, all that is required is for the representative to provide the Department of Motor Vehicles with a certified copy of the death certificate so that title can be transferred.

Finally, assets that are jointly owned—as in a husband and wife situation, or in a state that recognizes community property—become the property of the surviving spouse and therefore avoid probate.

This chapter discusses the formal probate process. Appendix C provides a state-by-state summary of probate laws. Chapter 13 discusses transferring assets by affidavit or summary probate proceedings. Chapter 18 discusses types of property that may be exempt from the probate process.

UNDERSTANDING THE NEED FOR A FORMAL PROBATE

Administration of a decedent's estate involves, among other things, probating the estate, collecting the decedent's assets, calculating and paying estate taxes, and distributing remaining assets.

An *estate* is the total property owned by the decedent prior to the distribution of that property in accordance with the terms of a will, or when there is no will, by the laws of inheritance in the state in which the decedent lived. The process known as probate was instituted for many reasons:

- to determine if a will is valid (The job of the probate court is to decide the validity of the will, which is generally a routine affair. However, if a court invalidates the document, persons who may have been beneficiaries under a will may not share in the estate. This becomes important if a person was omitted from a will that is now not valid.);
- to officially appoint the person named in a will to be the representative (It is a misconception that someone who is named as representative will be the representative. Instead, the court must determine if that person is the right person to serve. Also, heirs of the estate have the opportunity to challenge the person's appointment or to contest the will. A person who challenges a will, or part of a will, must file an objection with the court within a specified amount of time. Will contests are more fully discussed later in this chapter.);

- if there is no will, to appoint a person to administer the estate (Typically, a surviving spouse or child of the decedent will petition the court to be appointed.);
- to ensure that the property covered by the will is shown to be the decedent's;
- if there is no will, to distribute the property in accordance with the inheritance laws of the state where the decedent lived;
- to safeguard the estate from allowing a person to run free with the estate's assets to the detriment of the other heirs (Requiring court supervision ensures that assets cannot be distributed without court permission and approval first being obtained.);
- to distribute the assets of the estate;
- to ensure that the persons who may be receiving distribution are capable of receiving the distribution (Specifically, if there are minor children named in a will, courts will not allow children to receive money until they reach a certain age. Therefore, probate is necessary to protect the children's assets. Further, if a named individual is incompetent due to a mental disability, the court has the power to appoint someone on behalf of that person, again to safeguard the assets for the intended person.);
- to protect creditors and other entities that may be owed money from the estate (This is done by requiring the estate to put such creditors on notice so that they can file claims against the estate for payment.);
- to allow and approve fees for administration of the estate; and,
- to close the estate.

GETTING STARTED: INITIATING A PROBATE ACTION

There are four steps involved in initiating a probate action:

1. filing the petition;
2. locating and attaching the original will to the petition;
3. providing written notice; and,
4. having the court approve the petition.

PROBATE TIME LINE

The following time line is typical for a probate consisting of only real property.

- File Petition for Probate

4–5 Weeks

- Hearing on petition, at which court will:
    - issue letters and order and determine necessity for bond

Or

    - not approve appointment if a will contest is filed or a representative's qualifications are challenged

Next Four Months

- Creditor Claim Period
    - send notice to creditors
    - prepare Inventory and Appraisal form
    - make initial assessment of tax liability
    - allow or reject creditors' claims
    - may sell real property
    - may make initial distribution of specific gifts

After Four Months

- File petition for final accounting and distribution
- Apply for final hearing
- Final hearing, at which court approves accounting and distribution
    - assets are distributed to heirs
    - bond (if any) is terminated
    - final discharge order is signed

(NOTE: this time line is only an estimate. The complexity of issues can greatly effect how long the probate process will take.)

STEP ONE: FILING THE PETITION FOR PROBATE

Anyone who has an interest in the estate may file a petition for probate. This includes the person named in the will to be the representative, heirs of the decedent, and creditors. Although state laws vary as to the information required to be included in the petition, most states have court-approved forms. These forms are available from the clerk of the court.

Note that, with the exception of attaching the will to the petition, the filing process is the same whether or not the decedent had a will.

A typical probate petition includes the following information:
- a statement of your interest in the estate;
- a request that you be appointed as representative;
- your date of birth and Social Security number;
- names and addresses of the spouse and children of decedent, and of other heirs;
- where the decedent resided;
- date of the will; and,
- estimated value of the estate.

Almost all states have made their probate forms available online. To search, enter key phrases in online search tools, such as, "Missouri court probate forms." However, so that you have all the necessary forms before you file the papers with the court, it is worth your time to visit the clerk of the court, who will advise you as to all the required forms that you will need.

PRACTICAL POINT. The *Uniform Probate Code* reduces the complexity of a formal estate administration by developing user-friendly forms. The following states have adopted this code: Alaska, Arizona, Colorado, Florida, Hawaii, Idaho, Maine, Minnesota, Montana, Nebraska, New Mexico, North Dakota, South Carolina, South Dakota, and Utah.

Appendix C provides a summary of the probate codes for each state. To review your state's probate code online, visit **www.findlaw.com/casecode/#statelaw**.

THE ROLE OF AN ATTORNEY

Your decision to use an attorney or not is often based on the complexity or simplicity of the issues concerning the estate. If there is only one heir, or the estate consists of only a home and some bank accounts, it is common for a person to represent the estate without an attorney.

However, when there are major assets, or the distribution to heirs is not equal, it is advisable that you at least have a consultation with an attorney prior to filing the probate petition. The following are some additional scenarios where the assistance of an attorney may be in the best interest of the estate:

- there are assets of the estate that will be required to be sold to pay the creditors who have filed liens against the decedent during his or her lifetime;
- there is an ongoing business that needs to be managed;
- the decedent had filed a lawsuit or was being sued;
- the decedent's death may have been caused by the negligent act of another;
- the decedent has not filed personal tax returns for one or more years;
- the estate will owe federal taxes; or,
- you suspect that the will may be challenged by an heir or some other interested party.

PRACTICAL POINT. Sometimes, guiding an estate through the probate process and effectively administering the estate require a keen understanding of the probate and tax laws. If you need help in administering an estate, contact an attorney experienced in probate and estate administration to ensure that the most effective administration of the estate takes place. Please see Chapter 20, which more fully discusses the role of an attorney.

WHERE TO FILE THE PETITION

The petition must be filed in the county where the person resided at the time of his or her death. Unfortunately, determining residency is not always obvious. For example, imagine that the decedent had a home in Orange County, California but lived the last sixty days of his life in a nursing home in Los Angeles County. Should the petition be filed in Orange or L.A. County? Where to file is usually resolved by examining where the decedent intended to *permanently reside*. Such factors to be considered include:

- where the decedent received his or her mail;
- where the decedent voted;
- the address that the decedent used for employment;
- the address stated on the decedent's driver's license; and,
- the address the decedent used on tax returns.

For example, say the decedent lived half of the year in Palm Springs, California and the other half of the year in San Diego. Her driver's license, however, reflects the San Diego address. Accordingly, file the petition in San Diego.

> **PRACTICAL POINT.** On some forms, the petition asks, "where was the decedent domiciled at the date of death?" The word *domiciled* is synonymous with *resided*.

ANCILLARY PROBATE

If the decedent owned real estate in more than one state, it may be necessary to file what is known as an *ancillary proceeding* in order to probate property located in a state other than where the probate action is pending. This is because probate courts have *in rem jurisdiction*, or authority only over real property that is in the state where the court is located.

Ancillary probate is a scaled-down probate proceeding that governs only the assets located in that state. To initiate an ancillary probate, you will need to inquire with the probate court in the county where the real property is located as to that court's procedure. Typically, the ancillary probate court will require documentation to prove that there is an ongoing probate action in another state. This may include providing copies of the will along with any orders that the court has issued authorizing you to act. After you satisfy the probate court's requirements, the court will issue an order allowing the real property be transferred into the estate.

> **PRACTICAL POINT.** If you discover assets in another state but do not include these assets in the probate action, you will not be able to transfer the out-of-state asset at a later time without going back into court.

RICK'S STORY

Sam passed away in California and a probate action was commenced by his son Rick. The probate included Sam's home, but Rick elected not to include in the probate the lot that his dad owned in Bozeman, Montana, as he believed the value of the lot was nominal. Twenty years later, the lot was worth over $65,000. When he attempted to sell the lot, he learned that the property could not be transferred without a court order. Rick contacted my office and we coordinated with an attorney in Bozeman to file a probate solely for the purpose of allowing Rick to transfer the property.

STEP TWO: PRODUCING THE ORIGINAL WILL

If the decedent left a will, most states require that the original will, and not a copy, be attached to the petition. This is because the original will must be authenticated by the court to be valid. Along with the original will, you are required to attach what is commonly known as a *proof of subscribing witness*, which is a statement by one of the witnesses to the will who watched the testator sign his or her name to the will.

If All the Witnesses Are Deceasd or Cannot Be Located

What if you are unable to locate at least one of the witnesses? In these situations, if the will was prepared by an attorney, the courts will often accept a declaration from the attorney that he or she prepared the will. If the will was not prepared by an attorney, state laws vary as to other offers of proof that would be acceptable to validate the will.

When the Original Will Cannot Be Found

If you have located only a copy of the decedent's will, do not automatically assume that the original will does not exist. Refer to the following suggestions in your efforts to find the original will.

• Search the local probate court that may have accepted the will for safekeeping.

In some states, it is common practice to file the original will with the probate court. Upon filing, the court provides a receipt and stamps a copy of the will, known as a *conformed copy*, stating that the original will has been filed.

• Contact the lawyer whom you believe prepared the will.

Most wills, including copies, have the name of the attorney who prepared the will printed on the will or a will jacket. If you know the name of the attorney whom you believe prepared the will, contact his or her office. It is a common practice for attorneys to hold wills or copies of wills for an indefinite period of time. If the attorney has passed away, retired, or sold his or her practice, the state bar of each state has specific procedures in place to safeguard client files.

• If the decedent left a safe-deposit box, search the box.

If there is a safe-deposit box and you are on the signature card, you should examine the box as soon as possible. If you are not a signatory on the box, you will need to petition the probate court to gain access to the box. Please see Chapter 9 for a complete discussion about gaining access to a safe-deposit box.

• Publish a notice in the newspaper seeking information about the will.

The following is an example of a notice that you can publish in a newspaper seeking information about the decedent's will. Note that publishing a notice to find the will is not a legal proceeding, and therefore any notice that might lead to learning whether a will was signed is acceptable.

JAMES RONDELL, DECEASED

James Rondell died on March 1, 2007. His last known address was:

161 Franklin Boulevard, Long Beach, New York

If you have the original or copy of his will, please contact:

Dennis Berkowsky, Attorney at Law

68 West Park Avenue

Long Beach, New York 11561

PRACTICAL POINT. If all attempts to locate the original will have proved futile, you will need to check the court's policy for allowing a copy of the will to be admitted as a substitute for the original. Note, as part of the will validation process, the court will require testimony about how you came into possession of the copy, in order to prove your truthfulness. The court will then decide if the copy of the will should be allowed as a true substitute for the original.

STEP THREE: GIVING NOTICE

After you file the petition with the court, the court will assign a hearing date, which typically will occur within forty-five days of the day the petition was filed. As part of the probate process, you are required to provide *notice* to the heirs of the estate and all of the beneficiaries named in the will that a probate action has been commenced.

Giving notice requires more than simply telling someone that a petition has been filed. You must strictly follow the court-approved procedure for sending notice, which may include providing a copy of the probate petition and of the will to each heir and beneficiary. In addition, each heir and beneficiary must be advised as to the date, time, and place of the hearing.

Further, you are required to provide to the court the names and addresses of all of the persons to whom notice was sent. This is known as the *proof of notice*. If the court determines that a party did not receive proper notice, it will *continue* the hearing (postpone it until a later date) until you have complied with all of the court's notice requirements.

In addition to providing notice to the heirs and beneficiaries of the will, you must publish in a newspaper a copy of the court petition. This is what is known as a *legal notice*—providing notice to the world that a probate action has commenced. Providing such notice allows any person who may believe that he or she has a claim against the estate to have an opportunity to present his or her claim. Though these notices are often placed in the classified sections of newspapers and are rarely read by the general public, they are scrutinized by credit card companies and other creditors on the chance that the decedent owed money to the creditor.

Adhering to the court's procedures for providing proper notice can be very confusing. The following are common questions and answers concerning notice.

Is it always required to provide notice of a probate petition?
No. The notice procedures are required only when the value of the estate exceeds a certain amount as established by state law. Accordingly, if the estate's assets may be transferred by a summary probate procedure, as discussed in Chapter 13, notice is not required.

Who has the responsibility of sending notice of probate?
The person seeking court approval for appointment as the representative must send notice.

When does the proof of notice of probate have to be filed with the court?
You must provide the court with the names and addresses of all persons who received notice. This proof of notice typically must be filed with the court at least ten days prior to the hearing.

Who is entitled to receive notice?
The following persons are entitled to receive notice:
- the surviving spouse of the decedent, if any;
- all heirs at law of the decedent, whether or not there is a will and whether or not they are listed to receive a distribution; and,
- all living and ascertained beneficiaries named in the will and any beneficiaries of any trust created by the will.

STEP FOUR: THE INITIAL PROBATE HEARING

When the petition is filed, the court will assign a hearing date. At the hearing, the court will consider whether:
- the will is valid;
- you should be appointed as the representative;
- all persons who are entitled to receive notice have been properly notified; and,
- a bond should be required.

In addition, the court will consider any arguments from interested parties who object to your appointment or object to the will.

PROVING THE VALIDITY OF THE WILL

The validity of a will is dependent upon several elements being found in the will. Specifically, the will must be:
- in writing;
- signed and dated by the testator (maker of the will); and,
- signed in the presence of two or more impartial parties who also sign and date a declaration that they witnessed the testator place his or her signature on the document.

It is a common misbelief that a testator's signature must be notarized. Although some states require that the maker of the will have his or her signature notarized, having your signature notarized will not satisfy the requirements for a valid will if the state where the testator resides requires that the testator's signature be witnessed. Therefore, notarizing a document may not be a substitute for a will to be witnessed. Notarizing a document is not a substitute for a will to be witnessed.

Finally, most states require that the witnesses be at least 18 years of age and not named as beneficiaries in the will, so as to prevent a challenge to the will based on fraud. If witnesses are named as beneficiaries in the will, this may invalidate the will because they may have influenced the testator in making the will. As a result, the estate may have to be distributed as if the testator died without a will. This is known as *intestate succession* and is more fully discussed in Chapter 11.

HANDWRITTEN WILLS

The requirement that a will must be in writing typically means that it has to be typed or printed. However, some states allow a will to be admissible if it is handwritten and signed by the decedent. This is known as a *holographic will*. If a will is handwritten, it cannot be witnessed.

To be valid, a handwritten will should not contain the writing of anyone else on the face of the document. To illustrate, if the maker of the will writes on a piece of paper that also contained someone else's handwriting, many courts will invalidate the will if as it is not entirely in the handwriting of the maker of the will. However, handwriting does not include what is printed. Therefore, if a person used hotel stationery that bore the Hilton Hotel icon on the top of the page, it would not invalidate the handwritten will if the testator used the stationery to write his or her will.

Please refer to Appendix C, which lists those states that permit holographic wills.

IF THE MAKER OF THE WILL WAS PHYICALLY UNABLE TO SIGN HIS OR HER NAME

I have prepared many wills in which the maker of the will was unable to sign his or her name. Instead, the testator placed an "X" or some other marking on the signature line. It is acceptable for a testator to sign his or her name with a mark to validate the will, provided the testator's name is written by someone following the mark, the marking is witnessed, and the witnesses acknowledge that they watched the maker of the will place his or her mark.

JOSH'S STORY

Josh's dad passed away. He had made a will and the will was executed with a mark. When I filed the will with the probate court, it was rejected because there was no statement from the witnesses attesting that they saw him sign with a mark. In his will, Josh's dad specifically omitted his estranged son, Jason, with whom he had had no contact for over twenty years. As the will was not accepted, the estate was now governed by the laws of intestate succession, which meant that Jason shared the estate equally with Josh.

WHEN THERE ARE TWO OR MORE WILLS

It is not uncommon to discover two or more wills. This may occur if an earlier will was drafted many years before the most recent will was made. The testator may not remember that there was an earlier will, and so he or she makes another will. The problem occurs when the two wills are different. For example, say that the decedent was not married when he made his first will in 1975 and left his estate to his parents. He later married in 1982 and had two children. In his latest will, he leaves his entire estate to his spouse and children. Most wills include language that revokes all previous wills. If that language is not found, the general rule is that the document bearing the most recent date supersedes all previous wills.

WHETHER YOU SHOULD BE APPOINTED

Any *interested party* (someone with a stake in the decedent's estate) can object to your appointment as representative. Such arguments against your appointment could include that you are not financially responsible. To illustrate, if you have recently filed bankruptcy and have had a long history of being unable to handle your own financial affairs, the court will entertain testimony that you are not the right person for the job. Other commonly raised arguments against a representative's appointment include:

- he or she may not be available to perform his or her responsibilities and that could delay the closing of the estate, or
- his or her reputation for honesty is suspect as he or she has a criminal history of committing crimes involving the handling of money.

In addition, family jealousy often raises its ugly head when someone simply does not like you and wants to take away your opportunity to represent the family.

PRACTICAL POINT. In all matters concerning whether you should be appointed, the court will listen carefully to all arguments for and against you. In such situations, it is advisable to consider retaining an attorney, as the hearing is what is known as *evidentiary* that is, it is a hearing where attorneys call witnesses to take the stand and testify. Attorneys who practice in the probate courts are familiar with the proper objections that may be raised to testimony, as well as how evidence is to be presented. Unless you are familiar with the court process, you could be denied appointment based on your failure to comply with the court rules of procedure.

THE REQUIREMENTS OF A SURETY BOND

The purpose of a bond is to protect the estate from the representative's mismanagement of the assets. That is a nice way of saying it will insure the estate against any losses in case the representative decides to run off to Atlantic City and gamble away all of the money.

Most wills contain a statement that "a bond is not required," or that "the filing of a bond is waived." Attorneys often suggest to their clients that this language be inserted when the client chooses as his or her representative someone whom he or she personally knows and trusts. As a bond is an insurance policy for which premiums must be paid out of the assets of the estate, many people feel that it is an unnecessary expense of the estate that can be avoided by a waiver. If a bond is required, the amount of the bond will at least equal the value of the estate.

Regardless of whether the will waives the bond, the court may still require that a bond be posted if the heirs of the estate come forward and provide testimony to the court on their concerns about your ability to effectively manage the estate. For example, if you have had credit problems or filed a personal bankruptcy, or if there are some other facts that would lead to the court questioning your ability to manage money, a bond may be required.

In addition, if you reside in a different state from where the petition for probate has been filed, most courts will require that a bond be posted.

LEGALLY SPEAKING

If there is no will, courts almost always require that a bond be posted.

PRIOR TO THE HEARING

Most petitions for probate are routinely approved and often do not require a court appearance. This is because no objections to the appointment were filed with the court and the court is satisfied with the qualifications of the representative. Further, some courts have *probate notes* that the court issues in advance of the court hearing; these advise whether the petition is approved and therefore your appearance is not required. If the court does issue probate notes, they may be accessed by calling the court and listening to a recorded message that recites the list of approved cases. More technologically advanced courts placed the notes online on the court's website. Note that most petitions are not reviewed until a few days before the hearing. Accordingly, you should not call the court too far in advance of the hearing.

WILL CONTESTS

The fact that the decedent left a will does not guarantee that the decedent's property will be distributed according to the terms of the will. A court must provide an opportunity to allow others to object to the will, and a challenge may be brought by anyone who feels the will is inaccurate or invalid in some way. No matter how much care was taken in drafting the will, the law does not prevent someone from bringing such an action.

Will contests are commonly filed by the following:
- an heir of the decedent who was specifically omitted in the will;
- an heir who believes his or her portion of the inheritance is not fair when compared with the amounts other heirs received;
- an unwed person who lived with the decedent but was not named in his or her will;
- a close friend who was told by the decedent that he or she was named in the will; or,
- estranged stepchildren.

A *will contest* is a trial heard in probate court wherein a judge or jury is called upon to decide if there is sufficient evidence to rule in the favor of the person who is contesting the will. It is a very difficult and costly process. To contest a will, one or more of the following must be proven.

- The maker of the will was not mentally competent at the time that the will was created.

A valid will requires that the decedent was of sound mind at the time the will was made. The *sound mind* requirement typically requires proof that the decedent had the ability to generally understand the nature and extent of the property to be disposed, his or her relationship to those who would naturally claim a benefit from the will, and the practical effect of the will as executed.

Proving that the decedent was mentally ill, under the influence of alcohol or drugs, or taking pain medication at the time the will was made are ways to establish incapacity. Likewise, if the testator had made a previous will and made a subsequent will close to the time of his or her passing, the court will entertain arguments that the testator may have been unduly influenced in making the later will.

LEGALLY SPEAKING

If the maker of the will commits suicide, the will is not automatically invalidated. However, the will could be subject to a will contest, as the mental state of the decedent at the time he or she executed the will may be questioned, especially if the decedent signed the will close in time to the suicide. If the decedent signed the will many years prior to his or her death, and at that time was not acting under any mental incapacity, a court would most likely find that the will is valid.

- The maker of the will did not believe he or she was signing a will but some other document.
- The maker of the will was acting under threat of harm by some other person.
- The maker of the will was acting under the undue influence of another.

If, at the time a decedent made his or her will, the decedent did not exercise his or her own judgment in making the will but rather made the will according to the wishes of another, the will may be found invalid on the grounds of undue influence. Coercion, duress, and fraud are examples of undue influence.

- The will did not comply with state law in terms of being properly witnessed or signed, or in the proper form.
- The testator's signature, or portions of or the entire will is a forgery.

MARLON'S STORY

Marlon Brando died in 2004, leaving an estate estimated to be worth over $20 million. Immediately prior to his death, he allegedly signed an amendment to his will, known as a *codicil*, altering the will's terms as well as naming new co-executors. His personal assistant, who was given a home in the original will but was excluded in the codicil, filed a will contest alleging that Brando's signature on the codicil was a forgery. She contended that Brando always placed a secret code consisting of dots between various letters of his name to distinguish his true signature from fakes. The suit was settled out of court in January of 2007.

- There is evidence that there was a later will that supersedes the first will.

The consequences of a will contest are significant to all the parties involved. If there is the possibility of a will contest, contact an attorney experienced in probate and estate administration to ensure that your rights are protected throughout the process. Note that these types of cases are difficult and emotionally charged. Therefore, it is important to find an attorney with whom you feel comfortable.

PRACTICAL POINT. Many will contests are dismissed from the start if the court believes that the claim has no merit. A will contest is also a very expensive procedure, as the party bringing the action usually has to bear the financial responsibility of retaining an attorney.

If the person contesting the will is not successful, he or she will have no legal means of seeking reimbursement for expenses incurred. Also, since trials proceed extremely slowly through the court process, it is not unusual for a will contest to take several years before the case sees the four walls of a courtroom. For these reasons, attorneys often recommend to their clients to make every effort to resolve any conflict and reach a settlement. A will contest should only be a last resort after exhausting all efforts to settle.

ANNA NICOLE'S STORY

One of the most celebrated will contests involves Anna Nicole Smith. Her case had traveled all the way to the United States Supreme Court to consider her argument as to whether her husband of 14 months was competent when he redid his will leaving her 50% of her estate. His children have been challenging the amended will based on the argument that their dad was not of sound mind. Finally, in May 2006, the United States Supreme Court sided with Ms. Smith, agreeing that she is entitled to some portion of her late husband's estate. In doing so, the court sent the matter back to a lower federal court, when Judge Ruth Bader Ginsburg, writing for the court, said "Smith should have a fresh chance to pursue claims in federal court." However, as a result of Anna Nicole's death, it must first be decided who will be her representative to continue her battle on behalf of the estate. Stay tuned.

If the validity of a will is successfully contested, the probate court may:

- disallow only that part of the will that is successfully challenged;
- admit an earlier valid will (if one was made) in its place; or,
- determine that the decedent died intestate and distribute the assets according to the state's intestate succession laws. (See Chapter 11 for a discussion of intestate succession.)

If the person contesting the will is successful, you are no longer in charge of the estate and must relinquish all control. Any documents that you have obtained, as well as assets that you have acquired, need to be turned over to the person the court has appointed as the new representative.

You may petition the court as a creditor of the estate seeking compensation for the time that you performed services for the estate. This petition may or not be granted, and it is recommended that you seek legal representation to do so.

CHAPTER 10:

FORMAL PROBATE:
THE NEXT STEPS

After the court approves the petition for probate, the court will sign an order officially appointing you as the representative of the estate. In addition, the court will issue what is commonly known as *letters of administration*. These letters are the walking instructions that outline your duties and authorities to act on behalf of the estate. With these letters, institutions that hold assets in the name of decedent will, upon your request, transfer the assets into an estate account. The letters give you broad powers, including the ability to liquidate and invest assets and to sell real estate.

> **PRACTICAL POINT.** It is a good idea to obtain certified copies of the court order and the letters, as banks and other institutions may require a certified order and not a photocopy before they will release any assets.

ACKNOWLEDGMENT OF RESPONSIBILITIES

As part of your appointment, the court will require that you sign an acknowledgment of your duties and liabilities. The following form, issued by California courts, is similar in content to the forms found in other states.

DE-147

ATTORNEY OR PARTY WITHOUT ATTORNEY *(Name, state bar number, and address):*

TELEPHONE NO.:   FAX NO. *(Optional):*

E–MAIL ADDRESS *(Optional):*

ATTORNEY FOR *(Name):*

SUPERIOR COURT OF CALIFORNIA, COUNTY OF

STREET ADDRESS:

MAILING ADDRESS:

CITY AND ZIP CODE:

BRANCH NAME:

ESTATE OF *(Name):*

DECEDENT

**DUTIES AND LIABILITIES OF PERSONAL REPRESENTATIVE
and Acknowledgment of Receipt**

CASE NUMBER:

DUTIES AND LIABILITIES OF PERSONAL REPRESENTATIVE

When the court appoints you as personal representative of an estate, you become an officer of the court and assume certain duties and obligations. An attorney is best qualified to advise you about these matters. You should understand the following:

1. MANAGING THE ESTATE'S ASSETS

a. Prudent investments

You must manage the estate assets with the care of a prudent person dealing with someone else's property. This means that you must be cautious and may not make any speculative investments.

b. Keep estate assets separate

You must keep the money and property in this estate separate from anyone else's, including your own. When you open a bank account for the estate, the account name must indicate that it is an estate account and not your personal account. Never deposit estate funds in your personal account or otherwise mix them with your or anyone else's property. Securities in the estate must also be held in a name that shows they are estate property and not your personal property.

c. Interest-bearing accounts and other investments

Except for checking accounts intended for ordinary administration expenses, estate accounts must earn interest. You may deposit estate funds in insured accounts in financial institutions, but you should consult with an attorney before making other kinds of investments.

d. Other restrictions

There are many other restrictions on your authority to deal with estate property. You should not spend any of the estate's money unless you have received permission from the court or have been advised to do so by an attorney. You may reimburse yourself for official court costs paid by you to the county clerk and for the premium on your bond. Without prior order of the court, you may not pay fees to yourself or to your attorney, if you have one. If you do not obtain the court's permission when it is required, you may be removed as personal representative or you may be required to reimburse the estate from your own personal funds, or both. You should consult with an attorney concerning the legal requirements affecting sales, leases, mortgages, and investments of estate property.

2. INVENTORY OF ESTATE PROPERTY

a. Locate the estate's property

You must attempt to locate and take possession of all the decedent's property to be administered in the estate.

b. Determine the value of the property

You must arrange to have a court-appointed referee determine the value of the property unless the appointment is waived by the court. You, rather than the referee, must determine the value of certain "cash items." An attorney can advise you about how to do this.

c. File an inventory and appraisal

Within four months after Letters are first issued to you as personal representative, you must file with the court an inventory and appraisal of all the assets in the estate.

Form Adopted for Mandatory Use
Judicial Council of California
DE-147 [Rev. January 1, 2002]

DUTIES AND LIABILITIES OF PERSONAL REPRESENTATIVE
(Probate)

Probate Code, § 8404

American LegalNet, Inc.
www.USCourtForms.com

ESTATE OF *(Name):*	CASE NUMBER:
DECEDENT	

d. File a change of ownership

At the time you file the inventory and appraisal, you must also file a change of ownership statement with the county recorder or assessor in each county where the decedent owned real property at the time of death, as provided in section 480 of the California Revenue and Taxation Code.

3. NOTICE TO CREDITORS

You must mail a notice of administration to each known creditor of the decedent within four months after your appointment as personal representative. If the decedent received Medi-Cal assistance, you must notify the State Director of Health Services within 90 days after appointment.

4. INSURANCE

You should determine that there is appropriate and adequate insurance covering the assets and risks of the estate. Maintain the insurance in force during the entire period of the administration.

5. RECORD KEEPING

a. Keep accounts

You must keep complete and accurate records of each financial transaction affecting the estate. You will have to prepare an account of all money and property you have received, what you have spent, and the date of each transaction. You must describe in detail what you have left after the payment of expenses.

b. Court review

Your account will be reviewed by the court. Save your receipts because the court may ask to review them. If you do not file your accounts as required, the court will order you to do so. You may be removed as personal representative if you fail to comply.

6. CONSULTING AN ATTORNEY

If you have an attorney, you should cooperate with the attorney at all times. You and your attorney are responsible for completing the estate administration as promptly as possible. **When in doubt, contact your attorney.**

NOTICE:
1. **This statement of duties and liabilities is a summary and is not a complete statement of the law. Your conduct as a personal representative is governed by the law itself and not by this summary.**
2. **If you fail to perform your duties or to meet the deadlines, the court may reduce your compensation, remove you from office, and impose other sanctions.**

ACKNOWLEDGMENT OF RECEIPT

1. I have petitioned the court to be appointed as a personal representative.

2. My address and telephone number are *(specify):*

3. I acknowledge that I have received a copy of this statement of the duties and liabilities of the office of personal representative.

Date:

(TYPE OR PRINT NAME)   (SIGNATURE OF PETITIONER)

Date:

(TYPE OR PRINT NAME)   (SIGNATURE OF PETITIONER)

CONFIDENTIAL INFORMATION: If required to do so by local court rule, you must provide your date of birth and driver's license number on supplemental Form DE-147S. (Prob. Code, § 8404(b).)

Requirement of a Bond

If, as part of the court order, the court requires that you obtain a bond (see Chapter 9 for a further discussion), the court will approve your petition as representative, conditional upon your filing with the court proof that a bond has been issued.

Bonding companies are listed in the phone book under the category "insurance," and you can do an online search for "probate and bonding." In addition, bonding companies monitor new probate filings and will directly solicit your business. The premiums that are quoted are based on the estate value and the insurance policy is issued for one year. In the event that the probate is not completed within the year, you will be required to renew the policy and pay another premium. However, once the estate is completed, you can apply to the insurance company to have the policy prorated so that the estate receives a partial refund for the unused portion.

PRACTICAL POINT. Bonds are renewed automatically at the end of each year. Therefore, to avoid additional costs for the estate, you should notify the bonding company immediately once the estate closes to cancel the bond. You will need to supply the bonding company with a copy of the order from the court that the estate has closed.

Declining to Be the Representative After You Have Been Appointed by the Court

Your willingness to serve as representative may change, even after the court approves you in the position. Perhaps your personal workload does not permit you to put the time into the estate that is required, or you may be at odds with an heir and you do not see yourself being able to resolve your differences. Regardless, you may decline the appointment by asking the court to be relieved of your responsibilities. To do so, you must file a formal request with the court, which will then schedule a hearing.

> **PRACTICAL POINT.** The court may inquire as to your reason for stepping down; it cannot arbitrarily deny your request. As it is in the best interest of the estate to be represented by someone who wishes to act for the estate, the court will have to replace you with someone else.

Prior to the court accepting your resignation, you must account to the court for any assets that you have collected, sold, and distributed up to the time that your resignation is accepted. Further, until your resignation is accepted by the court, you are responsible to the estate for managing any assets.

JOE'S STORY

Joe called my office. He was representing the estate of his friend but became disillusioned by the legal process. He had been acting as the representative for six months and had told me that it was too much paperwork. However, instead of seeking court permission to resign, he stopped all of his efforts. One of the assets of the estate was a Ford Taurus, which a nephew of the decedent was driving. The nephew had not obtained car insurance and Joe never renewed the insurance on the vehicle. The car was involved in an accident that was the nephew's fault and the estate was sued. I told Joe that there was an excellent chance that he would be held personally liable for any judgment, as it was his responsibility to manage the assets of the estate and not abandon the estate. He did not accept my advice and was later sued.

OVERVIEW OF THE RESPONSIBILITIES OF A REPRESENTATIVE

Upon appointment of the court, the representative's job comes with many legal obligations. In general, the representative's role can be divided into five steps.

Step 1: Administer the estate.

Collect and manage assets, file tax returns, pay taxes and debts, and distribute any assets or make any distributions of bequests, whether personal or charitable in nature, as the deceased directed in his or her will.

Step 2: Manage the estate.

The representative takes legal title to the assets in the probate estate, and the probate court will sometimes require an accounting of the estate assets. The assets of the estate must be found and may have to be collected. As part of the asset management function, the executor may have to liquidate or run a business or manage a securities portfolio. To sell marketable securities or real estate, the executor will have to obtain stock power and tax waivers, file affidavits, and so on.

Step 3: Take care of tax matters.

The representative is legally responsible for filing necessary income and estate tax returns (federal and state) and for paying all estate and inheritance taxes. The representative can, in some cases, be held personally liable for unpaid taxes of the estate. Tax returns that will need to be filed can include the estate's income tax return (both federal and state), the federal estate tax return, the state estate and/or inheritance tax return, and the decedent's final income tax return (both federal and state). Taxes usually must be paid before other debts. In many instances, federal estate tax returns are not needed, if the size of the estate is be under the amount for which a federal estate tax return is required.

Step 4: Pay the debts.

The claims of the estate's creditors must be paid. Sometimes a claim must be litigated to determine if it is valid. Any estate administration expenses, such as attorneys', accountants', and appraisers' fees, must also be paid.

Step 5: Distribute the assets.

After all debts and expenses have been paid, the representative distributes the assets to the heirs and beneficiaries.

BANK ACCOUNTS

Upon approval of your appointment from the court, you will need to obtain a *taxpayer identification number* from the Internal Revenue Service (IRS) by filing federal Form SS-4. This form is available online from the IRS website at **www.irs.gov**. To access it, simply click on the link "online EIN application," which will take you to the form. Do not be confused that the form is titled "Application for Employer Identification Number," as the form is adaptable for estates. Note that question 8A requires that you provide the Social Security number of the decedent, but though you can no longer use that number when filing federal estate tax forms. A sample of Form SS-4 is found on page 118.

With this number, you will be able to open a checking account for the estate. In addition, depending upon the size of the estate, you may want to establish a savings or money market account so that the estate can earn interest. To open an account, the bank will require that you produce a certified copy of the death certificate and a copy of the court order, along with the taxpayer identification number of the estate.

Once the account is opened, you can deposit any checks that were issued to the decedent after his or her death, and you can pay for any expenses of the estate, which may include taxes, debts of the estate, and court-related fees. You may wish to consider consolidating all or some of the decedent's accounts into this one account in the name of the estate.

> **PRACTICAL POINT.** Prior to making any transfers, please refer to Chapter 14, which discusses when it may not be in the estate's best interest to disrupt investment accounts that were previously in place.

Form **SS-4** (Rev. February 2006) Department of the Treasury Internal Revenue Service	**Application for Employer Identification Number** (For use by employers, corporations, partnerships, trusts, estates, churches, government agencies, Indian tribal entities, certain individuals, and others.) ▶ See separate instructions for each line. ▶ Keep a copy for your records.	OMB No. 1545-0003 EIN

Type or print clearly.

1 Legal name of entity (or individual) for whom the EIN is being requested

2 Trade name of business (if different from name on line 1)	**3** Executor, administrator, trustee, "care of" name

4a Mailing address (room, apt., suite no. and street, or P.O. box)	**5a** Street address (if different) (Do not enter a P.O. box.)
4b City, state, and ZIP code	**5b** City, state, and ZIP code

6 County and state where principal business is located

7a Name of principal officer, general partner, grantor, owner, or trustor	**7b** SSN, ITIN, or EIN

8a **Type of entity** (check only one box)

☐ Sole proprietor (SSN) _____
☐ Partnership
☐ Corporation (enter form number to be filed) ▶ _____
☐ Personal service corporation
☐ Church or church-controlled organization
☐ Other nonprofit organization (specify) ▶ _____
☐ Other (specify) ▶

☐ Estate (SSN of decedent) _____
☐ Plan administrator (SSN) _____
☐ Trust (SSN of grantor) _____
☐ National Guard   ☐ State/local government
☐ Farmers' cooperative ☐ Federal government/military
☐ REMIC   ☐ Indian tribal governments/enterprises
Group Exemption Number (GEN) ▶ _____

8b If a corporation, name the state or foreign country (if applicable) where incorporated	State	Foreign country

9 **Reason for applying** (check only one box)

☐ Started new business (specify type) ▶ _____
☐ Hired employees (Check the box and see line 12.)
☐ Compliance with IRS withholding regulations
☐ Other (specify) ▶

☐ Banking purpose (specify purpose) ▶ _____
☐ Changed type of organization (specify new type) ▶ _____
☐ Purchased going business
☐ Created a trust (specify type) ▶ _____
☐ Created a pension plan (specify type) ▶ _____

10 Date business started or acquired (month, day, year). See instructions.	**11** Closing month of accounting year

12 First date wages or annuities were paid (month, day, year). **Note.** If applicant is a withholding agent, enter date income will first be paid to nonresident alien. (month, day, year) . . . . ▶

13 Highest number of employees expected in the next 12 months (enter -0- if none).	Agricultural	Household	Other

Do you expect to have $1,000 or less in employment tax liability for the calendar year? ☐ Yes ☐ No. (If you expect to pay $4,000 or less in wages, you can mark yes.)

14 Check **one** box that best describes the principal activity of your business. ☐ Health care & social assistance ☐ Wholesale–agent/broker
☐ Construction ☐ Rental & leasing ☐ Transportation & warehousing ☐ Accommodation & food service ☐ Wholesale–other ☐ Retail
☐ Real estate ☐ Manufacturing ☐ Finance & insurance ☐ Other (specify)

15 Indicate principal line of merchandise sold, specific construction work done, products produced, or services provided.

16a Has the applicant ever applied for an employer identification number for this or any other business? . . . . ☐ Yes ☐ No
Note. If "Yes," please complete lines 16b and 16c.

16b If you checked "Yes" on line 16a, give applicant's legal name and trade name shown on prior application if different from line 1 or 2 above.
Legal name ▶   Trade name ▶

16c Approximate date when, and city and state where, the application was filed. Enter previous employer identification number if known.

Approximate date when filed (mo., day, year)	City and state where filed	Previous EIN

Third Party Designee	Complete this section **only** if you want to authorize the named individual to receive the entity's EIN and answer questions about the completion of this form.	
	Designee's name	Designee's telephone number (include area code) ( )
	Address and ZIP code	Designee's fax number (include area code) ( )

Under penalties of perjury, I declare that I have examined this application, and to the best of my knowledge and belief, it is true, correct, and complete.

Name and title (type or print clearly) ▶	Applicant's telephone number (include area code) ( )
Signature ▶ Date ▶	Applicant's fax number (include area code) ( )

For Privacy Act and Paperwork Reduction Act Notice, see separate instructions.   Cat. No. 16055N   Form **SS-4** (Rev. 2-2006)

You should also use the money from this account to reimburse yourself and anyone else who advanced expenses on behalf of the estate prior to your appointment. The most common types of advances are:

- filing fees and other court-related costs;
- costs for surety bond premiums;
- funeral-related expenses;
- travel-related expenses for placement of minor children; and,
- ongoing expenses related to asset management, including mortgage payments, utility bills, and installment debts (such as a car).

Most important, you must maintain detailed records for each transaction in the bank account. The records should contain all information that will be needed when you prepare the final accounting for the court prior to the close of probate. Accordingly, all receipts, statements, invoices, and bills that are paid should be saved as supporting documentation.

LEGALLY SPEAKING

Though you have many broad powers and responsibilities, you specifically cannot take advantage of your position as representative by directly or indirectly purchasing assets of the estate for your own personal gain. In addition, you cannot use the assets of his estate to better your own business. Such acts will subject you to immediate removal by the court.

TOBY'S STORY

Toby was appointed by the court as his dad's representative. The heirs included Toby's niece and nephew. The major asset was his father's engraving business. Toby undervalued the business so that his friend, who was in a similar business, could buy it. The plan was that, after the probate closed, Toby and his friend would go into a partnership together. The nephew did not accept the accounting that Toby provided and called our office. In addition to having the business sold for its fair and real market value, the court replaced Toby with the nephew as representative.

INVENTORYING THE ESTATE

You are responsible for taking an inventory of the estate, which includes categorizing all of the assets, whether they are real estate or personal property. In addition, you must assign a value to each asset. This information is listed on a court form commonly known as an *Inventory and Appraisal Report*. If an asset value cannot be immediately determined, you will need to obtain an opinion from an appraiser as to the value. For example, if the decedent had an extensive stamp collection, the collection will have to be appraised by someone who is knowledgeable about stamp collections.

Once you complete the inventory, it must be reviewed by a court-appointed referee, who will appraise any real estate and confirm the values that you have placed on the items of personal property. If your values are too low or too high, the referee will adjust the amounts.

> **PRACTICAL POINT.** In states where the representative's fee is based on the value of the estate, it is the referee's stated value that will determine the amount of compensation.

The completed Inventory and Appraisal and Referee's Report is then filed with the probate court within a time period set by the court. Typically, an inventory must be filed within four to six months of your appointment. In addition, you may need to provide a copy of the report to each heir.

For a detailed explanation of valuing the estate's assets and completing the Inventory and Appraisal, please see Chapter 14. Chapter 8 provides a complete discussion of itemizing and organizing assets of the estate.

FORMAL NOTIFICATION TO CREDITORS

As representative, you must provide formal notice to all known creditors of the estate. The notice provides a deadline for any creditors of the estate to present a claim to you for payment. If the creditor presents a late claim, you are not required to pay the debt.

In addition, if the decedent received benefits provided by the state for medical care, the state agency for medical services must be put on notice so that the agency can submit a claim for repayment, as medical benefits are reimbursable to the state agency.

As laws vary from state to state, you will need to check with your court requirements to determine if there is a specified court form for providing notice to creditors. If there is not a form, you will need to determine what the court requires that you provide in the notice to the creditor. Typically, any notice will include the following:
- the name of the decedent;
- the date of his or her death;
- the case number;
- the address of the court;
- the decedent's last address;
- your name; and,
- your address.

In addition, you will need to include the time period in which a creditor has to file his or her claim. Again, each state has determined the time a creditor has to submit a claim.

Some states also require that the decedent's Social Security number be included in the notice. However, because of identity theft and credit card fraud, some states have removed this requirement. The notice also includes your name and address so that creditors can present you with claims for payment, and it includes the last day for which claims must be received to be considered for payment.

Depending on the state where the probate action is filed, notice must be provided either by publishing notice in a newspaper, by mailing notice to the creditors, or a combination of both.

Each state has set a specific deadline for the creditor to present its claim. Again, if the claim is not submitted in a timely manner, you can object to the claim as late and therefore not be obligated to pay it.

Chapter 9 includes a discussion of the legal requirement for providing notice. In addition, Appendix C provides a state-by-state summary of probate requirements, including the time limits in which creditors have to submit their claims for payment.

COLLECTING DEBTS OWED TO THE ESTATE

As the representative, you must also identify outstanding debts owed to the estate and pursue collection of these debts. Common types of debts that may be owing to the estate include:

- money that the decedent loaned to family, friends, or business associates for which there is a written agreement that includes terms for repayment, such as a promissory note;
- money that the decedent loaned and is secured by real estate; and,
- all rents owing on real estate owned by the decedent.

Any expenses incurred for collection of the debts, such as the costs involved for hiring a collection agency, are chargeable against the estate.

Gifts to Beneficiaries

If a beneficiary of the estate received money from the decedent prior to his or her passing, it must be determined if the money should be treated as a gift or as an advance against the amount he or she will receive as his inheritance. Accordingly, prior to making any distributions to the heir, you must review the will carefully to determine if any language is included that would clarify how the money should be treated. If the money was a loan and not a gift, that amount would be offset against what the beneficiary receives when the estate is distributed.

FILING THE ACCOUNTING AND CLOSING THE ESTATE

Prior to distributing the assets and moving to close the estate, you must file with the court an accounting. The accounting is:

- an itemization of all estate assets PLUS
- income that the estate has received during the probate process LESS
- expenses and debts.

In addition, the accounting states the amount of money you are seeking for compensation for your services. Finally, it lists the beneficiaries and their distributions. The accounting must also be accompanied by documented receipts from creditors who are entitled to payment, with proof that they have received payment.

After you file the accounting with the court, the court will schedule a hearing for approval. In most cases, providing that the accounting is in order, the accounting will be approved without the need for you to attend the court hearing. Please see Chapter 9, which discusses probate notes and how you can obtain notice in advance of the hearing of the court's decision.

The accounting must be accompanied by a court *final order*, which will be signed by the court upon approval of the accounting and the distribution. This is a very important document as, in the case of real estate, it will act as a substitute for a deed when property is being transferred to the beneficiaries. To illustrate, if the decedent left the family home to his or her three children, the court will sign an order transferring title to the three children. This order is then recorded against the property.

Appendix E contains a sample final accounting and a sample final order.

> **PRACTICAL POINT.** For your own protection, you should keep a copy of all records concerning the probate process for at least two years after the estate is closed.

DISTRIBUTING ASSETS TO BENEFICIARIES

After the order has been signed, you can then distribute the assets of the estate. However, prior to distribution, I advise my clients to obtain a receipt from the beneficiary that he or she has received his or her distribution. This receipt does not have to be elaborate. It can be as simple as sending a letter to the beneficiary. You may use the following as an example.

Re: Estate of Joshua Johnson

Dear Mary,

Enclosed please find a check in the amount of $20,000, which represents your distribution.
So that I may close the estate, I do require that you sign and date below that you acknowledge receiving the distribution.

Very truly yours,
Brian Shephard

I, Mary Rios, hereby acknowledge receipt of $20,000, which represents my share of the estate of Joshua Johnson.
Dated: _____

Early Distribution of Specific Gifts Prior to Closing of the Estate

Every will has a provision titled "distribution of property" or "distribution of assets." Included in that section may be a list of beneficiaries to whom the testator *bequeaths* specific items of personal property. These bequests may include jewelry, artwork, antiques, or other mementos that the decedent wanted to leave specifically to a named individual.

Chapter 7 discusses that unlike the movies, there is typically no formal reading of the will. Therefore, when you believe the time is right to make a distribution of a specific gift, you should do so. To illustrate, if your dad has passed away and a relative has flown in from out of state who you knew was to receive your father's gold ring, it is appropriate to give that item to the beneficiary while he or she is present. Likewise, if a beneficiary is aware that he or she is to receive a specific bequest, it would not be appropriate to hold out giving it to him or her, as it could only lead to family division.

PRACTICAL POINT. As a general rule, you are not faced with a timetable as to when to begin distribution of specific bequests. However, distribution must occur prior to the closing of the estate unless there is language in the will that provides otherwise.

FRANK'S STORY

Frank left his prized Harley Davison to his son-in-law, Jess. Laurie was Frank's daughter and the named representative. She despised her ex-husband Jess for having an affair when she was pregnant. Though Laurie and Jess divorced, Frank and Jess remained good friends. Frank told Jess that the Harley would someday be his, but Laurie was determined to never let Jess have it. Laurie did not appreciate my advice when I told her she could not withhold the bike from Jess.

PRACTICAL POINT. Items of value, unlike mementos that only have sentimental value, must be valued prior to distribution if a probate is required. Further, you must file an inventory with the court listing all assets and their values. Therefore, before you distribute items that have more than sentimental value, you must secure their monetary values.

Distribution of Nonmonetary Gifts to Organizations

Specific nonmonetary gifts to organizations may be distributed at any time. Again, however, you must ascertain the value of the gift prior to making the distribution. Accordingly, if your mom's will left her leather-bound collection of Nancy Drew books to her local library, the gift can be presented as soon as possible, provided that you record the value of the item.

Distribution of Charitable Monetary Gifts

A bequest to charities wherein the recipient is receiving a sum of money, as opposed to a specific item of personal property, is not considered an asset that would be subject to early disposition. A charity would receive the distribution at the time all distributions are made and the estate is closed.

Distribution of Personal Property When There Is No Will

If the decedent did not leave a will, chances are that there are items of personal property in addition to other assets (like real estate or bank accounts). As the representative, you have the authority to arbitrarily decide which of the heirs should receive these personal items. Beware, however, that you should make every effort to achieve an equal division of personal property amongst the heirs in order to avoid division within the family.

RUBIN'S STORY

Rubin was the representative of Leo's estate. Leo's wife had passed away a few years ago. They never had children. There were three nieces and one nephew. The nieces and nephew were entitled to inherit the estate, which consisted of Leo's home and its contents. In attempting to divide the personal property, Rubin informed me that he was having difficulty in arranging for an equal division. I advised Rubin that he could decide which niece or nephew would get any specific item of property so long as he placed a value on all of the items of personal property. Accordingly, he gave the jewelry to the nieces and the tools and Lionel train set to the nephew. (I think the nephew got the better deal.)

PRACTICAL POINT. If you do not see any logical way of dividing the items, you have the legal authority to arrange for an auction of all the items of personal property and then distribute the proceeds accordingly.

CHAPTER 11:
WHEN THERE IS NO WILL

Chapters 9 and 10 discuss the formal probate process when there is a will. However, if the decedent died leaving an estate without a will, every state has adopted a formula to determine who are the heirs of the estate under the laws of intestate succession.

UNDERSTANDING THE NEED FOR INTESTATE SUCCESSION

Although lawyers advise their clients to make wills and trusts, the concept of estate planning has never been overwhelmingly accepted. We know our car will run better if the oil is changed regularly and that dental checkups may prevent cavities, but most people die without making any type of provisions for after they are no longer here. Perhaps people expect their heirs to fight it all out. Unfortunately, too many times people with an estate do not understand the potential legal consequences of dying without a will.

However, all states do have in place very specific provisions laws for distributing an estate when a person dies without leaving a will. The intent of these laws is for the state to try and achieve what the decedent would have wanted had he or she left a will. As such, each state has identified who the *heirs at law* of the estate are and where they rank in receiving distributions of the estate.

Even though intestate succession laws vary from state to state, all states do recognize that a surviving spouse should receive the majority of the estate, followed by surviving children. If there are no children, the surviving spouse receives the entire estate. Only if there is no spouse or children would other relatives be next in line to inherit.

As to the amounts that each heir at law would be entitled to, this also varies from state to state. However, as referenced in Chapter 9, sixteen states have adopted the *Uniform Probate Code* (UPC), which specifies the order of distribution and the amount each heir would receive. For example, if the decedent resided in a state that follows the UPC, his surviving spouse and the two children would share as follows.

The surviving spouse would receive the first $150,000 plus one-half of the remaining balance of the estate; the children would share the balance.

Using the same example, if the decedent had no children with his spouse and is survived by his spouse and his parents, the estate would be divided as follows.

The surviving spouse would receive the first $200,000 plus three-fourths of the balance of the estate, and the parents would receive the balance.

Other states have adopted different formulas for distribution. Appendix C includes a state-by-state reference to the applicable code section for intestate succession.

LEGALLY SPEAKING

It is a common misconception that the state gets all your money when you die. Only when there are no surviving relatives, does the state receive the estate. In this situation, the property *escheats to the state.*

UNTANGLING THE LEGALESE INTO ENGLISH

In Chapter 1, I describe how the terminology used in probate law is probably the most confusing of all areas of law. Explaining intestate succession is even more frustrating, as words that we accept in everyday conversation take on a whole new meaning when it comes to intestate succession. The following explanation, however, should assist you in determining who the heirs at law of the estate are.

Determining Who the Spouse Is

The spouse is the wife or husband of the deceased, right? Well, maybe. Intestate succession laws refer to a spouse as someone who has survived the decedent and was legally married to him or her at the time of passing. However, state laws vary as to whether a spouse who was in the process of divorcing the decedent is considered a surviving spouse. Some states take an even more conservative view and hold that if the parties had separated, and one or both parties had considered divorce but had not filed a legal proceeding for divorce, the surviving spouse might not be a surviving spouse who is entitled to inherit from the decedent. In such situations, the courts will take testimony from any person who can help the court in making its decision.

Same-Sex Relationships

The District of Columbia, California, Hawaii, Maine, and New Jersey all have domestic partnership or reciprocal beneficiary laws. As a result, these states have extended the definition of a surviving spouse to include a same-sex partner. Provided the couple has registered with the state as domestic partners, the surviving partner would have the same rights of inheritance as if the couple had been married. Note that the state of Massachusetts acknowledges same-sex marriages, so a same-sex spouse would be recognized as a spouse by the state.

Marriage vs. Living Together

The definition of marriage includes the requirement that the parties be legally married; that is, a marriage ceremony was performed and a county clerk issued a marriage license. However, fifteen states and the District of Columbia recognize what is known as *common-law marriage*, in which courts will recognize a marriage based on the conduct of the parties. In such cases, someone who claims to be the survivor of such a relationship may have inheritance rights.

For a relationship to be recognized as a common-law marriage, state laws generally require that the parties do more than simply live together. Instead, they most hold themselves out to the world that they are husband and wife. Though each case is examined on its merits, "holding themselves out" has generally included:
• publicly referring to each other has husband and wife;
• having children and referring to each other as mother and father of the children; and/or,
• having a plan in place to become husband and wife.

Common-law marriage is recognized in Alabama, Colorado, the District of Columbia, Georgia, Idaho, Iowa, Kansas, Montana, New Hampshire, Ohio, Oklahoma, Pennsylvania, Rhode Island, South Carolina, Texas, and Utah.

LEGALLY SPEAKING

When presented with a claim based on common-law marriage, a probate court will carefully consider all the facts of the claim and analyze the conduct of the parties to determine if a common-law marriage did exist. Accordingly, it is your duty to present to the court any information that will assist the court in making a decision.

SOPHIE'S STORY

Sophie contacted my office and said she was the common-law wife of Jake, who died a few weeks after they moved to California. I told her that California did not recognize such relationships. After further questioning, she told me that they had recently moved from Colorado, that they still owned land there, and that their son was continuing to operate the family business. Jake had two sons from a prior marriage that had ended in a divorce. Under California law, Sophie would get nothing, but in Colorado, which does recognize common-law marriages, Sophie would be an heir at law and would inherit if she could prove that she and Jake held themselves out to the world as husband and wife.

Determining Community Property

The following states recognize the principle of community property:

- Arizona
- California
- Idaho
- Louisiana
- Nevada
- New Mexico
- Texas
- Washington
- Wisconsin

In these states, each spouse owns one-half of all property acquired during marriage that is not acquired through inheritance. As a result, if a decedent makes a will leaving more than one-half of his or her community property to someone other than his or her spouse, the spouse is still entitled to his or her one-half interest, regardless of what is stated in the will.

DETERMINING WHO THE CHILDREN ARE

Attorneys and other lawmakers have chosen the word *issue* to mean *children*. Wills and trusts also refer to the *issue of the marriage* rather than the *children of the marriage*. By definition, issue means direct descendants of the decedent, which is another way of saying related by blood.

In applying the laws of intestate succession, you must determine who the children of the marriage and descendants of the children are as opposed to those children who may only be related by a marriage or some other legal proceeding. The following scenarios are possible.

• Children legally adopted by the decedent

In all states, if a decedent has completed a legal adoption of a child, that child has all the rights of inheritance as if he or she were the naturally born child of the decedent. Likewise, if a child that was legally adopted predeceases the decedent, but leaves children, his or her children have the same rights of inheritance. To illustrate, if Brian adopted Gary, who died before Brian but left a child, Lois, then Lois has the same rights of inheritance as Gary would have had.

• Stepchildren of the decedent

In most states, unless adopted, stepchildren of the decedent do not have the intestate succession rights that natural or adopted children have.

• Foster children raised by the decedent

Similar to stepchildren, most states do not recognize foster children as having any legal rights of inheritance.

• Children placed for adoption by the decedent

In most states, if a decedent had placed a child for adoption and that adoption was completed, the adopted child has no legal rights of inheritance from the decedent.

SCOTT'S STORY

Scott was told at age five that he was adopted. When he turned 18 years old, with the assistance of an attorney, he learned the identity and whereabouts of his biological parents. Scott's real father had divorced his mother shortly after Scott was placed for adoption. Even though he attempted to make contact with his biological father, the father resisted all attempts to see Scott. When Scott learned that his father had died, leaving a sizeable estate, he contacted my colleague to assert his rights as his father's natural child. My colleague correctly advised him that he had no legal claim.

- Children born after the death of the decedent

In most states, a child who is born after the death of the decedent but conceived during his or her life has the same rights of inheritance as if he or she were born prior to the decedent's passing. To illustrate, assume that Sue is married to Jim. Jim is killed in a car accident. Sue delivers baby Sam seven months after Jim's death. Baby Sam is the issue of Jim.

LEGALLY SPEAKING

Because of advancements in *in vitro fertilization*, courts have had to reconsider whether a child born after a father's death but not conceived during his life has rights of inheritance. To illustrate, if a man had his sperm frozen, dies, and then his wife decides to become impregnated with his sperm, can the child inherit? Several state courts are now deliberating this and similar scenarios, so stay tuned. In cases in which a child is claiming rights of inheritance, these matters are best handled by an attorney who specializes in both estate planning and family law.

- Children born outside of marriage

In all states, if parents conceive a child but they are not married, the child always has rights of inheritance from his or her mother. However, proving inheritance rights from the father may be more difficult unless the court can find convincing evidence of paternity. *Paternity* can be established by blood tests and other DNA testing or a written acknowledgement by the father. However, without satisfactory proof, most courts will have a difficult time establishing a child's inheritance rights under the laws of intestate succession.

OTHER HEIRS AT LAW

Heirs of law, in order, after a surviving spouse and children, can include:
- parents;
- brothers and sisters;
- grandparents;
- uncles and aunts;
- nephews and nieces;
- cousins; and,
- all direct descendants of each group mentioned.

Accordingly, if a person dies unmarried and without children, but one of his or her parents is alive, the entire estate would go his or her parent. Even if he or she also had a surviving sister, the sister would not be in line to inherit as long as her parent was alive.

LEGALLY SPEAKING

In general, a person who murdered or was involved in the intentional death of the decedent cannot inherit from the decedent's estate. This policy applies both for persons who claim an interest through intestate succession as well as persons named in a will.

CHAPTER 12:
INTERPRETING AND ENFORCING THE LANGUAGE OF THE WILL

Chapter 9 discusses what is required to validate a decedent's will—it must be signed and witnessed, and the testator must have been of sound mind (able to understand the terms of the will) when he or she signed the will. If the will is determined to be valid, as representative you may be required to offer an explanation as to what the decedent intended by certain language that he or she used to express his or her wishes for the distribution of his or her assets. In other situations, the language that the testator used may be unenforceable. In those cases, you will have to seek guidance from the court as to whether certain portions of the will must be stricken.

Since the decedent is no longer with us, and employing a psychic to speak with the decedent is probably not an expense that the court will recognize, you may have to put on your detective hat to assist in interpreting the will. The following are common examples of areas needing interpretation.

INTERPRETING WHO RECEIVES SPECIFIC GIFTS

In a properly drafted will, the decedent may leave specific gifts to specifically named individuals. For example, a testator may write, "I leave my 1964 Red Mustang to my brother John." In this example, there is no confusion as to who is to receive the vehicle.

However, an explanation is required if the will reads, "I leave my entire German beer stein collection to my representative for him to distribute, at his discretion, to my buddies at work." In this situation, you would need to investigate what the decedent meant by his buddies, as opposed to other coworkers, so that the court has sufficient information to approve the distribution.

In another example, the testator could write, "I leave the rest and residue of my estate to all the guys in the bowling league." In this case, what if there are male and female league members? When the decedent chose the word "guys," was he limiting it to only males? Did the testator intend for distributions to be made to everyone in the league or just the members of his team? Again, your testimony along with others will help the court to interpret this provision.

Another problem occurs when the gift is not specifically described but the recipients are. For example, a will may include the clause, "I leave all my personal effects to my sisters and brothers." What are personal effects? Some states have held that personal effects are limited to only those items that you wear or can carry, while other states extend the meaning to include all items of personal property.

INTERPRETING CONDITIONAL GIFTS

As an attorney, I must limit my role in advising clients on the language they choose in their wills to what I know will be enforceable. It is not my role to dictate what they should say. On occasion, this has been a concern when a client chooses to make a gift conditional upon an event or a milestone occurring. Such conditions place an unreasonable burden on the representative because the event may never occur. Accordingly, if you are unable to resolve such language, it is best to seek an explanation from the court.

In extreme cases, the court will order that the estate be closed but will place any conditional monetary gifts in trust with the court, and a court-appointed trustee will be empowered to protect the asset. As a result of this court action, your responsibilities as representative will be relieved.

BILL AND SUE'S STORY

Bill and Sue died in an auto accident. They had three daughters and in their will they left their estate in three equal shares. However, before the girls could receive their inheritance, the will stated that each had to graduate from college with a B.S. degree. At the time of their death, two of the girls were in college, but the oldest was majoring in journalism, which would lead to a B.A. degree. The court stepped into the shoes of Bill and Sue and held that the only condition required for each girl to receive her share was that she needed to graduate from college with a B.A. or B.S.

INTERPRETING WHEN A CHILD IS NO LONGER A MINOR

Some wills leave gifts to minors under the *Uniform Transfer to Minors Act* (UTMA). In these cases, the will names the person who is to receive the gift on behalf of the minor. However, the recipient is only the holder of the gift until the minor reaches a certain age. To illustrate, a will may include language leaving "$5,000 to my daughter, Gretchen, as custodian for my grandson, Adam, under the UTMA." Gretchen is the manager of the money until Adam is no longer a minor. Most states interpret the age of majority as 21. Therefore, if Adam has reached his 21st birthday, he would be entitled to receive his inheritance. Note that the age of majority is determined by the law of the state where the decedent died, not where the minor resides. In Mississippi and the District of Columbia, the age of majority is 21, and in Nebraska, it is 19. In all other states, upon a minor reaching his or her 18th birthday, he or she is legally an adult.

LEGALLY SPEAKING

If the beneficiary is underage, the minor cannot receive the money until he or she reaches the age of majority, which is either 18 or 21, as the law of majority varies from state to state. As a result, you as the representative would hold the money in an invested account for the minor. Chapter 14 discusses managing and investing the assets of an estate.

INTERPRETING WHO IS THE CHILD OF THE DECEDENT

In many wills, children are often referred to as *issue*, as in the phrase, "I leave my entire estate to my issue in equal shares." Suppose, however, that the decedent had adopted an adult child (this could include the child of a spouse's first marriage who is now over the age 18). Unless the will specifies otherwise, the term *issue* includes adopted children. (See page 134 for more information on defining children of the decedent.)

Likewise, if the decedent had a child who was later adopted by someone unrelated to the decedent, most state laws hold that the adopted child is not considered to be a child of the decedent.

In some states, marriage is not required for a child to share in the estate. If a child was born from a relationship that did not include marriage, that child may still share. Therefore, if a will leaves property to "my children," this would include both children of a marriage and any children born out of wedlock.

Another problem might occur when the will refers to *children*, as in, "I leave my entire estate to my children in equal shares." Suppose that Patrick had three children from his first marriage and his second wife had two children. Under most state laws, Patrick's stepchildren would not be considered children and therefore would not share in the estate. Of course, if the will so specified to include the stepchildren, they would be included. The same general rule applies to foster children.

INTERPRETING GIFTS FOR PETS

Will provisions that include gifts to pets must be examined carefully to determine the decedent's intent. For example, a will that leaves "$20,000 to my friend Jane for the care of my dog Ernie," is subject to interpretation. Does it mean that Ernie lives with Jane? Who monitors how Jane spends the $20,000? What happens when the money runs out? In such situations, you will need to seek guidance from the court for interpretation prior to making any distributions.

INTERPRETING ASSETS LEFT TO A GROUP

Upon reviewing the language of a will, you may run across a provision in which the decedent's intentions are not clear as to whom he or she intended to be included as part of a group. For example, if Ryan had three sisters, "leaving my entire to my sisters" is clear, but a provision that states, "I leave the rest of my estate to my neighbors," would be unenforceable.

Children and grandchildren who are born after a will is made are generally viewed as being part of the original group of children. Therefore, if Steve left his estate to his grandchildren and two more grandchildren were born after he made his will, most states will conclude that Steve meant to leave his estate to all of his grandchildren, unless the will specified otherwise.

WHEN A WILL MAKES ILLEGAL PROVISIONS

If a will makes illegal provisions or provisions that are against public policy, those provisions are probably not enforceable. You will have to take the issue to court and ask the court to help you decide what to do. For example, my friend, who is an attorney in New York City, told me about an estate he was probating. In the will, the decedent left $20,000 to his brother "to assist in organizing an anti-Zionist rally in front of City Hall." Although our constitution provides for freedom of speech and such rallies are legal provided proper permits are first obtained, the court agreed that such a bequest was against public policy and struck that provision from the will.

WHEN THE MAKER OF THE WILL TRIES TO CONTROL FROM THE GRAVE

Many, many times I have been confronted by clients who would like to add provisions to their will whereby they maintain control after they are no longer here. The most common provisions usually involve a parent who has been disappointed by a child—a parent who wants to leave the child something while still punishing the child. Provisions in a will that impose unreasonable conditions on the beneficiary are subject to being stricken from the will as unenforceable.

Amber's Story

Amber despised her daughter's live-in boyfriend. Her will left the daughter one-third of the estate, provided that if Ellen ever married the boyfriend, she would have to give everything back. Sorry, Amber. You cannot control from the grave. Once it is in Ellen's pocket, it is hers.

The great magician Houdini once remarked that his greatest magic trick would be that he would come back from the grave to finish his magic act. Up until now, there has been no reappearing act, and as previously discussed, most provisions that try to control from the grave are unenforceable. However, I have had some clients who probably have had the last laugh based on the provisions they made in their wills.

Stan's Story

Stan was a great Dodger baseball fan, and he had two coveted season ticket seats to Dodger Stadium—four rows above the Dodger dugout. Stan also had two friends who were arch enemies; they got along with Stan, but they could not be in the same room together. Even at Stan's funeral, they remained far apart. When the will was read, Stan had awarded the seats to his two friends, fully knowing that each season they would have to communicate with each other in drawing up the schedule, as they would not attend the games together. Stan probably had the last laugh as he knew how difficult he had made the lives of his two friends—or perhaps this was Stan's way of trying to get these two guys together. I am sure every April Stan has a big grin on his face.

WHEN A WILL'S PROVISIONS ARE ILLOGICAL

Upon first reading, if a will provision seems illogical, it probably is. You may ask the court for assistance in determining whether a provision in a will is valid. To illustrate, a colleague of mine showed me the handwritten will of his client's mother. The woman collected porcelain dolls and had over one thousand dolls in her home. Her will included the provision that if she died, the home would be turned into a doll museum. Aside from the fact that she did not live on a commercial street and therefore a museum could not operate, there were no funds in the estate to even consider managing the collection. Accordingly, the provision was stricken by the court.

WHEN A WILL LEAVES PROPERTY THAT NO LONGER EXISTS

What happens when a will leaves a specific item of personal property to a named beneficiary but that item of property no longer exists? Is the intended beneficiary entitled to receive a replacement for the property? The answer depends on whether the decedent's state of residency has adopted the Uniform Probate Code (UPC). If the state has, the estate must replace the gift. (See page 95 for more about the UPC.)

IRENE'S STORY

Frances resided in Alabama. Her will left her ebony Baldwin grand piano to her friend Irene, but Frances sold the piano five years before she died. Alabama has not adopted the Uniform Probate Code. As a result, Irene is not entitled to a replacement of the piano. If Alabama had adopted the UPC, the gift would have to be replaced from the money in Frances's estate. If there were no bank accounts available to purchase the piano, the representative would have to sell an asset of the estate so that there would be available funds to purchase the piano.

WHEN THE WILL LEAVES NON-PROBATE ASSETS

Certain assets are, by law, exempt from probate and instead pass directly to the beneficiary of the asset. For example, life insurance proceeds flow directly to the beneficiary. Therefore, you may ignore a will provision on life insurance in its entirety if the named beneficiary on the insurance policy is different from the recipient named in the will.

LEGALLY SPEAKING

The state of Washington has a different law on the matter of non-probateable assets. Washington law allows a decedent's will to override the person named as beneficiary in certain documents, such as retirement accounts. It does not, however, allow a will to supersede the named beneficiary in a life insurance policy.

WHEN A WILL LEAVES PROPERTY TO A FORMER SPOUSE

As previously discussed, it is common for a decedent not to change his or her will after a major change in his or her life. As the representative, however, you must decide if a former spouse is entitled to receive his or her share even though the parties were divorced. Under most state laws, a divorce automatically revokes a divorced spouse's rights to inherit property, even if that spouse is left in a will. However, most states also hold the position that if the parties are only physically separated and a divorce proceeding has not been commenced or the parties are not legally separated, than that surviving spouse is probably entitled to receive his or her share as stated in the will.

WHEN A WILL EXCLUDES A SPOUSE'S LEGAL RIGHTS

As discussed in Chapter 8, if the decedent's death was the result of someone else's negligence, the estate may have a claim against the negligent party for what is known as a *wrongful death action*. However, even if a will makes reference to such a future claim and names a beneficiary of the claim, if there is a surviving spouse, most states view the surviving spouse as the proper party to go forward with a wrongful death action. Therefore, unless a divorce proceeding has been commenced or the parties are legally separated, such a claim may not be part of the estate and a probate court would most likely strike that provision from the will. If there is a surviving spouse, he or she can decide whether or not to go forward with the claim, as he or she is the *proper and moving* party. The court would separate this action from the probate and in a sense abandon it.

WHEN THE WILL LEAVES PROPERTY TO A TESTAMENTARY TRUST

If a will leaves all or part of the estate in a trust that comes into being after the decedent passes away, it is known as a *testamentary trust*. In this case, the representative must distribute the assets to the named trustee of the testamentary trust.

A testamentary trust is different from a revocable trust (discussed in detail in Chapter 19), since the assets of the decedent are not transferred into the trust until after the decedent's passing. As a result, the estate may still be subject to a formal probate action. When the decedent has stated that a testamentary trust is to be established, the representative must distribute the assets to the named trustee of the testamentary trust. If the language of the testamentary trust does not name a trustee or provide specific instructions for how the trustee is to manage the assets, you may have to consult a court for guidance.

PRACTICAL POINT. Upon reviewing the will, you can determine whether it was the intention of the decedent to establish a testamentary trust.

ABE'S STORY

Abe's will designated that upon his passing, a trust would be set up to take care of his grandchildren's education. Other than the reference to a trust, there was no language that would assist the trustee in managing the assets, including whether education includes college. As a result, we sought the court's guidance in crafting specific guidelines for how the assets would be applied.

WHEN THE WILL LEAVES PROPERTY TO A POUROVER TRUST

If the decedent left a living trust in addition to his or her will, the language of the will might state that "all the remaining assets of my estate shall pourover into the Robinson Family Trust." Chapter 19 more fully discusses trust management. In such cases, you must distribute all the assets that are in the name of the trust to the successor trustee.

Most pourover wills are designed to avoid probate. If the trust has been properly funded, with the assets being placed in the trust, there is no need for a probate. However, if there are assets that are not in the name of the trust, and the total value of these assets exceeds a certain amount, a probate may be required of these assets before they can be transferred to the trust. Accordingly, you must carefully examine how the assets are held to make sure they are in the name of the trust prior to any distribution.

JERRY'S STORY

My client Jerry loved boating and had a forty-foot cabin cruiser. When he died, he left a pourover will and trust. However, title to the yacht was never changed into the name of the trust. As a result, the yacht became probateable, because its value was over $100,000 and therefore not exempt from probate.

> **PRACTICAL POINT.** If an asset is not in the name of the trust, it cannot be transferred until it is determined that it is exempt from probate or until the court has issued you letters of administration (as discussed in Chapter 9).

ANDREW'S STORY

I did a will and trust for an elderly client. Three months before he died, Andrew called me to make sure everything was up to date. He assured me that he had transferred his savings account into the name of the trust. When he died, his son Robert called from the bank; he was trying to withdraw the funds. The account name was not changed over and the bank refused to honor his request despite the fact that he was the successor trustee. Robert was planning on using part of the money in the account to pay for Andrew's funeral and burial. Robert was angry with me and frustrated with the bank. The one who he should have been upset with was his dad, for not transferring the account into the name of the trust.

CHAPTER 13:
WHEN A FORMAL PROBATE IS NOT REQUIRED

Chapter 9 discusses when a formal probate may be required. However, whether the decedent died with or without leaving a will, not every estate is required to go through a formal probate process, as states have established guidelines that determine if a probate is required based on the value of the estate. For many states, this has been a recent change in response to public criticism that the probate process is very time-consuming and often benefits court personnel rather than the heirs of the estate.

As a result, courts have developed a streamlined or an informal process commonly known as *transfers by affidavit* and *summary probate* procedures. If the estate qualifies for one of these procedures, the entire process is sometimes reduced to weeks instead of months or years.

TRANSFER OF ASSETS BY AFFIDAVIT

As previously stated, probate laws differ from state to state. As the representative, one of your first tasks is to determine whether the assets can be transferred without the need for filing a probate petition with the court. This is commonly known as a *transfer by affidavit*. For the estate to qualify, the total value of the estate cannot exceed a certain amount. In California, that amount is $100,000. To illustrate, if Joe resided in California when he passed away and left three bank accounts that totaled $95,000, his estate would qualify as a small estate probate and therefore would be exempt from a formal probate. However, if any individual asset is valued at over $100,000, the estate must be probated.

Please refer to Appendix C for a complete state-by-state listing of the requirements for probate. In addition, **www.findlaw.com** provides an excellent explanation of state probate laws. Simply click on the link "Estate Planning." On the left side of your screen will appear a menu bar. Click "estate laws" and it will take you a listing of each state. You can then navigate to the probate laws of your state.

LEGALLY SPEAKING

If a decedent owned real estate, most states require a formal probate regardless of the value of the other assets.

This transfer by affidavit process is most often used when the decedent left bank accounts, stocks or brokerage accounts, or other assets and their total value does not exceed the threshold limit established by the state where he or she resided at the time of death. Further, as the decedent is no longer here and therefore cannot sign a withdrawal slip, the process allows a financial institution to release the assets to you.

Most banks and other financial institutions have preprinted affidavits available. In completing the affidavit, you will be required to state under oath that you and/or others are entitled to receive the money, that the value is as stated, and that a formal probate process has not been filed or anticipated. In addition, each state has established a time period before which assets may not be transferred by affidavit. For example, in California a transfer cannot take place until after the fortieth day of the decedent's passing. In addition to the affidavit, most states require that you complete a *statement of domicile*, stating the decedent's residence at the time of his or her death. The forms on pages 151 and 152 are typical of most affidavits. Note that both forms also require that your signature be notarized.

PRACTICAL POINT. Banks and other financial institution require affidavits to protect the assets from being transferred to someone who is not legally entitled to receive the assets.

Affidavit for Collection of Personal Property
Under California Probate Code 13100-13106
The undersigned state(s) as follows:

1. Marvin Ross Neas died on March 31, 2007, in the County of Los Angeles, State of California.
2. At least 40 days have elapsed since the death of the decedent, as shown by the attached certified copy of the decedent's death certificate.
3. No proceeding is now being or has been conducted in California for administration of the decedent's estate.
4. The gross value of the decedent's real and personal property in California, excluding the property described in Section 13050 of the California Probate Code, does not exceed $100,000.00.
5. There is no real property in the estate.
6. The following property is to be paid, transferred or delivered to the under-signed under the provisions of California Probate Code Section 13100:

   MetLife Insurance Policy No. 002-956-239 M

7. The successor of the decedent, as defined in Probate Code Section 13006, is: Kathleen Rach.
8. The undersigned is a successor of the decedent to the decedent's interest in the described property.
9. No other person has a right to the interest of the decedent in the described property.
10. The undersigned requests that the described property be paid, delivered or transferred to the undersigned.

I declare under penalty of perjury under the laws of the State of California that the foregoing is true and correct.
Dated: _____, 2007

KATHLEEN RACH

_____

AFFIDAVIT OF DOMICILE

STATE OF _____)

COUNTY OF _____)

    KATHLEEN RACH, being duly sworn, deposes and says:

That she resides at 19181 McCarthy Lane, Yorba Linda, County of Orange, State of California and is heir at law of Marvin Ross Neas, deceased, who died on the 31st day of March 2007.

That at the time of death the decedent's residence and domicile (legal residence) was in the City of La Mirada, County of Los Angeles, and State of California, and had been the same for the preceding 39 years; that the decedent's last federal income tax return showed his residence and domicile was in the City of La Mirada, County of Los Angeles, State of California; decedent last voted in the City of La Mirada, State of California.

That the decedent was not at any time during the year preceding the date of death a resident of or domiciled in any State within the United States of America other than the State of domicile shown above, and that the decedent executed no will or instrument within three years prior to death in which the decedent stated that he was a resident of any other State.

That this affidavit is made for the purpose of securing the transfer or delivery of the following described property owned by the decedent at the time of his death to a purchaser or the person or persons legally entitled thereto under the laws of the decedent's domicile.

MetLife Insurance Policy No. 002-956-239 M

In the State of California on the date of death.

Subscribed and sworn to before me this _____ day of _____, 2007

_____

KATHLEEN RACH

_____

NOTARY PUBLIC (affix seal)

LEGALLY SPEAKING

In most states, if the assets are eligible to be transferred by affidavit, creditors of the estate do not have to be paid.

PRACTICAL POINT. If you live in a state that recognizes community property, and the property is held as community property, the transfer by affidavit process is not necessary.

SUMMARY OR INFORMAL PROBATE

If a transfer by affidavit is not applicable, perhaps because the decedent owned real estate, the estate may still be exempt from the long formal probate process and instead qualify for a summary or informal probate.

Unlike the affidavit process, a petition for summary probate must be filed with the court and there is a hearing. The petition must be accompanied by an inventory of all the assets that have already been appraised by a probate referee. Similar to a formal probate, notice must still be given to all heirs of the estate. If the court approves the petition, it will issue an order that states the names of the beneficiaries and what property they are entitled to receive. In the event that there is real estate, the court will also sign a deed transferring title to the intended beneficiaries on behalf of the decedent.

LAWRENCE'S STORY

Lawrence died, leaving an undeveloped lot in the desert valued at $65,000 and no other assets. He had a son and two daughters. Under California law, the estate could not be transferred by affidavit because it consisted of real estate. However, because the overall value was less than $100,000, we filed a petition for summary probate, which allowed the court to step into Lawrence's shoes and sign a deed transferring the property to his children. The whole process took less than sixty days.

Where the summary process differs from a formal probate is that the entire estate is approved for distribution to the beneficiaries and is closed at the same hearing. This avoids the many, many months often associated with a formal probate proceeding. However, unlike a transfer by affidavit, the estate may have to remain open for a set period of time so as to allow creditors to present claims against the estate.

PRACTICAL POINT. Before commencing any type of probate proceeding, it is important that you identify how the asset is held. For example, if the asset is in the name of the decedent and someone else, a probate may not be necessary. Chapter 18 discusses several methods whereby property may be transferred without the need for any form of probate. For example, property that is held in joint tenancy automatically passes, without probate, to the surviving owner. Taking title in joint tenancy is most common when couples (married or not) acquire real estate, vehicles, bank accounts, securities, or other valuable property together.

Appendix C is a state-by-state guide for your use to determine whether the estate qualifies for a transfer by affidavit or a summary probate procedure.

CHAPTER 14:
MANAGING THE ASSETS AND LIABILITIES OF AN ESTATE

As discussed in Chapter 10, it may be necessary for you to inventory the assets of the estate. For most estates, once the assets are inventoried, the probate process moves along fairly quickly and you can soon thereafter close the estate.

However, in some cases, probates take longer than you may have anticipated. Meanwhile, there are assets that may lose their value or have maintenance expenses associated with them. Accordingly, the following is a guideline for managing the estate's assets and liabilities.

MANAGING ASSETS THAT DIMINISH IN VALUE

Assets that become less valuable as time passes are known as *diminishing* or *wasting assets*. The most common example of a diminishing asset is a motor vehicle that is not being used. In such cases, it is your responsibility to sell these assets so that you can maximize their value for the benefit of the estate. Typically, a court order is not required to sell these types of assets, as the letters of administration that the court issued at the time you were appointed the representative of the estate gave you the legal authority to sell and transfer assets. However, you must keep documentation of all such transactions, because you will have to provide an accounting to the court.

IVAN'S STORY

Ivan took over his father's printing business. Prior to his dad's death, he heard his dad complain that the business was changing and so many people were doing his job on their home computer. Sales were falling before his dad's death and only got worse after he died. Nevertheless, Ivan continued to run the business to the point where he was not even making enough money to pay his monthly expenses. Eventually, he was forced to close the business. His sister, from whom he was already estranged, filed a successful petition to have him removed as representative for wasting the assets of the estate.

MANAGING REAL ESTATE

If the decedent leaves behind real estate—whether a residence, income property, or a vacation home—you are now the property manager and are responsible for maintaining the property. For example, if the property is a rental, it is your responsibility to collect the rents and make sure that all repairs are made. In addition, you must pay all expenses related to the property, including:

• mortgage payments;
• real property taxes;
• homeowner's association dues (if applicable);
• utility bills; and,
• liability and fire insurance on the property in case a claim is presented.

PRACTICAL POINT. Chapter 10 discusses the legal process of obtaining letters of adminstration, which will allow you to open a bank account as well as pay for expenses on behalf of the estate or seek reimbursement for costs that you paid on behalf of the estate.

It is very important that you maintain adequate insurance on the property, which may require increasing the amount of the liability coverage to more than the decedent kept, as you can be held personally liable for any losses that occur if it is determined that the amount of insurance you kept was inadequate.

PETER'S STORY

Todd owned a four-plex apartment building and lived in one of the units. Todd's son, Peter, assumed management of the building when his father died. However, Peter did not inform the insurance company that Todd had died. He also did not realize that his father had received a lower insurance rate because he both owned and lived in one of the units. A claim was made by a tenant against Peter for injuries resulting from faulty wiring in the laundry room that caused the tenant to suffer burns on his leg and arm. The insurance carrier initially denied the claim, as the policy required that the company be informed upon the death of the insured. Fortunately for Peter, the insurance company reversed their decision and accepted the claim.

EVICITING A TENANT

If a tenant is not paying his or her rent, it is your responsibility to enforce collection of the rent or evict the tenant for nonpayment. However, to legally evict a tenant you will need to provide the court with your legal authority to step into the shoes of the owner so that you can go forward with an action for eviction. Because the estate includes real estate, some type of probate action is required. Accordingly, the letters of authority that you were issued upon your appointment will need to be presented to the court so that you can represent the estate in the eviction proceeding.

Evicting a Friend of the Decedent's

As anyone will attest, loneliness can be depressing. It is especially difficult for the elderly to be without companionship. A delicate situation arises when the decedent had a live-in companion. Your role is to examine if this person has any legal rights to remain in the residence after the decedent's passing. That is, you need to determine if he or she was mentioned in the will or trust and given what is legally known as a *life estate* to remain in the residence for his or her lifetime. If he or she was not, on behalf of the estate you will need to ask the friend to leave. If he or she does not go voluntarily, you will have to institute an eviction action.

If the decedent did leave a life estate, do not transfer title into the name of that person. Instead, title should remain in the name of the estate. However, depending upon how the language reads, the responsibility to pay the mortgage, insurance, and other maintenance of the property may be the responsibility of the estate or the person who was granted the life estate. If you have any question regarding interpretation, you should seek consultation with an attorney who specializes in estate planning.

BOB'S STORY

Bob and his wife had lived in their home for over thirty-five years. Shortly after Bob lost his wife to cancer, a widow who rented in the same complex became friendlier with Bob. Within a year, he asked her to move in together, as it would reduce their expenses. After his death, the widow claimed that Bob promised her that she could stay in the house as long as she wanted to. When I reviewed the will, she was not mentioned. The situation got messy when her children threatened Bob's son with a lawsuit if he did not agree to a monetary settlement. We called their bluff and filed an eviction action, and within days she was packing her bags.

PRACTICAL POINT. Being a representative requires that you employ diplomacy in carrying out your responsibilities, but at the end of the day, it is the estate that you represent and not anyone's individual interests. As I have often told my clients, you are not running for political office. Sometimes the decisions that you make may not be popular ones, but your loyalties are to the estate.

MANAGING PERSONAL PROPERTY

If the estate includes assets that have expenses required to maintain the property, you should decide whether the assets should be sold so as to avoid these expenses. Even if the asset will not diminish in value, you must decide if it is in the best interests of the estate to continue paying for its maintenance or whether the estate would benefit from sale of the asset and investment of the proceeds. For example, assume that the decedent had a motor home that was stored in a self-storage facility. Though the decedent does not owe any money on the motor home, to maintain it the estate would have to pay the monthly storage rental and other maintenance costs. While owning a motor home sounds like a lot of fun, unless it will be used on a regular basis so that the costs of its upkeep can be justified, it should be sold.

ADAM'S STORY

Forest died, leaving his son, Adam, and his daughter, Irene. Their mom had passed away previously. In the estate was a forty-five-foot boat that Adam often used with his family. Irene and her husband occasionally went out on the boat and did not want to sell but saw no other choice, as she did not think it was right to use other estate assets to pay for the upkeep. Adam did not have the money to buy her out of the interest. Being creative, Adam contacted a charter company that was used for burials at sea. He offered the use of the boat. Irene was reluctant but agreed so long as the revenue from the charters would cover the boat's expenses. Fortunately, the burial at sea business proved profitable and Forest's boat remained in the family.

> **PRACTICAL POINT.** As discussed in Chapter 10, assets that are specifically designated for an heir may be distributed prior to the close of probate. For example, if Johnny was specifically left a 1964 Ford Mustang that you are paying storage charges on, you should transfer the car to Johnny as soon as possible so as to avoid incurring further expenses for the estate.

MANAGING INVESTMENTS

Chapter 10 discussed opening bank accounts to transfer assets into the name of the estate. If the assets are in a checking account, the estate may gain little or no interest on the account. If the available funds in the account are significant, you may want to invest the money to achieve the highest return on your investment while at the same time maintaining the safety of the investment.

The will may include instructions that direct you to invest the assets for named beneficiaries for a certain period of time even after the probate has been closed. This situation most often occurs when there are minor children; the will or trust specifies a certain age a child must attain before he or she can receive his share.

Accordingly, the following advice is provided to assist you in making prudent financial decisions for the estate prior to distribution.

Sell, Transfer, or Leave it Alone

If the assets are already invested in a high-yielding interest-bearing account or some other investment that was designed to maximize the account's return, it may not be prudent to sell the assets. This is because there could be tax consequences or penalties for an early withdrawal, in addition to commissions and other costs related to the sale of the assets.

Further, as interest rates fluctuate, upon liquidation you may not be able to achieve the same investment result that the decedent had achieved. For example, if the decedent has the assets invested in high-yielding municipal bonds that are paying 10% interest, it would be extremely difficult for you to find a suitable investment that would achieve the same return.

Before making any decisions regarding liquidation, you should contact the bank or investment company that holds the assets. Typically, the name of the account executive who is managing the asset is listed on the account statement. That advisor will be able to explain the type of account that the funds are invested in. In addition, you should have a discussion with your tax professional concerning any potential tax liability to the estate for withdrawal of the funds.

Consult with a Financial Advisor

You may wish to consult with a financial advisor who is knowledgeable about estate administration. He or she will be able to evaluate the estate in terms of the types of assets involved and your investment goals. For example, if there are small children and it is your goal to have the assets grow so as to pay for college expenses, a financial advisor can make recommendations that will attempt to achieve this goal.

PRACTICAL POINT. Most financial advisors receive compensation based on the assets they sell. Similar to life insurance policies, investment companies pay the advisor in the form of commissions. However, some investments include up-front commissions that are paid directly from the investor. Make sure to ask the advisor how his or her commission is structured.

LOUISE'S STORY

During the time that I was handling Louise's mother's estate, Louise met with a financial advisor. He recommended investing $10,000 in a real estate trust that invested in apartment buildings. She was horrified, however, when she received her first statement, which showed the initial investment and a current balance of $8,500. That is because the advisor's commission of $1,500 came right off the top.

Questions to ask a financial advisor include the following.

- What is your experience in financial investing?
- Are you certified as a financial advisor?
- What are the charges associated with buying the investment?
- Is there an annual maintenance fee for the investment?
- If I decide to sell the investment, what are the charges associated with the sale?
- Must I own the investment for a certain period of time before I sell to avoid any sales charges?
- If I do sell before a set period of time, is there a penalty fee for the early sale?
- Is the fee that you receive for my purchase paid by the investment company or from me directly?

PRACTICAL POINT. Reputable financial planners are certified. That is, they have completed an extensive course of study and passed an examination. A great source for locating a certified financial planner is the Financial Planners Association website at **www.fpa.net**.

Prudent vs. Unwise Investments

As the representative, you are empowered to invest the assets of the estate. However, this statement is made with limitations. That is, you do not have free rein to invest assets in what might be considered an exercise of poor judgment. Typically, investments that are insured—such as government bonds, money market accounts, certificates of deposits, and timed deposits—are prudent investments. Investing in the stock market or in any speculative investment is generally not recommended unless you are knowledgeable and have experience. You can be held personally liable for any losses to the estate where it can be proved that you lacked the sophistication to make such investments.

JERRY'S STORY

Jerry was named the administrator of the estate. He had two brothers. Technology stocks were hitting new highs every day. With limited investing experience, he invested over $100,000 of the estate's assets in tech stocks. The tech stock meltdown occurred in 2000, but Jerry thought he could ride the wave and stayed in the market. The asset value plummeted more than 70%. When it came time to distribute the assets, he wrote checks to his brothers without any explanation. One of the brothers called my office as he had a pretty good idea of how much money his dad had at the time of his death. I referred him to a securities attorney who recommended suing Jerry personally for the estate loss. Jerry ended up settling by having a lien placed against his home.

MANAGING AN ONGOING BUSINESS

If the decedent owned a business, it must first be determined what type of entity the business was. Is the business a sole proprietorship, a partnership, a limited liability company, a corporation, or some other type of business entity? This is important, because there may be language in the formation agreement from when the business was organized that discusses disposition of the business upon the decedent's death. In the case of a partnership, the agreement may include a clause that states that the surviving partner has the right to buy out the interest of the decedent partner. Your task would be to negotiate a price for that interest.

If the business was owned solely by the decedent—that is, there were no partners, no shareholders, and no other individuals who claim an ownership interest in the business—you must then decide if it is in the best interests of the estate to continue the business or sell the asset. Unless you are familiar with the day-to-day operations and have experience in running this type of business, your decision will probably be to sell the business.

There are companies that market businesses for sale. Their services prior to listing the property will include doing a market analysis of the business to determine a reasonable asking price. However, as the sale of the business can be complicated, you are advised to seek consultation with a business attorney.

LEGALLY SPEAKING

Professional businesses, including law and medical practices, cannot be owned by persons who are not licensed doctors and lawyers and can only be sold to other like professionals.

MANAGING DEBTS OF THE ESTATE

In representing estates, the most frequently asked questions concerning debts of the estate by representatives include the following.

Dad had credit cards just in his name. Does my mom still have to pay them?

We don't have the money to keep making the mortgage payment on Mom's house. What happens if we don't pay?

Do we have to turn the car back in to the credit union or can we keep it?

The estate owed more money than there are assets. Can we file bankruptcy for the estate?

Will the estate owe money to the IRS?

Whether the estate is liable for the payment to creditors is determined by the type of debt, state law, and if a formal probate will be required, as discussed more fully in Chapters 10 and 13.

Most debts can be classified as either unsecured or secured. *Unsecured debts* are debts that are incurred but the creditor holds nothing as collateral. For example, charges made against a MasterCard or Visa for purchases are unsecured. *Secured debts* are debts for which the creditor holds a lien on the collateral or purchase. Until the debt is paid in full, the creditor retains control over the collateral.

Debts That Must Be Paid

Debts for which the creditor holds something as collateral must be paid. Such obligations are known as secured debts. Failure to pay the debt could result in the creditor taking legal action to reclaim the collateral.

The most common example is a real estate mortgage. Failure to pay mortgage payments could result in a foreclosure action. Accordingly, if the asset has *equity*—that is, after any loan securing the property was paid off there would still be value in the asset—you should make every effort to bring the delinquent payments current so as to preserve the assets of the estate.

BETTY'S STORY

Betty's mom passed away suddenly without a will. Her mom owned a three-unit apartment building. She lived in one unit and rented the other two. At the time of her death, one apartment was vacant. Betty's mom depended on the rental income to pay the mortgage. She had fallen three payments behind and the bank had begun a foreclosure action prior to her death. The property was worth a lot more than what she owed on the loan. Soon after Betty was appointed by the court as the representative, she listed the house for sale. An offer was quickly presented but the bank had already set a foreclosure sale date that would take place long before the buyer would complete the purchase. So as to not lose the sale and to protect Betty's equity, we sought immediate court relief to postpone the foreclosure sale and allow the house to sell. The bank agreed to extend their action for one week. Fortunately, Betty's buyer qualified for his loan and the sale closed.

Future payments owing on installment loans such as vehicles must also be paid or the creditor may exercise its rights to repossess the vehicle. To illustrate, my friend's dad passed away suddenly. He was driving a leased BMW. When he died, my friend called the leasing company and said that he wanted to return the vehicle. He misunderstood what they explained to him was the consequences of *early termination*. Within a month, he received a notice in the mail that the vehicle had been sold and that there was an $8,000 deficiency remaining on the account. I was sorry to inform my friend that the estate did owe the money.

> **PRACTICAL POINT.** Before paying mortgage and other installment-type payments, you should inquire as to whether the decedent had obtained insurance that pays the debt in the event of death. For real estate, it is known as *mortgage insurance*, as the loan will be paid in full by the insurance company upon presentation that the policy holder has passed away.

Certain installment debts also offer the debtor the option to pay for what is commonly known as *credit life insurance*, which will also pay off the debt upon one's passing. Many credit card companies offer the same options to their credit card holders. Though premiums are generally very expensive, if such policies were taken out by the decedent, it may result in a substantial savings of assets for the estate.

If there are insufficient assets available from the estate to make these payments, you should make the payments out of your own resources. Of course, once assets become available, you are entitled to reimburse yourself for such expenses. If you are unable to pay the expenses, you should inquire of any other heirs who can advance the estate the necessary funds so to avoid the loss of an asset.

Medical Reimbursement to State Agencies

If the decedent was receiving medical benefits that were being paid by the state through some form of welfare plan, the state is entitled to reimbursement in the event there are estate assets. Therefore, it is very important that you inquire with any state governmental agency that provided medical care to determine whether or not they will be claiming reimbursement for services provided. If a claim is presented, and there are insufficient assets to pay the claim, governmental agencies will negotiate the amount owing to them. However, you will need to provide the agency with a complete accounting of all of the assets and debts.

Payment of Credit Card and Other Debts

As stated in Chapter 13, the estate may not be liable for paying other debts. This may occur if the estate is not subject to probate or if the estate is eligible to transfer the assets to the beneficiaries by affidavit without the need for a formal probate. Accordingly, credit card obligations and other debts where the creditor holds nothing as collateral may not have to be paid.

Regardless of whether or not credit cards have to be paid, you should immediately destroy all credit cards in the name of the decedent and notify the creditor that the card holder has passed away. This will minimize the possibility of credit card fraud and identity theft. Likewise, to avoid annual credit card charges, you must advise the credit card company of the card holder's passing so that the account can be cancelled.

> **PRACTICAL POINT.** The decision to pay or not pay certain debts is one that should be made with caution. Though the estate should not have to pay debts it is not responsible for, you do not want to open yourself up to personal liability if the estate later must pay penalties and interest for a decision of yours that proves to be incorrect.

Regardless, under no circumstances are you required to pay debts of the estate out of your own personal assets. This is not to be confused with paying debts for which you are to be reimbursed. To illustrate, assume you represent your dad's estate, which consisted of only his home. Though it is your intention to sell the home, you may have to pay the utility bills and other expenses for the upkeep and maintenance of the home until it is sold. Once the home is sold, you are entitled to reimburse yourself for the utilities and maintenance expenses you incurred.

> **LEGALLY SPEAKING**
>
> The following are not considered assets of an estate and are therefore not subject to being used to pay debts:
> - life insurance proceeds;
> - proceeds from annuities;
> - proceeds from tax-deferred retirement plans including IRAs, IRA rollovers, and 401(k) plans; and,
> - property held in joint tenancy.

CREDITOR CLAIMS

If the estate must be probated, before any other debts are paid you will need to examine whether the creditor has timely submitted a *creditor's claim* for payment. This is because if claims are presented late, you may legally avoid payment of the debt. Again, laws vary from state to state as to the time restrictions imposed on creditors to present their claims. Appendix C provides the applicable probate codes for each state.

Finally, assuming the claim has been timely presented, debts are only payable from assets of the estate. Therefore, if there are insufficient assets available to pay the creditors in full, you may need to negotiate with the creditors forcing them to compromise the amount that is owing and having them agree to take a lesser amount.

Objecting to Creditor Claims

Chapter 10 discussed the role of the representative in providing notice to creditors for possible payment of claims. Your duties include determining whether or not a claim is valid and should be paid.

If you believe that a claim is not valid, you must file an objection to the claim with the probate court. In addition, you must provide notice to the creditor that you are objecting. The most common grounds for objecting to a claim are the following:

- the debt has already been paid;
- the claim was submitted late;
- the claim is for goods or services that the decedent ordered but never received or was not in good working order; or,
- the claim is for a debt that is so many years old that it is now uncollectible.

To object on the last ground, you will need to research the applicable law in your state to determine the statute of limitations in which to bring a claim. If the claim is large, you may wish to consult with an attorney for assistance.

Once you have filed your objection, the court will schedule a hearing to take testimony on the merits of your argument. Any written documentation that you believe supports your argument should be presented at that time. If the court rules in your favor, the court will disallow the claim. In the alternative, the court has the power to approve the claim in full or in part.

CHAPTER 15:
OBTAINING BENEFITS FOR THE ESTATE

The passing of a loved one may result in the temporary or long-term disruption of income that the survivors were depending on. To illustrate, if a spouse who had been working dies suddenly, the loss of his or her income could result in immediate financial difficulties for his or her spouse and family.

As the representative, you may be called upon to assist in obtaining benefits for family members and other beneficiaries of the decedent.

LIFE INSURANCE AND ANNUITIES

Life insurance and annuity proceeds become the property of the named beneficiary and as such are not subject to probate. The policy will include both the name of the decedent (who is listed as the insured) and the name of the beneficiary. It is also common for the insured to name more than one person as the beneficiary of the policy. Obtaining benefits, fortunately, is quite simple. After you contact the insurance company, the company will send you a beneficiary claim form, which must be signed by the beneficiary and returned with the original policy of insurance along with a certified copy of the death certificate. Some claim forms may also require that the beneficiary's signature be notarized.

If the original policy cannot be located, request that the insurance company send a form titled *declaration of lost policy* so that the insurance company can release the insurance benefits.

The decedent may have an annuity, which is both a policy on the life of the insured and a source of income for the decedent during his or her lifetime. If the decedent had an annuity, the procedure to claim benefits is the same as the procedure to claim life insurance benefits.

If the Policy is Not in Effect

Life insurance benefits are payable if the policy is in effect at the time of death. That is, providing insurance premiums have been paid and are up to date, the insurance carrier will make payment under the policy. Sometimes, due to an illness, a person may have forgotten to pay his or her policy premium. As a result, the policy lapsed. In such cases, the insurance carrier is not required to pay. However, the insurance company must provide the insured with written notice that the policy will be cancelled unless payment is made by a certain date, so the insured has a chance to keep the policy up to date.

If you find that the policy may not have all its payments up to date, do not accept the insurance carrier's word that the policy is no longer in effect. Demand that the company provide you with a copy of the cancellation notice. If it cannot, it must honor the policy. You may wish to consult with an attorney for all matters resulting from an insurance carrier refusing to pay benefits.

When a Former Spouse is the Beneficiary

It is not uncommon for an insurance policy to have been taken out by an insured many years ago naming his or her then-spouse as beneficiary. Over the years, there may have been changes in the insured's marital status, such as a divorce and remarriage. If the former spouse is listed as the beneficiary, state laws vary as to whether her or she would still be entitled to receive the insurance proceeds. Please refer to Chapter 11, which discusses the legal rights of a divorced spouse.

LEGALLY SPEAKING

Although life insurance proceeds are exempt from probate, the proceeds must still be included when the estate value is totaled, in order to determine whether the estate will owe federal and/or state taxes.

If the Beneficiary is the Trust

The beneficiary of a life insurance policy may be the decedent's trust as opposed to a named individual, perhaps because there are minor children involved. As minors cannot inherit property directly, any inheritance must be held in trust until the child reaches a certain age. Naming the trust as the beneficiary allows the proceeds to flow directly into the trust on behalf of the minor child.

In this instance, the insurance company will ask that you provide copies of the sections of the trust that appoint you as the trustee, along with the signature pages that the trustor signed. In addition, you will have to provide a certified copy of the death certificate.

MORTGAGE INSURANCE

Mortgage insurance is a type of insurance that pays off the loan against the real property in the event of a death. The theory is that if someone dies, the income that was available to make the mortgage payments is lost or decreased, making it more difficult to continue to make the payments. Mortgage insurance replaces that lost or decreased income. The same process for obtaining life insurance benefits applies to mortgage insurance.

PRACTICAL POINT. If you have reason to believe that the decedent had mortgage insurance but the policy cannot be located, carefully examine the monthly mortgage statement. It may include a reference to part of the monthly payment being applied to mortgage insurance. Also examine cancelled checks for names of insurance companies. This may lead you to the name of the mortgage insurance company.

WIDOW'S SOCIAL SECURITY BENEFITS

Regardless of whether a person was of retirement age and receiving Social Security at the time of his or her passing, the surviving spouse of the decedent is entitled to receive $255 as burial benefits from the government. All that is required to receive the benefit is proof of the decedent's Social Security number and verification that Social Security taxes were withheld from his or her paycheck. In addition, if the decedent was already receiving Social Security retirement benefits, his or her surviving spouse is entitled to receive those benefits. However, if the surviving spouse was also receiving Social Security retirement benefits, he or she is only entitled to receive the larger of the two monthly benefits. To illustrate, if Edgar was receiving $1,800 per month and dies, his widow Sue would now be entitled to receive his benefit. However, if Sue was already receiving $1,400 as her own Social Security retirement benefit, she would now receive Edgar's benefit of $1,800 per month, because it is the larger of the two benefit checks. Though it does seem unfair, Social Security retirement benefits were designed to provide income only during one person's lifetime.

WIDOW'S SOCIAL SECURITY DISABILITY BENEFITS

The surviving spouse may be entitled to receive *Social Security Disability* benefits if he or she is physically or mentally disabled and over the age of 50, and his or her disability prevents him or her from being gainfully employed. To qualify, the surviving spouse must prove that his or her spouse met the *earnings work credit* requirement.

To determine work credits, Social Security will examine the decedent's last ten years of employment. If he or she worked five of those last years, he or she would have earned twenty credits, since each year equals four credits. (The minimum number of work credits required to qualify for Social Security Disability is twenty.) In addition, the decedent had to have had Social Security withholdings taken from his or her paycheck. His or her age at the time of passing is not relevant.

Benefits may be applied for at any local Social Security office, by calling the Social Security Administration at 800-772-1213, or by visiting the website at **www.ssa.gov**.

EMPLOYMENT RETIREMENT PLAN BENEFITS

If the decedent had set up a retirement plan, either through his or her employer or as a self-employed individual, he or she named a beneficiary of the plan in the event of his or her death. You will need to contact the administrator of the retirement plan to determine the beneficiary of the plan.

Retirement plans, such as 401(k)s and IRAs, are exempt from probate and are designed to provide tax-deferred income. That is, the income that the plan produces is not taxed until the money is withdrawn. Under the Internal Revenue Service Code, withdrawals must start at age 59. However, what if the beneficiary is financially secure and does not need the money, let alone want to pay taxes that would be owing? In such cases, it might be wise for the beneficiary to decline the benefits and instead let it pass to the named alternate beneficiary, who might be in a lower tax bracket.

To illustrate, if Joe was married and left his widow Sarah sufficient income as well as other assets, she might decline to receive the retirement plan income and let it pass to her daughter, who is in a lower tax bracket. By doing do, the daughter would pay less in taxes as well as benefit from receiving the income.

LEGALLY SPEAKING

Before making any withdrawals, you should consult with a tax professional.

If a Trust is Named as the Beneficiary of the Retirement Plan

When a trust is named as the beneficiary of a retirement plan, the trust is entitled to receive a lump-sum distribution from the plan. However, if the plan is completely liquidated with no money remaining in the plan, the trust will have to pay taxes on the full distribution. Likewise, the trust will owe taxes on the income that the retirement plan produces. Accordingly, depending on the needs of the heirs, and the instructions to the successor trustee, it may be in the heirs' best interest to take minimal withdrawals from the plan. This may result in the trust not closing until all distributions from the retirement plan have been paid to the trust. Again, consult with a tax professional before making any withdrawals.

BANK ACCOUNT BENEFITS THAT ARE PAYABLE ON DEATH

Bank accounts that name a beneficiary are known as *payable on death* accounts or *Totten trusts*. The beneficiary of such an account is entitled to receive the money in the account, as long as he or she is able to provide the bank with a certified copy of the death certificate and personal identification proving he or she is the beneficiary.

PRACTICAL POINT. If the account is payable to more than one beneficiary, all of the beneficiaries would equally share the account, unless the account holder had named beneficiaries and assigned a percentage interest to each.

SAVINGS BOND BENEFITS

A savings bond that includes the phrase "payable on death" automatically becomes the property of the beneficiary named on the bond upon the death of the person who owned the bond. To redeem the bond, you will need to take the bond to a bank that sells savings bonds and provide the bank with a certified copy of the death certificate, along with documentation that establishes your legal authority to represent the estate.

If the beneficiary does not want to redeem the bond, but instead wishes to have it reissued in his or her name, he or she will need to complete Form 4000, "Request to Reissue United States Savings Bond." This form is available from banks that issue bonds. It can also be obtained online at **www.publicdebt.treas.gov/ sav/savreiss.htm**. Along with the form, the beneficiary must supply a certified copy of the death certificate.

REDEEMING TRAVELER'S CHECKS

With the acceptance of ATMs as a convenient way of obtaining cash, *traveler's checks* have lost their popularity. However, if you discover traveler's checks that the decedent had purchased, most issuing companies will redeem the checks. You will have to provide a certified copy of the death certificate along with some documentation establishing your legal relationship to the decedent.

REDEEMING UNUSED AIRPLANE TICKETS AND PREPAID TRAVEL

If a nonrefundable airplane ticket was purchased, it is the general policy of airline carriers to issue a credit to the surviving family member for future use. This credit usually must be used within one year of its issuance or it will expire. Occasionally, clients have reported to me success in having the ticket fully refunded. Accordingly, when contacting the airlines, request to speak to a supervisor as opposed to a ticketing agent. Make sure to also get the name of the person you are speaking with and to follow up your request with a certified letter.

Cruise lines and other vacation packagers have established policies regarding cancellation. The amount of any refund will depend on how close to the date of travel you notify the company of cancellation. Again, on a case-by-case basis, I have heard stories where full refunds were issued.

CHAPTER 16:
PERSONAL AND ESTATE TAXES

As the saying goes, there are only two things that are guaranteed in life—death and taxes. The obligation to pay taxes does not end when someone passes away. Your responsibility as the representative is to determine whether the decedent owed taxes personally, as well as whether the estate has a tax liability.

You carry the burden of making sure that tax returns are filed on time. Failure to comply with taxing requirements could expose you personally to penalties and other tax consequences. Further, if you distribute the assets of the estate and later learn that taxes are owing, you will be personally responsible to pay any taxes that might still be owing, and you cannot legally go back to the heirs to seek reimbursement.

LEGALLY SPEAKING

Taxes are classified as a *priority debt*. That is, taxes take precedence for payment over other debts and therefore must be paid first. Accordingly, if the assets of the estate are not sufficient to pay the creditors as well as taxes, the taxes must be paid and whatever is left over will go to the creditors.

FEDERAL AND STATE PERSONAL TAX RETURNS

The Internal Revenue Service (IRS) requires that personal income tax returns for the previous year be filed on or before April 15th. This requirement for filing does not change if a person has passed away. Therefore, if the decedent had income for a prior year, you must file a personal income tax return for the decedent by the 15th of April unless you obtain an extension by filing IRS Form 4868.

Note that filing an extension only extends the time to file the return. Taxes are still owing on April 15th and will accrue interest and penalties for every day that the taxes are not paid. Therefore, Form 4868 must be accompanied by a payment that represents a good faith estimate of the decedent's tax liability.

> **PRACTICAL POINT.** The final income tax return for the decedent covers that portion of the last calendar year that the decedent was alive. Therefore, if the decedent died on March 30th, a personal return would cover the income he or she earned from January 1st to March 30th. Income earned, such as interest and dividend income, that is earned after March 30th would be reported on the federal estate tax return Form 760.

Even if a tax return does not have to be filed, because the decedent had not earned enough taxable income for the previous year, if the estate is entitled to a tax refund, you will need to file a return.

Likewise, if the decedent resided in a state that requires a state tax return to be filed, the same rules apply. That is, you must file the state return in a timely manner and pay any taxes owing on behalf of the decedent.

LEGALLY SPEAKING

> **The requirement to file tax returns continues so long as the decedent has any income derived from the assets of his or her estate. For example, if a decedent owned a farm that produces crops, that income must be reported for each calendar year, and this may extend beyond the decedent's passing. If you have any questions concerning whether tax returns must be filed, consult with a tax professional.**

Filing a Joint Personal Return

If you are the surviving spouse, and you have always filed joint returns before, it is probably beneficial to file a joint return now, as filing jointly entitles you to more deductions. You should, however, discuss with a tax professional or the person who regularly prepares your returns whether it would be in your best interest to file a joint return.

LEGALLY SPEAKING

A representative of the estate can file a joint return with the surviving spouse of the decedent. Again, it is advisable that you consult with a tax professional as to what is in the estate's best interests.

FEDERAL AND STATE ESTATE TAX RETURNS

Estates are required to file a federal estate tax return if the value of the *gross estate* is above a certain dollar amount. For calendar years 2007–2008, the limit is $2 million. For calendar year 2009, the limit is $3.5 million. The gross estate includes the value of all property in which the decedent had an interest at the time of his or her death, including such items as real estate, stocks and bonds, mortgages, notes and cash, and insurance on the decedent's life. This return must be filed no later than nine months after the decedent's passing.

The estate tax return form is somewhat similar to the personal 1040 IRS forms, but there are many differences in what may be claimed as a deduction. For example, medical and dental expenses of the decedent are not deductible by the estate, though they are personal deductions that can be claimed on an individual return of the decedent's (provided that they were paid in the calendar year for which the tax return is filed). On the other hand, funeral expenses may not be deducted on a personal return but may be used as a deduction on the federal estate tax return.

To illustrate, assume the following:

Value of home $500,000
Value of commercial property 950,000
Value of vehicles 10,000
Life insurance proceeds 50,000
Funeral expenses 12,000

In determining the gross estate, you would add together the values of the real estate, vehicles, and life insurance proceeds, and then subtract the expenses for the funeral. In this illustration, the gross estate would be $2,448,000. Because the gross estate exceeds $2 million, the estate would be subject to federal estate taxes on the $448,000. Therefore, you would be required to file IRS Form 760.

Further, because the decedent is no longer here, you cannot use his or her Social Security number on the tax return for filing the estate tax return. Instead, you must apply for an *estate identification number*, which you use in place of the decedent's Social Security number.

The IRS form is SS-4 and can be applied for online at **www.irs.gov**. For a discussion on completing the form, please see Chapter 10.

LEGALLY SPEAKING

The following states also impose state estate taxes, provided the value of the estate exceeds exemptions as set by state law: Illinois, Massachusetts, Maine, Minnesota, New York, North Carolina, Oregon, Rhode Island, Vermont, Virginia, and Wisconsin. For all questions concerning estate tax liabilities, it is best to check with a tax professional.

PRACTICAL POINT. As the calculation and the procedure for the filing of both federal and state taxes is beyond the scope of this book, you are advised to consult with a tax professional.

Federal Estate Tax Guideline

Congress has imposed a stepped-up formula for the next several years whereby the limit on the value of the estate tax minimum will increase each year. So long as the estate value does not exceed this limit, the estate will not owe federal taxes.

Congress has done this is to deflect criticism from taxpayers who have argued that estate taxes are death taxes and the decedent already paid taxes during his or her lifetime for income and earnings. To tax the estate again represents double taxation, some say.

Under federal law as it now exists, there will be no federal estate tax in 2010, but in 2011 the estate limit drops back to $1 million unless the law is extended. Therefore, it is important to check the law for the year of the decedent's death to determine any tax liability.

For a complete discussion of federal tax liabilities, you can review Internal Revenue Service Publication 559, "Guide for Survivors, Executors, and Administrators," and Publication 950, "Introduction to Estate and Gift Taxes." These publications are also available online at **www.irs.gov**.

GIFT TAX RETURNS

If the decedent made monetary gifts prior to his or her death in excess of the annual exclusion allowed, a *gift tax* return must be filed. The gift tax annual exclusion is the amount the IRS excludes from reporting and taxing requirements. Currently, the annual gift tax exclusion amount is $11,000 per recipient per year (but this amount is subject to change based on an inflation adjustment formula under federal tax law). Check the decedent's financial records to find out if you are responsible for the filing of the decedent's final gift tax returns.

> **PRACTICAL POINT.** Determining whether an estate or the decedent owes taxes is sometimes best determined by a tax professional. If the decedent had his or her taxes prepared by an accountant or a tax preparation service, you may want to contact them for assistance.

CHAPTER 17:
YOUR RIGHT TO COMPENSATION

Your time has value, and often the actual work that you perform on behalf of the estate is more extensive than what you originally anticipated. Accordingly, unless you decide to waive your right to compensation, you are entitled to be paid for your services. What you may be entitled to receive as compensation is governed by state law.

COMPENSATION FOR ADMINISTERING AN ESTATE

Probate codes in all states allow for compensation based on what is deemed *reasonable*, or they allow a fee that is calculated on a percentage value of the estate. To illustrate, California allows for statutory fees as follows:

4% of the first $100,000 of estate value
3% of the next $100,000 of estate value
2% of the next $800,000 of estate value

Therefore, if the estate value was $1,000,000, your compensation would be $23,000.

In addition, you are entitled to be reimbursed for all expenses you may have incurred on behalf of the estate. These expenses could include:
- money paid for the funeral;
- court filing fees and other court costs;
- insurance bond fees;

- fees paid to real estate brokers;
- appraisal fees;
- storage fees;
- travel fees directly related to the estate; and,
- consultation fees with attorneys and other professionals.

CHLOE'S STORY

Sherri was a single mom living in California. She died, leaving two minor daughters. Her will appointed her sister Chloe, who lived in New Jersey, to be her representative and the guardian of her children. At the time of Sherri's death, Chloe flew to California to pick up her nieces. The plane tickets for Chloe and her nieces would be an expense reimbursable from the estate.

Note that regardless of the fee compensation allowed by law, probate fees must be approved by the probate court before the representative can receive compensation. Accordingly, though there may be assets available from which you can take your compensation, you may not do so until the court order is signed.

Appendix C includes a state-by-state summary of how compensation is awarded to the representative of an estate.

WHEN THERE ARE NO AVAILABLE ASSETS TO PAY COMPENSATION

If an estate consists solely of real estate, unless the real estate is sold, there is no means to receive compensation. As a result, if you are seeking compensation for the work that you have performed, the court will not be able to award you fees, since fees can only be awarded from available liquid assets.

TAMARA'S STORY

Tamara had five sisters. Her mother's only assets were a savings account worth about $10,000, a very old car, and the family residence. Tamara was named representative. Her siblings did not want to sell the home. Further, her mom had credit card and tax debt, which were paid from the savings account. Tamara sought compensation, but the sisters chose to have title to the home transferred into all of their names. When the judge signed the order closing the estate, he addressed the issue of compensation by stating that "the representative is entitled to compensation limited to the liquidated assets available of the estate." Because the real estate was not considered a liquid asset, Tamara was unable to be compensated for her work.

WAIVING COMPENSATION

There is no requirement that you take compensation; you may waive your right to be compensated. Obviously, if you are the only heir and all assets are to be distributed to you pursuant to the will, whether you receive compensation is irrelevant as it will eventually all go into the same pocket.

However, if the estate is small, and the time that you have worked has not been significant, you may wish to waive your right to compensation. If you think that taking compensation may cause bad blood with the other heirs (who may already be upset that you were chosen as representative over them), waiving compensation may be the best choice. Regardless, if you have worked diligently, you are entitled to be paid.

PETITIONING FOR EXTRAORDINARY FEES

Depending on the complexity of the issues, your role as the representative may be greater than in a typical estate. For example, if the decedent left a business that had to be operated for a period of time before a buyer could be found, and you were involved in the daily operations of managing and running the business, you are justified in seeking extraordinary fees, which may exceed the statutory or reasonable fees set by your state's probate code.

To illustrate, assume you ran a tool and die business for one year. Through your efforts, the business was sold for $250,000 and the total value of the estate was $300,000. Under California law, you would only be entitled to compensation in the amount of $9,000. However, by submitting to the court very detailed time records with explanations of your time spent in running the business, the court would consider your fee petition for your extraordinary work. Specifically, records that document your actual time, along with performance records that chart increased sales, will justify your request for additional fees. Arguably, the court does not expect you to work at a job without reasonable compensation.

LEGALLY SPEAKING

Prior to the court's consideration of your fee petition, you must provide all heirs with a copy of your request for additional fees so that they have time to object if they feel that your request is not reasonable.

IMPORTANCE OF KEEPING ACCURATE RECORDS

In states where fee compensation is based on the reasonable value of your services, it is important that you accurate records of your time. The records should include the work that was performed. The following are two samples of time records.

Date: May 1, 2007
Work performed: met with accountant to value decedent's business
Time spent: 1.5 hours

Date: May 3, 2007 to December 14, 2007
Work performed: supervised rehabilitation of decedent's home in preparation
of listing for sale. Contracted for new roof, carpeting, painting, new backyard
fence, and replacement of heating unit; replaced upstairs bathroom fixtures.
Time spent: 20 hours

In documenting "time spent," you can record your time using accurate minutes
or hours, such as 1 hour, 15 minutes. You can also use the method preferred by
most courts and used by attorneys, in which time is recorded in increments of six
minutes. For example, .2 would equal six minutes, and .5 would equal thirty
minutes. To calculate your compensation, you would total the time spent and
multiply by the hourly rate. For example, 1.5 times $25 per hour equals $37.50.

PRACTICAL POINT. As previously stated, in states where probate fees are
statutory and are therefore calculated based on the value of the estate,
time records are usually not required. However, if you are petitioning the
court for extraordinary fees, you will need to provide accurate records of
your time.

LEGALLY SPEAKING

**Money earned as a representative is categorized by the IRS as taxable
income. You will need to report any income earned when you prepare
your tax returns. However, it may be wise to waive any compensation if
you are also an heir, as inheritances are generally not subject to taxation.**

CHAPTER 18:
YOUR ROLE AS AN ADVISOR

Family members and other beneficiaries may seek your advice for their own estate planning needs. This is especially true if the decedent passed away without leaving a will or trust, as there is now a greater urgency for survivors to create such documents. Issues brought up may include:

- whether to place inherited assets into a revocable living trust, which avoids probate;
- whether to place assets into joint tenancy with another person;
- whether to transfer assets into a *payable on death* account; and,
- which documents need to be revised as a result of the decedent's death.

The following are the most common types of assets that avoid probate. Since some of these methods could result in federal tax consequences, you should refer all specific questions to an attorney so that a proper plan for estate planning is in place before any transfers are made.

In addition, if the beneficiary's inheritance is substantial, you should refer the beneficiary to a tax professional before assets are inherited, as the beneficiary will need to evaluate his or her own personal income or estate tax liability before accepting ownership of the inheritance.

PAYABLE ON DEATH BANK ACCOUNTS

Payable on death bank accounts offer one of the easiest ways to keep money out of probate. The account owner fills out a simple form (provided by the bank) naming the person that he or she wants to inherit the money in the account at his or her death.

During the account owner's lifetime, the person named to inherit has no rights to the money. Likewise, if the owner needs the money or changes his or her mind as to the name of the beneficiary, he or she may do so. The funds can also be withdrawn and the account closed.

At the account owner's death, the beneficiary simply goes to the bank, shows proof of the death and of his or her identity, and collects whatever funds are in the account. The probate court is never involved.

RETIREMENT ACCOUNTS

Funds in retirement accounts such as IRAs and 401(k)s do not have to be probated after your death. The beneficiary named simply claims the money directly from the account custodian.

When an IRA or 401(k) account is initially opened, the account holder names a beneficiary as well as an alternate beneficiary, in case the first beneficiary named does not survive or does not wish to claim the funds.

LEGALLY SPEAKING

In community property states, a spouse owns a one-half interest in any retirement account that was set up and funded during the marriage. Therefore, even if someone other than a surviving spouse was named as the beneficiary, a surviving spouse would have community property rights to claim the asset. The states that have community property laws are Arizona, California, Idaho, Louisiana, New Mexico, Nevada, Texas, Washington, and Wisconsin.

TRANSFER ON DEATH REGISTRATION OF SECURITIES

Many people have sizable amounts of money invested in corporate and government securities instead of on deposit in bank accounts. Similar to payable on death accounts, these corporate and government securities can be left to named individuals and avoid probate.

Further, almost every state has now adopted the *Uniform Transfer-on-Death Security Registration Act*, which lets the owner of the securities name someone to inherit the stocks, bonds, or brokerage accounts and avoids probate.

When the account is registered with a stockbroker or the securities company itself, the owner makes a request to take ownership in what is called a *beneficiary form*. When the papers that show ownership are issued, they will also show the name of the beneficiary.

After the account is registered this way, the beneficiary has no rights to the stock as long as the account owner is alive. The account owner is free to sell it, give it away, or name a different beneficiary.

However, on the owner's death, the beneficiary can claim the securities, without filing for probate, simply by providing proof of death and some identification to the broker or securities company.

TRANSFER ON DEATH REGISTRATION FOR VEHICLES

Only two states, California and Missouri, allow car owners the option of naming a beneficiary to inherit the vehicle on the registration form.

The registration lists the name of the beneficiary (or more than one), who will automatically own the vehicle after your death. The beneficiary you name has no legal rights as long as you are alive. You are also free to sell or give away the car, or to name someone else as the beneficiary.

If you own the vehicle with someone else, such as a spouse, you can still designate a beneficiary. However, the beneficiary will inherit the vehicle only after both owners have died.

JOINT TENANCY

Joint tenancy allows an owner to avoid probate when one of the owners dies. The most attractive feature of this strategy is its simplicity. Property owned in joint tenancy automatically passes, without probate, to the surviving owner. Taking title in joint tenancy is most common when couples (married or not) acquire real estate, vehicles, bank accounts, securities, or other valuable property together.

REVOCABLE LIVING TRUSTS

Living trusts were invented to avoid probate. The advantage of holding property in trust is that after death, the trust property is not part of the estate for probate purposes, because a trustee owns the trust property. After the trustor's death, the trustee can easily and quickly transfer the trust property to the family or friends that the trust leaves the assets to and thus avoid probate. For a more complete discussion of trusts and trusts management, please see Chapter 19.

LEGALLY SPEAKING

Though assets placed in a trust avoid probate, the estate may still owe federal and state taxes if the total value of the estate exceeds a certain amount. In the year 2007, the amount an estate cannot exceed if it is to avoid federal estate taxes is $2 million.

GIFTS

Giving away property during your lifetime helps avoid probate for a very simple reason: if you do not own it when you die, it does not have to go through probate. Gifting your estate lowers probate costs because the higher the monetary value of the assets that go through probate, the higher the expense. Under current law, a person may make gifts from his or her estate not to exceed $11,000 per recipient per year in order to avoid reporting to the IRS and paying gift taxes.

LIFE INSURANCE

Life insurance benefits become the property of the beneficiary named in the policy. However, the amount of the proceeds is included in determining the total value of the estate for federal estate tax purposes. To illustrate, if Sam had a home worth $700,000, a rental property valued at $300,000, a savings account containing $750,000, and a $500,000 policy naming Bill as his beneficiary, his estate has a total value of $2,250,000. Under current law, the estate would owe federal taxes, as it is over $2 million.

However, to avoid including the life insurance proceeds as part of the total value, Sam could transfer ownership of the policy to Bill or someone else. Although he can still make the premium payments due on the policy, at Sam's death the proceeds would not be added to the total value. Accordingly, heirs should consult their insurance agent or company, which can prepare a form known as an *assignment of ownership* or *incident of ownership*.

Same-Sex Relationships

If the beneficiary is in a same-sex relationship, as mentioned in Chapter 11, some states do recognize the relationship, giving the survivor of such a relationship the same rights of inheritance as a surviving spouse. To qualify, however, the parties have to register with the state wherein they reside as *domestic partners*. Before making any decisions regarding estate planning, the beneficiary should research the applicable laws of his or her state.

CREATING AND REVISING WILLS AND OTHER DOCUMENTS FOR SURVIVING SPOUSES

In addition to recommending methods of avoiding probate, you may be asked to make or revise estate planning documents after the decedent's passing.

Almost all husband and wife estate planning documents appoint the other spouse to be the representative as well as the power of attorney for health and financial decisions. These documents are known as *reciprocal estate planning documents*. Upon the death of a spouse, the survivor's documents should be revised naming someone else to be the representative and to have authority to make health and financial decisions.

In addition, if real estate was held in joint tenancy, the surviving spouse will need to transfer the title into his or her name. To illustrate, assume that a deed to a home was in the names of Todd and Arlene Woods as joint tenants. If Todd has passed away, Arlene must record a new deed transferring title into her name alone. If this is not done, upon her passing, a probate will be required, because there will be no one alive to sign a deed transferring title.

Transferring title from joint tenants to the surviving tenant is quite simple. All states have forms for this task, often available online by searching the website of the county in which the property is located. They can also be obtained, usually free of charge, from a title company or escrow company. Though the names of the forms vary from state to state, the most common titles of the forms are *Affidavit of Death of Joint Tenant* and *Transfer by Surviving Joint Tenant*.

The sample forms on pages 197 and 198 are for California, but they are representative of similar affidavits in other states. Note that both forms require that a certified copy of the death certificate be attached and that the signer's signature be notarized.

AFFIDAVIT—DEATH OF JOINT TENANT

_____, of legal age, being first duly sworn, deposes and says:

_____ is the decedent mentioned in the attached certified copy of Certificate of Death, and is the same person who is named as one of the parties in that certain deed dated _____, executed by _____ to _____ as joint tenants, recorded on _____, as Instrument No. _____, Official Records of _____ County, California, describing the following real property:

Dated: _____

Subscribed and sworn to (or affirmed) before me on this _____ day of _____, _____, by _____, personally known to me or proved to me on the basis of satisfactory evidence to be the person(s) who appeared before me.

Signature_____

(This area for notary stamp)

AFFIDAVIT
Surviving Spouse Succeeding to Title to Community Property
(Section 13540 Probate Code of the State of California)

STATE OF CALIFORNIA   )
COUNTY OF   ) SS.

_____, of legal age, being first duly sworn, deposes and says: that _____, the decedent mentioned in the attached certified copy of Certificate of Death, is the same person as ___ _____ named as one of the parties in that certain Grant Deed dated _____ executed by _____ to _____, husband and wife as community property, recorded as Instrument No._____ on _____ in Book _____, Page _____, of Official Records of _____County, California, covering the following described property situated in the City of _____, County of _____, State of California, legally described as follows:

   That _____ was married to _____ at the time of the death of the decedent.

   That the above-described property has been at all times since acquisition considered the community property of him/her and decedent. More than forty (40) days have passed since the death of the above named decedent, and no notice has been recorded pursuant to Section 13541 of the Probate Code.

   That, with respect to the above-described property, there has not been nor will there be an election filed pursuant to Probate Code Sections 13502 or 13503 in any probate proceedings in any court of competent jurisdiction.

   That the above-described property has not passed to someone other than the affiant under the decedent's will or by intestate succession. That the property has not been disposed of in trust under the decedent's will. That the decedent's will does not limit the affiant to a qualified ownership.

   That this Affidavit is made for the protection and benefit of the surviving spouse, his/her successors, assigns and personal representatives and all other parties hereafter dealing with or who may acquire an interest in the above-described property.

Dated:

Signature: _____

_____

Name

(Please print)

State of California

County of _____

Subscribed and sworn to (or affirmed) before me on this _____ day of _____, 20___ by _____, personally known to me or provided to me on the basis of satisfactory evidence to be the person(s) who appeared before me.

_____

Notary Public in and for said State

(This area for official notarial seal)

REVISING THE NAMED GUARDIAN

If there are minor children and a spouse passes away, as representative you should examine the surviving spouse's will to determine if the name of the guardian should be revised. Relationships may have changed or circumstances changed as a result of the spouse's death.

LAURIE'S STORY

Laurie's husband Dan died suddenly. She had two small children. Her parents had passed away several years ago and the rest of her family lived back East. In their wills, Laurie and Dan named Dan's sister and brother-in-law as guardians of their children. Laurie was never happy with that decision, as she never really got along with her sister-in-law. After Dan's passing, she changed her will and named her sister as guardian.

CONTINUED EMOTIONAL SUPPORT

Chapter 6 discusses your role in providing emotional support to family members. Sometimes, emotional support may be required long past the grieving period. If this is the case for you or for a beneficiary, your local community may have programs that offer support groups and grievance counseling.

DAILY LIVING ASSISTANCE

As the representative, you may be called upon by the surviving spouse to assist in making arrangements for his or her daily assistance. Your community may offer programs such as Meals on Wheels, in which a hot meal is delivered daily to persons who are unable to attend to their own needs. In addition, if the surviving spouse has decided that his or her home is too large for one person and that he or she no longer wishes to live alone, options such as assisted living should be considered. Please see Chapter 4, which includes a complete discussion of assisted living.

CHAPTER 19:
REVOCABLE TRUSTS AND TRUST MANAGEMENT

Part 2 of this book discusses the role of a representative in managing an estate in which the decedent left a will or was appointed by the court. If the decedent also made a trust naming you as the successor trustee, your responsibilities and duties are spelled out in the trust document. However, similar to wills, trusts have their own unique language.

TRANSLATING TRUST TERMINOLOGY INTO ENGLISH

The *grantor* is the person who makes or creates the trust. He or she may also be referred to as the *settlor* or *trustor*.

The *trustee* is the person who manages the trust assets. During the trustor's lifetime, he or she is also the trustee. However, upon his or her death, the person named as his or her successor takes over the management of the trust and is known as the *successor trustee*.

The *beneficiary* is the person named in the trust to benefit from the assets that are placed into the trust. A beneficiary can also be a charity or an animal.

Trusts that are created during the lifetime of the trustor are known as *revocable trusts*, because so long as the trustor is alive, he or she can make changes to the trust. The testator has control over the assets during his or her lifetime. Revocable trusts are also commonly known as *revocable living trusts* or *inter vivos trusts*. If the trust was created as part of a will and is not in effect until after the decedent died, it is known as a *testamentary trust*. (see p. 145.)

PRACTICAL POINT. Because a living trust is set up during the lifetime of the trustor, he or she can, and usually does, name him- or herself as the trustor and trustee. Unless he or she elects to appoint someone to succeed him or her as trustee during his or her lifetime, it is only at the time of his or her death that someone steps into his or her shoes to be the successor trustee.

BEN'S STORY

I was named by my uncle as his successor trustee. Shortly after his 90th birthday, it was apparent that he was having difficulty managing his business affairs. Accordingly, he asked me to step into his shoes at that time. I continued to manage the trust during his lifetime and after his passing.

The trust is funded by transferring the trustor's assets into the trust during the lifetime of the trustor. Any assets that are not placed into the trust may become subject to probate unless they are the type of assets that, by design, avoid probate. The most common assets that avoid probate are:

- assets held in joint tenancy;
- IRA, Keogh, 401(k) accounts; and,
- life insurance and annuity contracts.

A/B BYPASS TRUSTS

The most common type of trust prepared for a husband and wife is known as a *revocable A/B trust* or a *bypass trust*. In addition to avoiding probate, this type of trust may also prevent the estate from owing federal estate taxes, because upon the passing of one of the spouses, the trust assets are split into two trusts, with each trust having equal value. As a result, each trust may claim the maximum estate limitation before federal estate taxes are owed.

To illustrate, suppose an estate has a total value of $3 million. Under present law, the maximum exemption allowed is $2 million. Therefore, the estate would owe taxes on $1 million upon the first spouse's passing. By distributing the assets into two trusts when the first spouse passes away, each trust would be entitled to a $2 million exemption. Therefore, upon the first spouse's passing, there would be no tax liability, because his or her trust is valued at $1.5 million, which is less than the exemption. Likewise, upon the second spouse's passing, unless his or her trust's value exceeded $2 million, that trust would not have any tax exposure.

PRACTICAL POINT. My office has prepared hundreds of living trusts for our clients. However, we emphasize at all client meetings that it is the responsibility of the client to *fund* the trust. (That is, the client must decide which assets are to be transferred into the trust or remain outside of the trust.) Otherwise, all of our efforts are self-defeating. As part of our practice, and to protect our office from liability, we require that the client sign a document acknowledging it is his or her responsibility. Still, we have received too many calls from family members who later discovered that the trust was not funded. Unfortunately, once death has occurred, it is too late. As a result, the assets must be probated before they can be distributed to the beneficiaries.

GUNTER'S STORY

I did a trust for a very nice older gentleman. Gunter's estate included a home and $50,000 in a bank account. I told him he must go to the bank and change the name on the account to the name of the trust. Three years later he called me and told me he was terminally ill. I pulled his file and asked him if he had funded the trust with the account at Washington Mutual. He said he did. A month later his son called me from the bank branch. Gunter had passed away. Gunter had told him about the account and he was there to withdraw the money. However, the bank informed him that the change of ownership was never made. Accordingly, they could not release the money without a court order. Unfortunately, the son was planning on using part of the money to pay for Gunter's funeral expenses. There was nothing I could offer to his son that resolved his immediate dilemma. All of this could have been avoided had Gunter made one single trip to his bank.

LEGALLY SPEAKING

Living trusts are revocable at any time during the trustor's lifetime. However, upon the trustor's passing, the terms of the trust are irrevocable and therefore cannot be changed or altered by the successor trustee.

THE ROLE OF THE TRUSTEE

Whether you are assuming your role during the trustee's lifetime or at his or her passing, your primary obligation as trustee is to carry out the trust purposes in accordance with the terms of the trust. The duties of a trustee are usually delineated in the trust instrument. Generally, the trustee is expected to do the following:

- *accept*, or take possession, and control the trust assets;
- perform initial administrative functions;
- invest the trust assets prudently to generate a stream of income for the benefit of the beneficiaries;

- fulfill mandatory directions as outlined in the trust instrument, and exercise discretionary duties with impartiality and discretion;
- enforce all claims and suits that the trust has against other parties, and defend actions against the trust;
- keep careful records and render accounts when required to do so;
- obtain a taxpayer identification number and pay all taxes and reasonable expenses of administration;
- distribute income and/or principal according to the terms of the trust;
- ensure confidentiality; and,
- do all acts regarding the property that an owner of the property could do.

The trustee is expected to refrain from self-dealing, commingling the assets with his or her own assets, pledging the trust assets as collateral for his or her benefit, and generally treating the trust assets as his or her own.

Note that the above list is a generalized presentation of some of the more common duties and responsibilities of a trustee. It is not intended to be exhaustive or technical. The specific details of a trustee's duties and responsibilities often vary from state to state. Furthermore, many of the steps that a trustee must take in administering a trust depend on the provisions of the trust document.

LEGALLY SPEAKING

A trustee is a *fiduciary*. By accepting the position, the trustee accepts certain strictly defined legal duties and responsibilities, and exposes him- or herself to substantial penalties if he or she fails to discharge his or her duties properly or violates the high standards prescribed for trustees. The law imposes these high standards in order to protect the trust assets, and ultimately, the trust beneficiaries. Even though the trustee's duties are detailed in the trust instrument, if any court should later find that the trustee did not act in a prudent manner with the trust assets, the trustee is liable, regardless of whether or not the particular situation that triggered the court action was a specific violation of a detailed duty or not.

CHUCK'S STORY

Celebrated *Top Gun* pilot Chuck Yeager set up a family trust many years ago, naming his daughter as successor trustee. Shortly before he remarried, he placed the management of the trust with the daughter. After she was sued in her capacity as successor trustee by her family members, who were also named as beneficiaries of the trust, a court found that she had sold the trust her interest in a family ranch at an inflated price. In addition, she had diverted other trust assets for her personal benefit. As a result, she was found personally liable and was ordered to reimburse the trust for its losses.

WHEN THE TRUST NAMES COTRUSTEES

Often, the grantor names two persons to serve as cotrustees. Both trustees must be able to work together harmoniously. The following are suggested guidelines for cotrustees.

- Trusteeship imposes a duty on each trustee to ensure that the actions of his or her fellow trustee comply with the trust and with the law.
- Although day-to-day management may be, and sometimes practically must be, delegated, overall supervision lies with the trustees as a whole. Trustees are not entitled—through good nature, embarrassment, indolence, or ignorance—to allow cotrustees free rein to do as they see fit.
- Allowing a cotrustee to commit a breach of trust, whether that allowance is expressed or implied, will involve both trustees in the consequences of the breach of trust.
- Trustees are entitled to have their own opinions, but they must distance themselves from these and not allow them to undermine the trust. They cannot allow themselves to be influenced by matters extraneous to the terms and purposes of the trust; they must uphold trust strategy.

It is the duty of trustees to take advice and then make their own decisions in the light of the advice. Trustees must separate their own interests and personality from the interest and personality of the trust. If a trustee finds he or she cannot do that, he or she should abstain from participating in relevant decisions, and if it goes further than just a few issues, he or she should resign as a trustee.

Trustees must not allow a conflict of interest to develop between themselves and the trust—to do so is a breach of trust. *Breach of trust* can involve dishonesty but can also consist of failure to observe the law or failure to seek proper advice. It includes any form of bad management or neglect, or any act that goes against the purposes of the trust. Allowing a cotrustee to commit a breach of trust is itself a breach of trust.

DECLINING YOUR APPOINTMENT AS TRUSTEE

If you decide to decline your appointment as trustee, a letter should be addressed as soon as possible to the person named as the alternate trustee. A copy of the letter should also be sent to all of the beneficiaries of the trust. The following is the language that should be incorporated in the letter:

To _____, alternate trustee of the John Doe Trust.

After careful consideration, it is my decision to resign as trustee of the John Doe Trust.

By this resignation, I am forwarding to you any and all records, documents, or other papers that I have accumulated on behalf of the trust. I am also providing an accounting of all assets from the time that I collected assets to the present.

(Add the following if you are claiming compensation for your work.)

In addition, enclosed please find an itemization of the time that I have performed services on behalf of the trust. Pursuant to the trust, I hereby request that I be compensated for my time.

Dated: _____

COMPARISON OF TRUSTEE AND EXECUTOR

Unlike in a probate action, a trustee does not require court permission to begin serving as trustee. Likewise, the trustee does not need authority to sell, transfer, and manage the trust assets. The trustee's authority is found in the language of the trust. As a result, the beneficiaries of the trust can sue the trustee directly if they suspect that the trustee has mismanaged any of the trust funds.

AARON'S STORY

I received a frantic call from Aaron. He was the trustee of his father-in-law's estate. There were three beneficiaries—his wife and her two sisters. He was being sued for embezzling trust assets. Specifically, he took $50,000 from a trust account and used it as a down payment on a vacation home for him and his wife. He probably would have gotten away with it had he and his wife not filed for divorce a year after he bought the house. In the divorce proceedings, his wife's attorney traced the down payment to the trust account.

STEP-BY-STEP GUIDELINE FOR TRUSTEES

The following is a guideline of the steps that you need to follow in carrying out your responsibilities as trustee of a decedent's trust.

Step One: Locate and Inventory the Assets of the Trust

Similar to estate management, one of your first tasks as trustee is to locate the trust document and then inventory the assets of the trust. The discussion found in Chapter 8 equally applies to the assets of a trust. Note that when inventorying assets, you will want to first determine whether the asset is held in the name of the trust.

For example, if Theodore Gordon had a $100,000 bank account with Wells Fargo that was supposedly in his trust, the bank account statement could read, "The Gordon Family Trust"or, "Theodore Gordon, as trustee of the Gordon Family Trust." If the account reads simply "Theodore Gordon," with no reference to his trust, there is a very high probability that the asset was not transferred into the trust and therefore will be subject to probate.

You must separate assets that are not part of the trust. For example, if you locate a life insurance policy that names a beneficiary other than the trust, this is not a trust asset and it becomes the property of the beneficiary.

> **PRACTICAL POINT.** For simplicity, most attorneys include an exhibit to the trust, usually found as the last page of a trust document or attached to the document, that lists the assets of the trust. However, you should not assume that this exhibit is accurate or complete, as the trustor may have made changes since the date that he or she signed the trust.

The most common assets that are placed in a trust are:
- real estate including a residence, vacation homes, and rental properties;
- bank accounts;
- investment accounts;
- motor vehicles; and,
- businesses.

Step Two: Collect Money Owing to the Trust

The trust may be the beneficiary of assets, and it is your job to collect these assets. For example, the trustor may have named the trust as the beneficiary of his or her life insurance policy or work-related retirement plan. If so, you will need to contact the holder of the asset and request a claim form. Along with the form, you will be asked to provide a certified copy of the death certificate and some proof of your authority to act. Usually, this is satisfied by submitting a copy of the signature page of the trust along with a photocopy of the trust section that names you as successor trustee.

Step Three: Value the Trust Assets For Possible Tax Liabilities

The IRS requires that the estate file a federal estate tax return, known as IRS Form 706, if the estate value exceeds a certain amount. For the year 2007, that amount is $2 million. Accordingly, as trustee you are required to value all of the assets of the trust, including assets that are collected on behalf of the trust. For valuation purposes, this includes proceeds from life insurance policies. Refer to the discussion in Chapter 10 for more information on asset valuation.

Step Four: Notifying the Beneficiaries of the Trust

As soon as is practical, you should notify all of the beneficiaries listed in the trust that they have been named. In addition, they should be provided with information regarding the expected value of their distribution. It is also recommended that you provide some timetable for distribution. In most trust estates, unless tax returns have to be filed or real estate sold, it is not uncommon to distribute a trust estate within a few months of the passing of the trustor.

LEGALLY SPEAKING

If the trustor died in a state that has adopted the Uniform Probate Code (UPC), you must provide the beneficiaries with the following:
- your name and address (within thirty days of your assumption of the role as successor trustee);
- if requested, a copy of the trust to the requesting beneficiary; and,
- if requested, an accounting to the requesting beneficiary.

Please see Chapter 9 for a list of those states that have adopted the UPC.

> **PRACTICAL POINT.** Keeping the beneficiaries informed will avoid future questions by the beneficiaries as to your role and the length of the process.

Step Five: Reimburse Expenses and Pay the Debts of the Trust

Unlike a formal probate, in which debts owing from the estate must be paid, you may be under no obligation as trustee to pay debts of the trust estate for the assets that were placed into the trust. You will, however, need to review the law of the decedent's state of residence to determine if the estate is liable for payment to creditors.

Regardless, the trust is responsible for the payment of any obligations due from trust assets, which would include mortgage payments and installment contract payments for trust assets. The trust must reimburse you or any other party who paid for expenses on behalf of the trust. To illustrate, if the trustor's brother paid for the mortgage on the trustor's residence, he is entitled to be reimbursed from the trust assets.

Step Six: Distribute the Assets

Provided you have located all of the assets of the trust, paid any expenses and debts (if required) of the estate, and paid any federal and state taxes, you may distribute the assets to the beneficiaries as named in the trust.

Along with the actual distribution, you should send a letter to each named beneficiary asking the recipient to sign an acknowledgement that he or she has received the distribution. The letter should contain the following information.

Trust of Robert Jones

Dear Sally,

As trustee of the trust of Robert Jones, I am now in a position to make a final distribution to you as beneficiary of the trust.

Accordingly, enclosed please trust account check number 412 in the amount of $42,000, payable to you.

Prior to depositing this check, you are required to sign and date below your acknowledgment that you have received the distribution. You are also acknowledging that this is the final distribution you will receive from the above trust.

Yours very truly,

James Jones

I, Sally Combs, hereby acknowledge that I am in receipt of check number 412 in the amount of $42,000, which represents my final distribution from the trust of Robert Jones.

Dated: 6/12/07

Step Seven: Provide the Beneficiaries With An Accounting

Depending upon your state law, you may also be required to provide each beneficiary with an accounting of all of the trust assets, less expenses, debts, and any trustee fees. It is also advisable that you have each beneficiary sign an acknowledgment that he or she has received the accounting.

INVESTING THE ASSETS OF THE TRUST

Depending on the language of the trust, you may be required to invest some or all of the assets for the benefit of a beneficiary who is not entitled to receive an immediate distribution. For example, the trustor may have minor children and the trust provides for investing the assets on behalf of the child until he or she obtains a certain age. In addition, the trust language may make provisions that a certain percentage of the assets be set aside to pay for college expenses of the minor child. Please refer to the material presented in Chapter 14, which discusses managing and investing assets.

COMPENSATION FOR MANAGING A TRUST

A properly drafted trust will include provisions for compensation of the trustee. However, the specific amount that a trustee is entitled to may not be spelled out. Instead, the language may read that the trustee is entitled to *reasonable compensation*. A reasonable amount will differ from state to state, as the cost of living differs. In California, for example, it is reasonable to charge an estate $25 per hour for work performed as a trustee. In Alabama, the commonly charged rate is $15 per hour. Some states have established a fee schedule for compensation.

If the trust that you are managing does not specify an amount, you should consult with an attorney, who can provide you with information regarding the suggested hourly rate for compensation in your state.

PRACTICAL POINT. Unless otherwise specified in the trust, you may receive compensation on a monthly basis or less frequently. Also, remember that once you assume role the role of trustee, you are entitled to begin billing for your time. Accordingly, if the maker of the trust has become disabled, your right to receive compensation begins at the moment that you step into the shoes of the trustee and begin work on behalf of the trust.

BILL'S STORY

Bill's uncle passed away in August of 2004, but he had sought Bill's assistance in 2002, when he began having difficulty managing his own affairs due to his failing eyesight. Accordingly, he placed Bill's name on his checking account so that Bill could pay his monthly expenses. As time passed, Bill's role increased to arranging doctor visits and home health care. At the time that Bill's uncle passed away, Bill was managing all of his uncle's personal and legal affairs. When Bill consulted with me in 2004, he informed that he had not taken any compensation to date. I advised him that, pursuant to the terms of the trust, he was well within his rights to compensate himself beginning in 2002.

PRACTICAL POINT. Before taking a fee, you may wish to consider waiving your fee if you are also a beneficiary, because any fee that you take as compensation must be reported as income when you file your tax returns, while distributions from a trust to you as a beneficiary are not taxable.

SEEKING PROFESSIONAL ADVICE

The main reason why persons elect to make a trust as opposed to a will is to avoid probate. By avoiding probate, the estate often will not have to engage an attorney, which saves the estate a lot of money.

If the trust was properly drafted, and was funded by the assets of the trust, in almost all cases it will not be necessary to engage an attorney. Instead, you will simply follow the instructions provided in the language of the trust and then make the distributions to the beneficiaries as stated in the trust.

However, if the estate is required to file a tax return, it is advisable that you seek the assistance of an attorney or tax professional. Note that legal and accounting fees are expenses of the estate and can be deducted on the estate tax returns.

CHAPTER 20:
DO I NEED AN ATTORNEY?

It is uncommon today to find an attorney who is truly a *general practitioner*—that is, one who handles all types of legal matters. Similar to the practice of medicine, attorneys specialize in different areas of the law. This is partly because the practice of law is often dictated by local court requirements in addition to state codes and laws. As a result, though an attorney may be somewhat familiar with the probate process, unless he or she actively files probate cases, he or she would have difficulty navigating through the legal system, as opposed to someone who regularly appears in probate court.

The legal process can be very intimidating. This is not to say that a person cannot act as the estate's representative competently. In fact, many states have directed their courts to design forms that are very user-friendly. For example, some courts have installed self-serve kiosks from which a person can easily obtain copies of court forms (which include simple instructions for filing). However, clerks of the court cannot give legal advice, as that would constitute practicing law without a license. Still, clerks can be helpful in directing you to the location of certain forms.

Whether to represent the estate yourself, known as acting *in pro per*, or to retain an attorney will often depend on the simplicity or complexity of the estate. The following factors should be considered.

What is the size of the estate and will there be any taxes owing?

Do you have any indication that an heir may challenge your appointment as representative?

Are there assets that must be maintained, such as a business?

Do you have any indication that any person may challenge the estate and file a will contest?

Are all of the assets located in the state where the decedent passed away or are there assets in other states?

If there is a will, will there be an outright distribution to the heirs named or are the assets to be invested for distribution as a later time?

Is there available cash in the estate to pay attorney fees?

Was the decedent's death the result of an illness or was it caused by the act of someone else?

Did the decedent leave a revocable living trust that avoids probate or a trust that requires ongoing court supervision?

Generally, when there is a will that directs equal and immediate distribution to the heirs, a representative should have little difficulty in representing the estate without assistance. Provided the court rules of procedure are followed, the petition should sail through the legal process.

Representatives get into trouble when they confront complex tax issues or when there are challenges to the estate. Also, if the decedent left real property and the title to the property was held by the decedent and others, courts need to make a determination as to how the property should be divided. As courts cannot give advice, these issues are usually resolved with the assistance of an attorney.

ATTORNEY FEES

Even if you decide that it would be in the best interest of the estate to retain an attorney, there must be sufficient assets in the estate to pay the attorney fees, or an arrangement has to be in place for the fees to be paid from some source other than from the assets of the estate. In some states, the fee is based on the value of the estate. For example, a California estate with a value of $400,000 would allow an attorney to petition the court for a fee of $11,000, from the following guidelines.

- 4% of the first $100,000 of the gross value of the estate

- 3% of the next $100,000

- 2% of the next $800,000

- 1% of the next $9 million

Of course, if the estate exceeds $9 million, it would seem almost petty to worry about attorney fees.

BILL'S STORY

Bill's dad passed away and his brother hired an attorney. The estate consisted only of the dad's home, valued at $550,000, which was left to the brothers. Bill's brother was living in the home. Neither brother wanted to sell the home or buy out the other's interest. However, when the attorney filed the final accounting with the court as required before the estate could close, he included in his accounting a request for attorney fees in the amount of $14,000, which was based on the value of the estate. Neither brother had personal funds to pay the bill, and they had to sell the home to satisfy the attorney's fee.

If you have any reservations about whether to proceed with or without an attorney, I recommend that you at least consult with an attorney before proceeding on your own. Most attorneys offer a free consultation. When you make the appointment, inquire if there is a consultation fee so that you are prepared.

PREPARING FOR YOUR APPOINTMENT

Most attorneys have their own checklist that will cover the important issues to be discussed at the initial meeting, but there may be something unique to the estate that the attorney would not know to ask about. Accordingly, so that you can get the most out of the consultation, come prepared with a list of questions particular to the estate. In addition, you should ask the following questions.

- How is the attorney fee calculated?
- What are the estimated court costs?
- Is the client billed for postage, photocopying, and other office expenses?
- If an heir contests the will, are there additional attorney fees?
- What is the estimated timetable to complete the probate?
- What will be expected of you, the representative, in regards to your time?

In discussing attorney fees, you may wish to ask if the attorney will accept the case on a *flat fee* bases. That is, the attorney would agree to perform all services based on a negotiated amount rather than what is provided by the court fee schedule. If the estate does not require filing of tax returns, there are no unique issues, and you do not anticipate any challenges by heirs, you may wish to propose such a fee arrangement.

LEGALLY SPEAKING

Regardless of the fee arrangement, make sure that the attorney puts in writing the terms of his or her representation. In addition, review the agreement to verify that the attorney fee is stated and other costs are explained.

DO'S AND DON'TS FOR YOUR FIRST MEETING WITH THE ATTORNEY

DO:

- Be punctual
- Take notes
- Allow the attorney to ask any informational questions before you begin to ask your questions

DON'T:

- Be intimidated—ask for an explanation of anything you do not understand
- Give the attorney any documents to hold unless you are sure you are going to retain him or her
- Interrupt
- Insult

On more than one occasion, I have been asked what I would charge to prepare all the paperwork necessary but not to put my name on the documents. Such a request is tantamount to reducing a law practice to a typing service and is insulting. Attorney fees are based on the attorney's time and experience.

FINDING A PROBATE ATTORNEY

The best way of finding an attorney is from a personal referral, assuming that person was pleased with the representation. You may be a member of a legal plan offered through your employee. If you are, most plans offer a discounted rate. In addition, members of AARP are entitled to a 20% reduction in attorney fees. Their website, **www.aarp.org**, has a link to their attorney network. Phone book directories list attorneys by their specialties. Typically, the categories are "Wills and Trusts" and "Probate." Similar searches may be conducted online. Finally, your local attorney bar association will refer you to attorneys in your community that specialize in probate law.

CHAPTER 21:

WORDS OF THANKS

Everyone who passes through your life leaves you with something, especially the ones who have given so much joy.
—Anonymous

Books about a representative's role in managing an estate are written because someone left this world with something to give. It was that person's last wishes that his estate be distributed in a manner that he chose. Laws were made to follow those wishes. Although there are other books written to assist representatives, this is the chapter you will not find anywhere else.

When a loved one passes away, we must cope with our emotions while attempting to apply logic. Sometimes the two blend together, making it difficult to see tomorrow. Yet all too often, after the funeral and the many emotional months that pass, we sometimes forget about the person who left his gift and what his life meant. While the assets have been itemized, the mementos distributed, and the checks issued, what sometimes gets fuzzy is the reason that brought us here.

Yes, life must go on for the survivors, but wouldn't it be nice to be able to say thanks to the person for his generosities? Of course, that's not possible (and if it was, Hallmark would have a section in their stores just for such occasions).

So how do we properly thank the person who thought enough about us? How do you properly thank the decedent who has given niece Susan the money for the down payment on the home that she and her husband have struggled to acquire?

Or the financial opportunity for brother Brian to open his own business? Or the college education that granddaughter Amy had previously only dreamed of?

In Jewish tradition, within the first year after passing, family and friends gather at the gravesite to dedicate or *unveil* the grave marker. It is not a solemn occasion, as enough time has passed for the tears to have dried. A few remarks are shared by those who wish to be heard, followed by a religious leader who says a prayer. Upon leaving, each member places a small stone on the grave marker as a symbolic gesture to the deceased that he was visited. The occasion represents both closure and the opportunity to say thank you to your loved one for all the things that he has done for you.

As the representative, sometime between the start of your role and the time that you distribute assets, you may want to arrange a gathering of the beneficiaries in celebration of the decedent's life. Whether it is at the gravesite, at the beach, toasting to his favorite red wine, or sharing a quart of ice cream, it is an opportunity to collectively say thank you for your loved one's kindness, thank you for his gift, and thank you for passing through your life.

GLOSSARY

A

administrator. A person appointed by the probate court to manage an estate during probate when a person has died without a will.

annuity. Issued by an insurance company and purchased to accumulate funds for retirement. It is also used to pay an income for a specified number of years in a specified amount, or for the rest of the annuitant's life. Other annuities provide income in exchange for money or another asset.

asset. Any item that adds value to an estate or to someone's personal financial situation, such as a house, a car, bank accounts, and stocks.

B

beneficiary. A person or organization who receives the benefits from a trust, bank account, investment, life insurance policy, or retirement plan.

C

creditor. A person or business to whom money is owed.

D

death benefits. Money that is received upon the death of another person.

decedent. The person who has died with or without leaving a will.

E

estate. The decedent's property, including real estate, personal property and any other assets owned or controlled by the decedent at the time of his or her death.

estate tax. Taxes that are payable to the federal government or the state when assets are transferred at a person's death to someone other than his or her spouse. Generally affects only large estates.

executor. The person named in a will to manage an estate during probate.

F

fair market value. A reasonable value established between a knowledgeable buyer and willing seller.

fiduciary. A person in a position of trust with respect to another's property; a general term used to refer to a representative, executor, administrator, or trustee.

G

grantor. The person who creates and funds a trust.

H

heirs. The persons who would inherit the estate assets if there were no will. Sometimes also referred to as *heirs at law*.

I

intestate. A person who died without leaving a will. This person's estate is distributed by the laws of the state where the person lived.

intestate succession. The order in which the heirs of the decedent receive the distribution of assets when he or she dies without a will.

inventory. A complete list of a person's property and belongings. The fair market value of each item usually is listed also.

J

joint tenants with rights of survivorship. A way of holding property. Often, both spouses are named as owners. Accounts held jointly in this way automatically belong to the survivor after the death of one person. These properties do not need to go through probate.

L

liabilities. Any debts that reduce the value of an estate or a personal financial situation, such as a mortgage loan, car loan, credit card bills, and medical expenses.

P

personal representative. Another name for an executor.

petition. A formal request made to a court.

post a bond. To put a large sum of money with the probate court as a guarantee that an estate will be managed carefully. Sometimes a representative is asked to post a bond.

probate. The legal process that determines if a will is legally valid and administers an estate until the property is distributed.

probate court. The court that oversees the process of probate. It also appoints guardians for children under the age of 18, if needed. The probate court is in the same county where the person lived.

R

representative. Either the executor or the administrator of the estate.

S

securities. Typically stocks, which indicate ownership in a company; bonds, which represent a loan made to a company or government entity; and, mutual funds, which may own a combination of stocks and/or bonds.

settling an estate. The process of paying a decedent's debts and taxes and dividing his or her estate among survivors according to the laws of the state where the person lived.

T

testate. A decedent who had a will.

testator. A decedent who created a trust through his or her will.

W

will. A legal document that says how a person wishes his or her estate to be divided among survivors. A will also should say who will take care of children under age 18.

APPENDIX A:
REPRESENTATIVE'S CHECKLIST

The passing of a loved one creates a very stressful situation for his or her survivors. At the time of passing, you will need to prioritize your duties so that you can perform your role effectively. The following checklist is intended to serve as a road map to assist as you navigate through the first few days after the decedent's passing.

❏ Notify family members, friends, employers, and any organizations that the decedent was active in
❏ Arrange, if necessary, for emotional support for family members and loved ones
❏ Locate the will and any other estate planning documents
❏ Make interim arrangements for care of minor children and notify the children's schools
❏ Arrange for care of pets
❏ Contact the decedent's employer
❏ Notify any appointee under a power of attorney of the decedent's passing
❏ Contact any home health care providers to pick up home aid equipment
❏ Discontinue any home care services, such as Meals on Wheels
❏ Locate any documents that might express the decedent's last wishes for organ donation, his or her funeral, and final interment

Make funeral arrangements:
  ❏ Contact the funeral home
  ❏ Order certified copies of death certificates from the funeral home
  ❏ Arrange for publication of an obituary

❏ Arrange for the funeral service and after-service reception
❏ Discuss arrangements with the family and any religious advisors
❏ Make lodging arrangements for out-of-town family and guests
❏ Keep accurate records of all expenses related to the funeral

If the decedent lived alone:
❏ Dispose of perishable food
❏ Secure the residence
❏ Cancel home deliveries
❏ Arrange with the post office to have mail held

APPENDIX B:
NOTIFICATION

The following is a list of contacts to notify upon the decedent's passing. Cancel all subscriptions, services, and orders.

❏ Mail service
❏ Fire department (if home will be unoccupied)
❏ Newspaper delivery
❏ Magazines
❏ Utilities:
    ❏ Electric
    ❏ Gas
    ❏ Telephone
    ❏ Water
    ❏ Trash
    ❏ Cellular phone
    ❏ Cable/satellite

❏ Home maintenance:
    ❏ Alarm company
    ❏ Gardener
    ❏ Pool service
    ❏ Pest control
    ❏ Home cleaning services
    ❏ Homeowner's association

❏ Internet providers
❏ Health clubs and other memberships
❏ Library
❏ Other home deliveries

APPENDIX C:

STATE-BY-STATE SUMMARY OF PROBATE LAWS

The following is a summary of the probate laws for each state, followed by a state-by-state listing of the applicable probate codes.

To review each state's codes online, visit Gavel2TGavel, which is an Internet resource providing each state's codes and statutes. The direct link is **www.request.net/g2g/codes/state/index/htm**. Simply click on your state's name, and you will be directed to the codes for your state.

Also, please be aware that laws do change. Therefore, you should not rely on the following information without first checking online or at your local courthouse to see if it is up-to-date.

ALABAMA

Holographic will	Not valid unless valid state where signed
State inheritance tax	No
State estate tax	No
Transfer by affidavit	No
Summary probate	Yes, if no real estate and total value of estate is less than $3,000
Time limit for creditors' claims	Six months after letters issued
Adopted Uniform Probate Code	No
Compensation	Reasonable

ALASKA

Holographic will	Valid
State Inheritance tax	No
State estate tax	No
Transfer by affidavit	Yes, if value of estate does not exceed homestead allowance as per Alaska §§13.16.690 and 695
Summary probate	Yes
Time limit for creditors' claims	Four months after publication
Adopted Uniform Probate Code	Yes
Compensation	Reasonable

ARIZONA

Holographic will	Valid
State inheritance tax	No
State estate tax	No
Transfer by affidavit	Yes, if value of all real estate is less than $50,000, all debts and taxes are paid; value of all personal property is less than $50,000
Summary probate	Yes, if value of entire estate does not exceed homestead allowance as per Arizona §3974
Time limit for creditors' claims	Four months after publication
Adopted Uniform Probate Code	Yes
Compensation	Reasonable

ARKANSAS

Holographic will	Valid
State inheritance tax	No
State estate tax	Yes
Transfer by affidavit	No
Summary probate	Yes, if value of all property does not exceed $50,000 with additional allowances for widow, Arkansas §§28-41-101
Time limit for creditors' claims	Three months after publication
Adopted Uniform Probate Code	No
Compensation	Yes, statutory, §§28-48-108

CALIFORNIA

Holographic will	Valid
State inheritance tax	No
State estate tax	No
Transfer by affidavit	Yes, if personal property value is less than $100,000 and no real estate
Summary probate	Value up to $100,000
Time limit for creditors' claims	Four months after letters are issued
Adopted Uniform Probate Code	No
Compensation	Yes, statutory, §§10810

COLORADO

Holographic will	Valid
State inheritance tax	No
State estate tax	No
Transfer by affidavit	Yes, if no real estate and total value is less than $50,000, see §§15-12-1201
Summary probate	Yes, if total value is less than $50,000
Time limit for creditors' claims	Four months after publication
Adopted Uniform Probate Code	No
Compensation	Reasonable

CONNECTICUT

Holographic will	Not valid unless valid in state where signed
State inheritance tax	Yes, but phased out in 2008
State estate tax	No
Transfer by affidavit	No
Summary probate	Yes, if no real estate and total estate value is less than $20,000
Time limit for creditors' claims	Time determined by court
Adopted Uniform Probate Code	No
Compensation	Reasonable

DELAWARE

Holographic will	Not valid unless valid in state where signed
State inheritance tax	No
State estate tax	No
Transfer by affidavit	Yes, if estate value, exclusive of Delaware real estate, is less than $20,000
Summary probate	No
Time limit for creditors' claims	Eight months after death
Adopted Uniform Probate Code	No
Compensation	Reasonable

DISTRICT OF COLUMBIA

Holographic will	Not valid
State inheritance tax	No
State estate tax	Yes
Transfer by affidavit	Only if total estate consisted of two or fewer vehicles
Summary probate	Yes, if estate value is less than $40,000
Time limit for creditors' claims	Six months after publication
Adopted Uniform Probate Code	No
Compensation	Reasonable

FLORIDA

Holographic will	Not valid
State inheritance tax	No
State estate tax	No
Transfer by affidavit	No
Summary probate	Yes, if no real estate or if total estate value is less than $75,000, see §§735.201
Time limit for creditors' claims	Three months after publication
Adopted Uniform Probate Code	Yes
Compensation	Yes, statutory, see §§733.6171

GEORGIA

Holographic will	Not valid
State inheritance tax	No
State estate tax	No
Transfer by affidavit	No
Summary probate	Yes, if no real estate and total estate value is less than $75,000
Time limit for creditors' claims	Three months after publication
Adopted Uniform Probate Code	Yes
Compensation	Yes, statutory, see §§733.6171

HAWAII

Holographic will	Valid
State inheritance tax	No
State estate tax	No
Transfer by affidavit	Yes, if total value of estate is less than $100,000
Summary probate	Yes, if total value of estate is less than $100,000
Time limit for creditors' claims	Four months after publication
Adopted Uniform Probate Code	Yes
Compensation	Reasonable

IDAHO

Holographic will	Valid
State inheritance tax	No
State estate tax	No
Transfer by affidavit	Yes, if total value of estate is less than $75,000
Summary probate	Yes, providing total value is less than homestead limit
Time limit for creditors' claims	Four months after publication
Adopted Uniform Probate Code	Yes
Compensation	Reasonable

ILLINOIS

Holographic will	Not valid
State inheritance tax	No
State estate tax	Yes
Transfer by affidavit	Yes, if total value of estate is less than $100,000
Summary probate	Yes, if total value of estate is less than $100,000
Time limit for creditors' claims	Two months after mailing of notice
Adopted Uniform Probate Code	No
Compensation	Reasonable

INDIANA

Holographic will	Not valid
State inheritance tax	Yes
State estate tax	No
Transfer by affidavit	Yes, if total value of estate is less than $25,000
Summary probate	Yes, if value of estate, subject to probate is less than $25,000
Time limit for creditors' claims	Three months after publication
Adopted Uniform Probate Code	No
Compensation	Reasonable

IOWA

Holographic will	Not valid unless valid in state where signed
State inheritance tax	Yes
State estate tax	No
Transfer by affidavit	Yes, if no real estate and total estate value is less than $25,000
Summary probate	Depending who are decedent's survivors
Time limit for creditors' claims	Four months after publication
Adopted Uniform Probate Code	No
Compensation	Yes, statutory

KANSAS

Holographic will	Not valid
State inheritance tax	No
State estate tax	Yes
Transfer by affidavit	Yes, if total estate value is less than $20,000
Summary probate	Upon approval from court
Time limit for creditors' claims	Four months after publication
Adopted Uniform Probate Code	No
Compensation	Reasonable

KENTUCKY

Holographic will	Valid
State inheritance tax	Yes
State estate tax	No
Transfer by affidavit	No
Summary probate	Yes, if there is a surviving spouse and estate value is less than $15,000
Time limit for creditors' claims	Six months after issuance of letters
Adopted Uniform Probate Code	No
Compensation	Reasonable

LOUISIANA

Holographic will	Yes
State inheritance tax	No
State estate tax	Yes
Time limit for creditors' claims	Thirty days
Adopted Uniform Probate Code	No

MAINE

Holographic will	Valid
State inheritance tax	No
State estate tax	Yes
Transfer by affidavit	Yes, if total estate value is under $10,000
Summary probate	Yes, providing estate value does not exceed homestead allowance, see §§3-1203
Time limit for creditors' claims	Four months after publication
Adopted Uniform Probate Code	Yes
Compensation	Reasonable

MARYLAND

Holographic will	Valid if made by person in armed forces while outside of U.S.
State inheritance tax	Yes
State estate tax	Yes
Transfer by affidavit	No
Summary probate	Yes, if total value of estate is less than $50,000 with surviving spouse, or $30,000 if no spouse
Time limit for creditors' claims	Nine months after death
Adopted Uniform Probate Code	No
Compensation	Reasonable

MASSACHUSETTS

Holographic will	Not valid
State inheritance tax	No
State estate tax	Yes
Transfer by affidavit	No
Summary probate	Yes, if no real estate and total value is less than $15,000
Time limit for creditors' claims	Four months after executor's bond is posted
Adopted Uniform Probate Code	No
Compensation	Reasonable

MICHIGAN

Holographic will	Valid
State inheritance tax	No
State estate tax	No
Transfer by affidavit	Yes, if no real estate and total value is less than $15,000
Summary probate	Yes depending who the survivors are
Time limit for creditors' claims	Four months after publication
Adopted Uniform Probate Code	No
Compensation	Reasonable

MINNESOTA

Holographic will	Not valid unless valid in state where signed
State inheritance tax	No
State estate tax	Yes
Transfer by affidavit	Yes, if total estate value is $20,000 or less
Summary probate	Yes, if no property is subject to creditors' claims
Time limit for creditors' claims	Three months after publication
Adopted Uniform Probate Code	Yes
Compensation	Reasonable

MISSISSIPPI

Holographic will	Valid
State inheritance tax	No
State estate tax	No
Transfer by affidavit	No
Summary probate	Yes, if estate is $5,000 or less
Time limit for creditors' claims	Three months after publication
Adopted Uniform Probate Code	No
Compensation	Reasonable

MISSOURI

Holographic will	Not valid
State inheritance tax	No
State estate tax	No
Transfer by affidavit	No
Summary probate	Yes, if entire estate value is less than $40,000
Time limit for publication	Six months after publication
Adopted Uniform Probate Code	No
Compensation	Statutory, see code §§473.153

MONTANA

Holographic will	Valid
State inheritance tax	No
State estate tax	No
Transfer by affidavit	Yes, if total estate value is less than $20,000
Summary probate	Yes, if total estate value does not exceed homestead allowance, see §§72-3-1103
Time limit for publication	Four months after publication
Adopted Uniform Probate Code	Yes
Compensation	Statutory, see code §§72-3-631 to 633

NEBRASKA

Holographic will	Valid
State inheritance tax	Yes
State estate tax	Yes
Transfer by affidavit	Yes, if entire estate value is less than $25,000
Summary probate	Yes, if entire estate value does not exceed homestead allowance, see code §§30-24, 127
Time limit for publication	Two months after publication
Adopted Uniform Probate Code	Yes
Compensation	Reasonable

NEVADA

Holographic will	Valid
State inheritance tax	No
State estate tax	No
Transfer by affidavit	Yes, if surviving spouse and/or children, estate must be less than $20,000
Summary probate	With court approval, providing estate is less than $200,000, other provisions for surviving spouse
Time limit for creditors' claims	90 days after mailing of creditor notice
Adopted Uniform Probate Code	No
Compensation	Reasonable

NEW HAMPSHIRE

Holographic will	Not valid
State inheritance tax	No
State estate tax	No
Transfer by affidavit	No
Summary probate	Yes, if no real estate and total estate value is less than $10,000
Time limit for publication	Six months after letters issued
Adopted Uniform Probate Code	No
Compensation	Reasonable

NEW JERSEY

Holographic will	Valid
State inheritance tax	Yes
State estate tax	Yes
Transfer by affidavit	No
Summary probate	Yes, if there is no will and whether there is a spouse, see §§3b:10-4
Time limit for creditors' claims	Six months after publication
Adopted Uniform Probate Code	No
Compensation	No

NEW MEXICO

Holographic will	Not valid unless valid where signed
State inheritance tax	No
State estate tax	No
Transfer by affidavit	Yes, there is a if surviving spouse and estate value is less than $100,000
Summary probate	Yes, if estate value does not exceed state allowances, see §§45-3-1203
Time limit for creditors' claims	Two months after mailing of notice
Adopted Uniform Probate Code	Yes
Compensation	Reasonable

NEW YORK

Holographic will	Yes, if made by member of armed services during period of conflict
State inheritance tax	No
State estate tax	Yes, if estate is greater than $1 million
Transfer by affidavit	No
Summary probate	Yes, if no real estate and total value is less than $20,000
Time limit for creditors' claims	Three months after publication
Adopted Uniform Probate Code	No
Compensation	Reasonable

NORTH CAROLINA

Holographic will	Valid only if the will was found after death and in a place intended for safekeeping
State inheritance tax	No
State estate tax	Yes
Transfer by affidavit	No
Summary probate	Yes, if value of estate is less than $10,000 or $20,000 if surviving spouse
Time limit for creditors' claims	90 days after mailing of creditor notice
Adopted Uniform Probate Code	No
Compensation	No

NORTH DAKOTA

Holographic will	Valid
State inheritance tax	No
State estate tax	No
Transfer by affidavit	Yes, if value of estate is less than $15,000
Summary probate	Yes, if value of estate is less than homestead allowance, see code §§30.1-23-03
Time limit for creditors' claims	Three months after publication
Adopted Uniform Probate Code	Yes
Compensation	Reasonable

OHIO

Holographic will	Not valid
State inheritance tax	No
State estate tax	Yes
Transfer by affidavit	No
Summary probate	Yes, depending if there is surviving spouse
Time limit for creditors' claims	Three months after letters issued
Adopted Uniform Probate Code	No
Compensation	Reasonable

OKLAHOMA

Holographic will	Valid
State inheritance tax	No
State estate tax	Yes
Transfer by affidavit	No
Summary probate	Yes, if estate value is less than $60,000
Time limit for creditors' claims	Two months after mailing notice
Adopted Uniform Probate Code	No
Compensation	Reasonable

OREGON

Holographic will	Not valid
State inheritance tax	No
State estate tax	Yes
Transfer by affidavit	No
Summary probate	Yes, if estate value is less than $140,000 and not more than $50,000 is personal property and not more than $90,000 is real estate
Time limit for creditors' claims	Four months after publication
Adopted Uniform Probate Code	No
Compensation	Reasonable

PENNSYLVANIA

Holographic will	Valid
State inheritance tax	Depending on value of estate
State estate tax	No
Transfer by affidavit	No
Summary probate	Yes, if no real estate and total estate value is less than $25,000
Time limit for creditors' claims	One year after death
Adopted Uniform Probate Code	No
Compensation	Reasonable

RHODE ISLAND

Holographic will	Not valid unless valid where signed
State inheritance tax	No
State estate tax	Depending on size of estate
Transfer by affidavit	No
Summary probate	Yes, if no real estate and value is less than $15,000
Time limit for creditors' claims	Six months after publication
Adopted Uniform Probate Code	No
Compensation	Reasonable

SOUTH CAROLINA

Holographic will	Not valid unless valid where signed
State inheritance tax	No
State estate tax	No
Transfer by affidavit	Yes, if estate value is less than $10,000 and approved by judge
Summary probate	Yes, if estate value is less than $10,000
Time limit for creditors' claims	Eight months after publication
Adopted Uniform Probate Code	Yes
Compensation	Reasonable

SOUTH DAKOTA

Holographic will	Valid
State inheritance tax	No
State estate tax	No
Transfer by affidavit	Yes, if estate value is less than $50,000
Summary probate	Yes, regardless of value
Time limit for creditors' claims	Four months after publication
Adopted Uniform Probate Code	Yes
Compensation	Reasonable

TENNESSEE

Holographic will	Valid
State inheritance tax	Depending on value of estate
State estate tax	No
Transfer by affidavit	No
Summary probate	Yes, if value of estate is less than $25,000
Time limit for creditors' claims	Six months after publication
Adopted Uniform Probate Code	No
Compensation	Reasonable

TEXAS

Holographic will	Valid
Intestate succession codes	§§38
State estate tax	No
Transfer by affidavit	Yes, if there is no will and estate value is less than $50,000
Summary probate	Yes, if requested in will and all beneficiaries agree
Time limit for creditors' claims	Four months after publication
Adopted Uniform Probate Code	No
Compensation	Reasonable

UTAH

Holographic will	Valid
State inheritance tax	No
State estate tax	No
Transfer by affidavit	Yes, if value of estate is less than $25,000
Summary probate	Yes, if value of estate does not exceed the homestead allowance
Time limit for creditors' claims	Three months after publication
Adopted Uniform Probate Code	Yes
Compensation	Reasonable

VERMONT

Holographic will	Not valid
State inheritance tax	No
State estate tax	Depending on value of estate
Transfer by affidavit	No
Summary probate	If surviving spouse or children, no real estate and value is less than $10,000
Time limit for creditors' claims	Four months after publication
Adopted Uniform Probate Code	No
Compensation	Reasonable

VIRGINIA

Holographic will	Valid
State inheritance tax	No
State estate tax	Yes
Transfer by affidavit	Yes, if value of estate is less than $15,000
Summary probate	No
Time limit for creditors' claims	One year after publication
Adopted Uniform Probate Code	No
Compensation	Reasonable

WASHINGTON

Holographic will	Not valid unless valid where signed
State inheritance tax	No
State estate tax	Yes
Transfer by affidavit	Yes, if value of estate is less than $60,000
Summary probate	Yes
Time limit for creditors' claims	Four months after publication
Adopted Uniform Probate Code	No
Compensation	Reasonable

WEST VIRGINIA

Holographic will	Valid
State inheritance tax	No
State estate tax	No
Transfer by affidavit	No
Summary probate	Yes, if value of estate is less than $100,000
Time limit for creditors' claims	Three months after publication
Adopted Uniform Probate Code	No
Compensation	Reasonable

WISCONSIN

Holographic will	Not valid unless valid where signed
State inheritance tax	No
State estate tax	Yes
Transfer by affidavit	Yes, if value of estate is less than $20,000
Summary probate	Yes, if value of estate is less than $50,000 and there is a surviving spouse or minor children
Time limit for creditors' claims	Four months after publication
Adopted Uniform Probate Code	No
Compensation	Reasonable

WYOMING

Holographic will	Valid
State inheritance tax	No
State estate tax	No
Transfer by affidavit	Yes, if value of estate is less than $150,000
Summary probate	Yes, if value of estate including real estate is less than $150,000
Time limit for creditors' claims	Three months after publication
Adopted Uniform Probate Code	No
Compensation	Statutory, see §§2-7-804

STATE-BY-STATE LISTING OF PROBATE CODES

ALABAMA	Title 43 Chapter 2 Administration of Estates Title 43 Chapter 8 Probate Code
ALASKA	Title 13 Decedents' Estates, Guardianships, Transfers and Trusts Title 13 Chapter 16 Probate of Wills and Administration
ARIZONA	Title 14 Trusts, Estates and Protective Proceedings
ARKANSAS	Title 28 Wills, Estates and Fiduciary Relationships
CALIFORNIA	California Probate Code
COLORADO	Title 15 Probate, Trusts and Fiduciaries
CONNECTICUT	Title 45 Probate Courts and Procedure
DISTRICT OF COLUMBIA	Division III Title 18 Wills Division III Title 19 Descent Distribution and Trusts Division III Title 20 Probate and Administration of Decedents' Estates
FLORIDA	Title XLII Estates and Trusts
GEORGIA	Title 53 Wills, Trusts, and Administration of Estates

HAWAII	Title 30A Uniform Probate Code
IDAHO	Title 15 Uniform Probate Code
ILLINOIS	Chapter 755 Estates Chapter 760 Trusts and Fiduciaries
INDIANA	Title 29 Probate Title 30 Trusts and Fiduciaries
IOWA	Title XV Chapter 633 Probate Code Title XV Chapter 634 Private Foundations and Charitable Trusts Title XV Chapter 635 Administration of Small Estates Title XV Chapter 636 Sureties-Fiduciaries-Trusts-Investments
KANSAS	Chapter 59 Probate Code
KENTUCKY	Chapter 140 Inheritance and Estate Taxes Chapter 386 Administration of Trusts—Investments Chapter 391 Descent and Distribution Chapter 394 Wills Chapter 395 Personal Representatives Chapter 396 Claims Against Decedents' Estates
LOUISIANA	Book III, Title I Of Successions Uniform Probate Law
MAINE	Title 18 Decedents' Estates and Fiduciary Relations Title 18A Probate Code
MARYLAND	Titles 1 to 16 Estates and Trusts

MASSACHUSETTS	MGL Part II, Title II Descent and Distribution, Wills, Estates
MICHIGAN	Chapters 701 to 713 Probate Code
MINNESOTA	Chapters 524-532 Estates of Decedents; Guardianships
MISSISSIPPI	Title 91 Trusts and Estates
MISSOURI	Title XXXI, Chapters 456-475 Trusts and Estates of Decedents
MONTANA	Title 72 estates, Trusts and Fiduciary Relationships
NEBRASKA	Chapter 30 Decedents' Estates; Protection of Persons and Property
NEVADA	Title 12 Wills and Estates of Deceased Persons Title 13 Guardianships; Conservatorships; Trusts
NEW HAMPSHIRE	Title 56 Probate Courts and Decedents' Estates
NEW JERSEY	Titles 3A and 3B Administration of Estates — Decedents and Others
NEW MEXICO	Chapter 45 Uniform Probate Code Chapter 46 Fiduciaries and Trusts
NEW YORK	Chapter 17-B Estates, Powers and Trusts
NORTH CAROLINA	Chapter 41 Estates Chapter 47 Probate and Registration

NORTH DAKOTA	Title 30.1 Uniform Probate Code
OHIO	Title XXI Courts - Probate - Juvenile
OKLAHOMA	Title 58 Probate Procedure Title 84 Wills and Succession
OREGON	Chapter 111 Probate Law Chapter 112 Intestate Succession and Wills Chapter 113 Initiation of Estate Proceedings Chapter 114 Administration of Estates Chapter 115 Claims, Actions, and Suits Against Estates
PENNSYLVANIA	Title 20 Decedents, Estates and Fiduciaries
RHODE ISLAND	Title 33 Probate Practice and Procedure
SOUTH DAKOTA	Title 29A Uniform Probate Code Title 55 Fiduciaries and Trusts
SOUTH CAROLINA	Title 21 Estates, Trusts, Guardians and Fiduciaries Title 62 Probate Code
TENNESSEE	Title 30 Administration of Estates Title 31 Descent and Distribution Title 32 Wills

TEXAS	Texas Probate Code Texas Probate Code Chapter V Estates of Decedents Texas Probate Code Chapter IV Execution and Revocation of Wills Texas Probate Code Chapter XIII Guardianship
UTAH	Title 30.1 Uniform Probate Code
VERMONT	Title XXI Courts - Probate - Juvenile
VIRGINIA	Title 58 Probate Procedure Title 84 Wills and Succession
WASHINGTON	Chapter 111 Probate Law Chapter 112 Intestate Succession and Wills Chapter 113 Initiation of Estate Proceedings Chapter 114 Administration of Estates Chapter 115 Claims, Actions, and Suits Against Estates
WEST VIRGINIA	Title 20 Decedents, Estates and Fiduciaries
WISCONSIN	Title 33 Probate Practice and Procedure
WYOMING	Title 29A Uniform Probate Code Title 55 Fiduciaries and Trusts

APPENDIX D:
UNCLAIMED PROPERTY

The following addresses and websites are provided for you to search for unclaimed property. Remember, you will need the decedent's Social Security number to conduct a search. Further, if property is discovered, you will be required to produce a certified copy of the death certificate and other documentation that establishes your authority to act on behalf of the estate. For a further discussion, see Chapter 10.

ALABAMA
State Treasury
Unclaimed Property Division
P.O. Box 302520
Montgomery, AL 36130
www.treasury.state.al.us

ALASKA
Department of Revenue
Tax Division
Unclaimed Property Section
P.O. Box 110420
Juneau, AK 99811
www.tax.state.ak.us/
  UnclaimedProperty

ARIZONA
Department of Revenue
Unclaimed Property Unit
P.O. Box 29026
Phoenix, AZ 85038
www.azunclaimed.gov

ARKANSAS
Unclaimed Property Division
Auditor of State
1400 W. 3rd St., Suite 100
Little Rock, AR 72201
www.state.ar.us/auditor

CALIFORNIA
State Controller
Division of Collections - Bureau of
Unclaimed Property
3301 C Street, Suite 712
P.O. Box 942850
Sacramento, CA 94250
www.sco.ca.gov/

COLORADO
Unclaimed Property Division
1120 Lincoln Street
Suite 1004
Denver, CO 80203
www.colorado.gov/treasury

CONNECTICUT
Unclaimed Property Division
Office of State Treasurer
55 Elm Street
Hartford, CT 06106
www.state.ct.us/ott/

DELAWARE
Bureau of Abandoned Property
P.O. Box 8931
Wilmington, DE 19899
www.revenue.deleware.gov

DISTRICT OF COLUMBIA
Office of Finance & Treasury
Unclaimed Property Unit
1275 K Street, NW
Suite 500B
Washington, DC 20005
http://cfo.washingtondc.gov

FLORIDA
Department of Financial Services
Bureau of Unclaimed Property
Post Office Box 1990
Tallahassee, FL 32302
www.fltreasurehunt.org

GEORGIA
Georgia Department of Revenue
Local Government Services
Unclaimed Property Program
4245 International Parkway
Suite A
Hapeville, GA 30354
www.etax.dor.ga.gov/ptd/ucp/index.shtml

HAWAII
Department of Budget and Finance
Unclaimed Property Program
P.O. Box 150
Honolulu, HI 96810
http://pahoehoe.ehawaii.gov/lilo/app

IDAHO
Idaho State Tax Commission
Unclaimed Property Section
P.O. BOX 70012
Boise, ID 83707
http://tax.idaho.gov/unclaimed.htm

ILLINOIS
Office of State Treasurer
Unclaimed Property Division
P.O. Box 19495
Springfield, IL 62794
www.state.il.us/treas

INDIANA
Attorney General's Office
Unclaimed Property Division
P.O. Box 2504
Greenwood, IN 46142
www.indianaunclaimed.com

IOWA
Michael L. Fitzgerald, State Treasurer
The Great Iowa Treasure Hunt
Lucas State Office Building
321 East 12th Street
Des Moines, IA 50319
www.greatiowatreasurehunt.com

KANSAS
Unclaimed Property Division
900 Jackson Suite 201
Topeka, KS 66612
www.kansascash.com/prodweb/up/
index.php

KENTUCKY
Office of State Treasurer Jonathan Miller
Unclaimed Property
1050 US Highway 127 South
Suite 100
Frankfort, KY 40601
www.kytreasury.com

LOUISIANA
John Kennedy, State Treasurer
Unclaimed Property Division
P.O. Box 91010
Baton Rouge, LA 70821
www.treasury.state.la.us/

MAINE
State Treasurer's Office
Unclaimed Property Division
39 State House Station
111 Sewall Street, 3rd FL
Augusta, ME 04333
www.maine.gov/treasurer/
unclaimed_property/

MARYLAND
Unclaimed Property Unit
301 W. Preston Street
Baltimore, MD 21201
www.marylandtaxes.com/default.asp

MASSACHUSETTS
Abandoned Property Division
1 Ashburton Place, 12th Floor
Boston, MA 02108
www.state.ma.us/treasury/

MICHIGAN
Department of Treasury
Unclaimed Property Division
P.O. Box 30756
Lansing, MI 48909
www.michigan.gov/treasury

MINNESOTA
Minnesota Department of Commerce
Unclaimed Property Division
85 7th Place East, Suite 600
St. Paul, MN 55101
www.state.mn.us

MISSISSIPPI
Treasury Department
Unclaimed Property Division
P.O. Box 138
Jackson, MS 39205
www.treasury.state.ms.us/Index.asp

MISSOURI
State Treasurer
Unclaimed Property Division
P.O. Box 1004
Jefferson City, MO 65102
www.showmemoney.com

MONTANA
Department of Revenue
Unclaimed Property Division
Sam W. Mitchell Bldg.
125 N. Roberts, 3rd Floor
Helena, MT 59604
www.discoveringmontana.com

NEBRASKA
Nebraska State Treasurer
Unclaimed Property Division
5800 Cornhusker Highway
Building 2, Suite 4
Lincoln, NE 68507
www.treasurer.org

NEVADA
Office of the State Treasurer
Unclaimed Property Division
555 E Washington Avenue
Suite 4200
Las Vegas, NV 89101
http://nevadatreasurer.gov/

NEW HAMPSHIRE
Treasury Department
Unclaimed Property Division
25 Capitol Street
Room 205
Concord, NH 03301
www.state.nh.us/treasury/

NEW JERSEY
Department of the Treasury
Unclaimed Property
P.O. Box 214
Trenton, NJ 08695
www.state.nj.us/treasury

NEW MEXICO
Taxation & Revenue Department
Unclaimed Property Division
P.O. Box 25123
Santa Fe, NM 87504
https://ec3.state.nm.us/ucp/

NEW YORK
State Comptroller
New York State Office of Unclaimed
Funds
110 State Street
8th Floor
Albany, NY 12236
www.osc.state.ny.us/

NORTH CAROLINA
Department of State Treasurer
Unclaimed / Escheats Division
325 N Salisbury Street
Raleigh, NC 27603
www.NCCash.com

NORTH DAKOTA
State Land Department
Unclaimed Property Division
P.O. Box 5523
Bismarck, ND 58506
www.land.state.nd.us

OHIO
Department of Commerce
Division of Unclaimed Funds
77 South High Street
20th Floor
Columbus, OH 43215
www.unclaimedfundstreasurehunt.
ohio.gov/

OKLAHOMA
Oklahoma State Treasurer's Office
Unclaimed Property Division
4545 North Lincoln Boulevard
Suite 106
Oklahoma City, OK 73105
www.treasurer.state.ok.us

OREGON
Department of State Lands
Unclaimed Property Division
775 Summer Street NE Suite 100
Salem, OR 97301
www.oregonstatelands.us/

PENNSYLVANIA
Pennsylvania Treasury Department
Unclaimed Property Bureau
P.O. Box 1837
Harrisburg, PA 17105
www.patreasury.org

RHODE ISLAND
Department of Treasury
Unclaimed Property Division
P.O. Box 1435
Providence, RI 02901
www.treasury.ri.gov

SOUTH CAROLINA
Office of the State Treasurer
Unclaimed Property Division
P.O. Box 11778
Columbia, SC 29211
www.state.sc.us/treas

SOUTH DAKOTA
Office of the State Treasurer
Vernon L. Larson
500 East Capitol Avenue
Pierre, SD 57501
www.sdtreasurer.com

TENNESSEE
Treasury Department
Unclaimed Property Division
Andrew Jackson Building
9th Floor
500 Deaderick Street
Nashville, TN 37243
www.treasury.state.tn.us/unclaim/

TEXAS
Texas Comptroller of Public Accounts
Unclaimed Property Division
P.O. Box 12019
Austin, TX 78711
www.window.state.tx.us/up

UTAH
State Treasurer's Office
Unclaimed Property Division
341 South Main Street
5th Floor
Salt Lake City, UT 84111
www.treasurer.state.ut.us/

VERMONT
State Treasurer's Office
Unclaimed Property Division
133 State Street
Montpelier, VT 05633
www.vermonttreasurer.gov/

VIRGINIA

Department of Treasury

Unclaimed Property Division

P.O. Box 2478

Richmond, VA 23218

www.trs.virginia.gov

WASHINGTON

Department of Revenue

Unclaimed Property Section

P.O. Box 47477

Olympia, WA 98504

http://ucp.dor.wa.gov

WEST VIRGINIA

Office of State Treasurer

One Players Club Drive

Charleston, WV 25311

www.wvtreasury.com

WISCONSIN

State Treasurer's Office

Unclaimed Property Division

P.O. Box 2114

Madison, WI 53701

www.ost.state.wi.us

WYOMING

Office of the State Treasurer

Unclaimed Property Division

2515 Warren Avenue, Suite 502

Cheyenne, WY 82002

http://treasurer.state.wy.us

APPENDIX E:
SAMPLE FORMS

This appendix contains a sample final accounting report and a sample order on accounting. You can use these as reference for how to set up your own final accounting and what to expect when the court hands down its order on your accounting.

Sample Final Accounting Report 264
Sample Order on Accounting 271

Pages 264–270 contain a sample of a typical final accounting report that is submitted to the court prior to closing the estate. In addition to the accounting, you may be required to produce documentation, such as receipts, to verify the statements made in the accounting.

Most courts require that you also prepare the order for the judge's signature that will close the estate. Upon review of the sample order, found on pages 271–274, you will discover that the order is a summary of the accounting, includes the names of each beneficiary and what they are to receive, specifies what creditors were paid, if any, and approves the attorney fees. Finally, if you are seeking compensation for your services, the court will approve the fee.

Note that these forms have been reduced in size for publication purposes. Also, most courts require that the information be double-spaced.

Benjamin H. Berkley
A Professional Law Corporation
1440 N. Harbor Blvd., Suite 250
Fullerton, CA 92835
Telephone: (714) 871-6440
Facsimile: (714) 871-9714

Attorney for Administrator

SUPERIOR COURT OF CALIFORNIA, COUNTY OF ORANGE

The Estate of   RUSSELL OWEN SONG   Case No. A214583)

) FIRST AND FINAL ACCOUNT AND REPORT
) OF ADMINISTRATOR AND PETITION FOR
) ITS SETTLEMENT, ALLOWANCE OF
) ADMINISTRATOR'S COMMISSION,
) ALLOWANCE OF STATUTORY ATTORNEY'S
Deceased.) FEES, AND FINAL DISTRIBUTION.
_____)

Petitioner, Mike Kim, is the Administrator of the Estate of Russell Owen Song, deceased.

Petitioner states:

1. Date and Place of Death.

Russell Owen Song died intestate on June 17, 2002, in Anaheim, California, and was a resident of the County of Orange and the State of California.

2. Appointment of Personal Representatives.

Petitioner qualified as Administrator and letters of administration were issued to Petitioner on October 10, 2006. Petitioner was granted full authorization to administer the Estate under the Independent Administration of Estates Act and Petitioner is still theAdministrator of the Decedent's Estate.

3. Administration Completed.

The time period covered by this accounting is from June 17, 2006 to March 31, 2007, inclusive. Petitioner has performed all duties required of him as Administrator of the Estate of Decedent. Except as hereinafter set forth, all debts of the Decedent and this Estate, and all expenses of administration incurred to date, including costs of publication, have been paid.

The Estate was administered under the Independent Administration of Estates Act. Petitioner did the following without Court supervision after having sent a notice of proposed action to all persons entitled:

A . Sold the real property located at 1361 Schooner Lane, Anaheim, California for $260,000.00.

Petitioner did the following things without Court supervision and without sending notices of proposed action:

    Sold decedent's personal property as follows:

1. Household furniture and furnishings - $665.00.

2. Mitsubishi - $15,200.00

3. Toyota - $6,850.00

4. Time for Filing Creditors' Claims.

More than four (4) months has elapsed since issuance of letters and the time for filing Creditors' Claims expired on February 10, 2003. All known and reasonably ascertainable creditors of the Estate described in Probate Code Section 9050 received the notice described in Probate Code Section 9052 or are within the class of creditors described in Probate Code Section 9054. Probate Code Section 9001 et seq. is not applicable in this Estate. Petitioner reviewed the decedent's personal records and files, the decedent's bank records, and the decedent's mail in order to ascertain the names of the decedent's creditors. The decedent did not apply for nor receive any health care under the provisions of Chapter 7 or Chapter 8, Part

3, Division 9, Welfare and Institution Code of the State of California. Probate Code Section 9001 et seq. is not applicable in this Estate. Notice was given to the Director of Health Services, who declined to file a claim in this matter.

5. Creditors' Claims.
Union Bank of California filed a Creditor's Claim in the sum of $12,729.93 which was paid from the proceeds from the sale of the 1997 Mitsubishi 300 GT SL Coupe.

6. Inventory and Appraised Value of the Estate.
An Inventory and Appraisal of the Estate was filed on June 2, 2003, showing the value of said Estate to be the sum of $227,000.00. An additional Inventory and Appraisal was filed on or about July 23, 2004, showing additional property of $65,105.67.
Petitioner alleges that the Inventory and Appraisal lists all of the assets of Decedent's Estate that have come into Petitioner=s knowledge or into his possession.

7. Personal Property Taxes.
No personal property taxes were owed by the Estate.

8. Income Taxes.
No California or federal income taxes are payable by the Estate.

9. California Inheritance Tax or Estate Tax.
No California Estate tax return has been or will be filed, because the Estate is of insufficient size to require one.

10. Federal Estate Tax.
No federal Estate Tax return is required and no federal Estate Tax is due or payable.

11. Summary of Account.
Petitioner has kept all cash in his possession in interest bearing accounts or other investments authorized by law except what was needed to administer the Estate.

Petitioner has attached hereto supporting schedules for the following summary of account.

Charges

Amount of Inventory and Appraisal	$292,105.67
Receipts during accounting period	17,288.06
Gain on Sales	36,017.40
Other receipts	141,409.59
Total charges	486,820.72

Credits

Disbursements during accounting period		71,901.49
Sale of Real Property		$143,480.80
Losses of Sales		835.00
Distributions		0.00
Other Credits		0.00
Property on Hand		$184,802.79
As of July 22, 2004	TOTAL CREDITS	$515,994.67

Character of Estate Property.

The whole of the Estate is Decedent's separate property.

Heirs and Beneficiaries.

Said decedent died intestate and all of the property remaining in said Estate should be distributed according to the laws of intestate succession. The decedent's intestate heirs are: Mike Kim, Steven Kim, Melissa Kim and Kenneth Kim, the children of Kenneth Kim and Ralph Kim, son of Ralph Kim.

14. Preliminary Distributions.

No preliminary distributions have been made.

Proposed Distributions.

Therefore, the property of the Estate, together with any other property of the decedent or the Estate not known or discovered, should be distributed as follows: The Estate insofar as is known, consists of the assets listed in as of April 23, 2004.

Statutory Fees for Ordinary Services.

The statutory attorney's fees and Administrator's commission, payable to each for their ordinary services are $9,953.64 computed on a compensation base of $347,682.13 arrived at as follows:

Fee Base

Inventory and Appraisement	$292,105.67
Receipts	19,559.06
Gains on Sale	36,017.40
Total	$347.682.13

Fee Computation

4% on first $100,000.00	$4,000.00
3% on next $100,000.00	$3,000.00
2% on next $147,682.13	$2,953.64
TOTAL	$9,953.64

17. Extraordinary Commissions and Fees.

Petitioner waives any extraordinary commissions to which he may be entitled. Petitioner's attorney waives any extraordinary fees to which he may be entitled.

18. Required Statements.

a. There were no sales, purchases, changes in the form of assets, or other transactions occurring during the period of the account that are not otherwise readily understandable from the schedules.

b. There are no unusual items in the account.

c. There was no compensation paid to the attorney not the Administrator.

d. There is no relationship between the fiduciaries or the attorney for the fiduciaries and any agent hired by the fiduciaries during the accounting period.

19. Request for Special Notice.
No request for special notice has been filed in this matter. Although the decedent was not a MediCal beneficiary, the California State Department of Health Services was given notice of the proceedings and no claim or request for special notice was filed.

20. The property available for distribution is subject to the disbursements.
21. Subject to such disbursements and retention the Estate should be distributed as follows:

Name of Distributee Description of Property

Mike KIM The rest and residue of the Estate
 consisting of the MetLife Account #404-5572083 and checking account at Wells Fargo Bank Account #011-1908299

WHEREFORE, Petitioner prays for an Order of this Court that:
1. The Administration of this Estate be closed;

2. The First and Final Account of Petitioner as Administrator be settled, allowed, and approved as filed;

3. All the acts and proceedings of Petitioner as Administrator be confirmed and approved;

4. Petitioner requests the sum of $9,953.64 be allowed and ordered paid to him as and for statutory Administrator's commission, the computation of which is set forth in Schedule A; and finding that Petitioner has waived any extraordinary commissions to which he may be entitled;

5. Petitioner be authorized to pay to Benjamin H. Berkley attorney for Petitioner, the sum of $9,953.64 as statutory fees for his services to Petitioner; and finding that attorney for Petitioner has waived any extraordinary fees to which he may be entitled;

6. Distribution the Estate of the decedent in Petitioner's hands and any other property of the decedent or Estate not now known or hereafter discovered be made as set forth above in Paragraph 21; and

7. Such further Order be made as the Court considers proper.

Dated: July 22, 2007

_____ MIKE KIM, PETITIONER

SAMPLE ORDER ON FINAL ACCOUNTING

BENJAMIN H. BERKLEY
A PROFESSIONAL LAW CORPORATION
1440 North Harbor Boulevard, Suite 250
Fullerton, CA 92835
(714) 871-6440
Bar No. 79974
Attorney for Petitioner, Mike Kim

SUPERIOR COURT OF THE STATE OF CALIFORNIA
COUNTY OF ORANGE

Estate of   Case No. A214583
RUSSELL OWEN SONG,
) ORDER ON FIRST
)AND FINAL
) ACCOUNT
)
)
)February 23, 2005
)Time: 9:00 a.m.
)Dept.: L-73

_____)

MIKE KIM, as Administrator of the Estate of RUSSELL OWEN SONG, having filed his First and Final Account and Report of Administrator and Petition for its Settlement, and the same having come on for hearing this 24th day of February 2005, in Department L-73 of the above-entitled Court, the Honorable Judge _____ presiding, the Court, after examining the petition and hearing the evidence, finds:

Due notice of the hearing of the Petition has been regularly given as required by law.

All of the allegations of the Petition are true.

Decedent died on June 17, 2002, in Anaheim, California, and was a resident of the County of Orange, and the State of California.

Decedent died intestate. Petitioner qualified as the Administrator of the Estate, and letters of administration were issued to Petitioner on October 10, 2002, and at all times since then they have been and now is the Administrator of the decedent's Estate.

Notice of death has been duly given, published, and filed together with an affidavit showing due publication thereof and the time for filing or presenting claims has expired.

Petitioner has performed all duties required of him as Administrator with respect to the administration of the Estate, the Estate is ready for distribution and is in a condition to be closed.

An inventory and appraisement of the Estate has been duly returned and filed herein showing the value of the Estate to be $300,529.79.

No personal property taxes are due and payable by the Estate.

No California or federal Estate taxes are due.

No California state or federal income taxes are payable in the Estate.

The whole of the Estate is separate property of the decedent.

The commissions provided by law for the ordinary services of the Petitioner is $10,076.53. Benjamin H. Berkley, attorney at law, has rendered ordinary legal services to petitioner, and the fee provided by law for such services is the sum of $10,076.53. The payment of such funds by the beneficiary should be approved in discharge of the statutory commissions and fees.

IT IS THEREFORE ORDERED THAT:

1. The administration of the Estate is brought to a close.

2. The First and Final Account of Petitioner as Administrator be settled, allowed, and approved as filed.

3. All acts and proceedings of the Petitioner as Administrator be confirmed and approved.

4. The payment of the statutory commissions to Administrator in the amount of $10,076.53 is approved; and any extraordinary fees to which Petitioner may be entitled is waived.

5. Statutory fees in the amount of $10,076.53 to Benjamin H. Berkley is approved.

6. Notice of Death has been duly given as required by law.

7. The personal representative shall be discharged upon the filing of proper receipts and an Affidavit for Final Discharge.

8. The following described property on hand for distribution is distributed as follows:

Name of Distributee	Description of property
Mike Kim	One-sixth (1/6th) of the rest and residue of the Estate.
Steven Kim	One-sixth (1/6th) of the rest and residue of the Estate.
Melissa Kim	One-sixth (1/6th) of the rest and residue of the Estate.
Kenneth Kim	One-sixth (1/6th) of the rest and residue of the Estate.
Ralph Kim, Jr.	One-sixth (1/6th) of the rest and residue of the Estate.
Kimberly Michelle Harris	One-sixth (1/6th) of the rest and residue of the Estate.

The residue of the Estate, insofar as is now known, consists of the following property:

1.   MetLife account number 404-5572083;

2.   Wells Fargo Checking account number 011-1908299.

All the rest, residue and remainder of the Estate, hereinafter, more particularly described, together with any property of the Estate not now known or discovered which may belong to the Estate, or in which the decedent or the Estate may have an interest, is hereby distributed to Mike Kim, Steven Kim, Melissa Kim, Kenneth Kim, Ralph Kim, Jr. and Kimberly Michelle Harris, in equal shares, share and share alike.

Dated:

_____
JUDGE OF THE SUPERIOR COURT

APPENDIX F:

BLANK FORMS

This appendix contains blank forms that you may find useful in preparing your own estate planning, or when advising others on their own estate planning. These are also examples of the kind of forms you should be looking for at the time of passing, as they will help you immensely in organizing the affairs of the estate. The deceased may have discussed some or all of these with you when he or she asked you to be the representative of his or her estate. Note also that forms 1, 2, and 3 are only applicable during the decedent's lifetime.

When you photocopy these forms, be sure to enlarge them to fit an 8.5" x 11" page.

form 1: Power of Attorney for Health Care 276
form 2: Living Will 284
form 3: Durable Power of Attorney 286
form 4: Accounts and Debts Organizer 292
form 5: Personal Data and Record Locator 295

FORM #1

EXPLANATION

You have the right to give instructions about your own health care. You also have the right to name someone else to make health care decisions for you. This form lets you do either or both of these things. It also lets you express your wishes regarding donation of organs and the designation of your primary physician.

Part 1 of this form is a power of attorney for health care. Part 1 lets you name another individual as agent to make health care decisions for you if you become incapable of making your own decisions, or if you want someone else to make those decisions for you now even though you are still capable. You may also name an alternate agent to act for you if your first choice is not willing, able, or reasonably available to make decisions for you. (Your agent may not be an operator or employee of a community care facility or a residential care facility where you are receiving care, or your supervising health care provider or employee of the health care institution where you are receiving care, unless your agent is related to you or is a coworker.)

Unless the form you sign limits the authority of your agent, your agent may make all health care decisions for you. This form has a place for you to limit the authority of your agent. You need not limit the authority of your agent if you wish to rely on your agent for all health care decisions that may have to be made. If you choose not to limit the authority of your agent, your agent will have the right to:

a. Consent or refuse consent to any care, treatment, service, or procedure to maintain, diagnose, or otherwise affect a physical or mental condition.

b. Select or discharge health care providers and institutions.

c. Approve or disapprove diagnostic tests, surgical procedures, and programs of medication.

d. Direct the provision, withholding, or withdrawal of artificial nutrition and hydration, and all other forms of health care, including cardiopulmonary resuscitation.

e. Make anatomical gifts, authorize an autopsy, and direct disposition of remains.

Part 2 of this form lets you give specific instructions about any aspect of your health care, whether or not you appoint an agent. Choices are provided for you to express your wishes regarding the provision, withholding, or withdrawal of treatment to keep you alive, as well as the provision of pain relief.

Space is also provided for you to add to the choices you have made or for you to write out any additional wishes. If you are satisfied to allow your agent to determine what is best for you in making end-of-life decisions, you need not fill out Part 2 of this form.

Part 3 of this form lets you express an intention to donate your bodily organs and tissues following your death.

Part 4 of this form lets you designate a physician to have primary responsibility for your health care.

After completing this form, sign and date the form at the end.

The form must be signed by two qualified witnesses or acknowledged before a notary public. Give a copy of the signed and completed form to your physician, to any other health care providers you may have, to any health care institution at which you are receiving care, and to any health care agents you have named. You should talk to the person you have named as agent to make sure that he or she understands your wishes and is willing to take the responsibility.

You have the right to revoke this advance health care directive or replace this form at any time.

POWER OF ATTORNEY FOR HEALTH CARE

PART 1

(1.1) **DESIGNATION OF AGENT**: I, _____,
presently   a   resident   of   _____   County,   state   of
_____, designate the following individual as my agent to make health
care decisions for me: _____, presently a resident of
_____ County, state of _____.

(1.1a) If I revoke my agent's authority or if my agent is not willing, able, or reasonably available to make a health care decision for me, I designate as my first alternate
agent _____, presently a resident of
_____ County, state of _____.

(1.2) **AGENT'S AUTHORITY**: My agent is authorized to make all health care decisions for me, including decisions to provide, withhold, or withdraw artificial nutrition and
hydration and all other forms of health care to keep me alive, except as I state here:

_____

_____

_____

(Add additional sheets if needed.)

(1.3) **WHEN AGENT'S AUTHORITY BECOMES EFFECTIVE**: My agent's
authority to make health care decisions for me takes effect immediately.

(1.4) **AGENT'S OBLIGATION**: My agent shall make health care decisions for me in
accordance with this power of attorney for health care, any instructions I give in Part 2
of this form, and my other wishes to the extent known to my agent. To the extent my
wishes are unknown, my agent shall make health care decisions for me in accordance
with what my agent determines to be in my best interest. In determining my best interest, my agent shall consider my personal values to the extent known to my agent.

(1.5) **AGENT'S POST-DEATH AUTHORITY**: My agent is authorized to make anatomical gifts, authorize an autopsy, and direct disposition of my remains, except as I state here or in Part 3 of this form.

_____

_____

_____

(Add additional sheets if needed.)

(1.6) **NOMINATION OF CONSERVATOR**: If a conservator of my person needs to be appointed for me by a court, I nominate the agent designated in this form. If that agent is not willing, able, or reasonably available to act as conservator, I nominate the alternate agents whom I have named, in the order designated.

PART 2

INSTRUCTIONS FOR HEALTH CARE

If you fill out this part of the form, you may strike any wording you do not want.

(2.1) **END-OF-LIFE DECISIONS**: I direct that my health care providers and others involved in my care provide, withhold, or withdraw treatment in accordance with the choice I have initialed below:

_____(a) Choice Not To Prolong Life. I do not want my life to be prolonged if (1) I have an incurable and irreversible condition that will result in my death within a relatively short time, (2) I become unconscious and, to a reasonable degree of medical certainty, I will not regain consciousness, or (3) the likely risks and burdens of treatment would outweigh the expected benefits, OR

_____(b) Choice To Prolong Life. I want my life to be prolonged as long as possible within the limits of generally accepted health care standards.

(2.2) **RELIEF FROM PAIN**: Except as I state in the following space, I direct that treatment for alleviation of pain or discomfort be provided at all times, even if it hastens my death:

_____

_____

_____

(Add additional sheets if needed.)

(2.3) **OTHER WISHES:** (If you do not agree with any of the optional choices above and wish to write your own, or if you wish to add to the instructions you have given above, you may do so here.) I direct that:

_____

_____

_____

(Add additional sheets if needed.)

PART 3
DONATION OF ORGANS AT DEATH
(OPTIONAL)

(3.1) Upon my death (initial applicable):

_____(a) I give any needed organs, tissues, or parts, OR

_____(b) I give the following organs, tissues, or parts:

_____

_____

_____

_____ OR

_____(c) My gift is for the following purposes (strike out any of the following you do **not** want):

　　　　(1) Transplant

　　　　(2) Therapy

　　　　(3) Research

　　　　(4) Education

_____(d) I do not wish to donate my organs.

PART 4
PRIMARY PHYSICIAN
(OPTIONAL)

(4.1) I designate the following physician as my primary physician:

_____

(name of physician)

_____

(address)   (city)   (state)   (zip)

_____

(phone)

OPTIONAL: If the physician I have designated above is not willing, able, or reasonably available to act as my primary physician, I designate the following physician as my primary physician:

_____

(name of physician)

_____

(address)   (city)   (state)   (zip)

_____

(phone)

PART 5

(5.1) **EFFECT OF COPY:** A copy of this form has the same effect as the original.

(5.2) **SIGNATURE:** Sign and date the form here:

_____

Date _____

(5.3) **STATEMENT OF WITNESSES**: We declare under penalty of perjury under the laws of _____ (1) that the individual who signed or acknowledged this advance health care directive is personally known to me, or that the individual's identity was proven to me by convincing evidence, (2) that the individual signed or acknowledged this advance directive in my presence, (3) that the individual appears to be of sound mind and under no duress, fraud, or undue influence, (4) that I am not a person appointed as agent by this advance directive, and (5) that I am not the individual's health care provider, an employee of the individual's health care provider, the operator of a community care facility, an employee of an operator of a community care facility, the operator of a residential care facility for the elderly, or an employee of an operator of a residential care facility for the elderly.

Print Name:

_____

Signature:

_____

Address:

_____

Dated:

_____

Print Name:

_____

Signature:

_____

Address:

_____

Dated:

_____

    (5.4) **ADDITIONAL STATEMENT OF WITNESSES**: At least one of the above witnesses must also sign the following declaration. I further declare under penalty of perjury under the laws of the state of _____ that I am not related to the individual executing this advance health care directive by blood, marriage, or adoption, and to the best of my knowledge, I am not entitled to any part of the individual's Estate upon his or her death under a Will now existing or by operation of law.

_____

(signature of witness)

    (5.5) STATE OF _____   )

           COUNTY OF _____   )

On this _____ day of _____, 20_____ before me, a notary public in and for said county and state, residing herein, duly commissioned and sworn, personally appeared _____, personally known to me (or proved to me on the basis of satisfactory evidence) to be the person whose name is subscribed to the within instrument and acknowledged to me that he/she executed the same in his/her authorized capacity, and that by his/her signature on the instrument the person, or entity upon behalf of which the person acted, executed the instrument.

WITNESS my hand and official seal.

_____

(Signature of Notary Public)

FORM #2

LIVING WILL (A DIRECTIVE TO MY PHYSICIAN)

I, _____, being of sound mind, willfully and voluntarily make known my desire that my dying not be artificially prolonged under the circumstances set forth below, and declare that:

If at any time I should have an incurable injury, disease, or illness certified to be a terminal condition by two physicians who have personally examined me, one of whom is my attending physician, and the physicians have determined that my death will occur unless life-sustaining procedures are used, and if the application of life-sustaining procedures would serve only to artificially prolong the dying process, I direct that life-sustaining procedures be withheld or withdrawn and that I be permitted to die naturally and with only the performance of medical procedures deemed necessary to provide me with comfort and care.

I further direct that if at any time I should be in a permanent vegetative state or an irreversible coma as certified by two physicians who have personally examined me, one of whom is my attending physician, and the physicians have determined that the application of life-sustaining procedures, including artificially administered food and fluid, will only artificially prolong my life in a permanent vegetative state or irreversible coma, I direct that these procedures, including the administration of food or fluids, be withheld or withdrawn, and that I be permitted to die naturally with only the administration of medication to alleviate pain or the performance of medical procedures necessary to provide me with comfort and care.

In the absence of my ability to give directions regarding the use of life-sustaining procedures, it is my intention that this Declaration be honored by my family and attending physician as the final expression of my legal right to refuse medical or surgical treatment and accept the consequences of such refusal.

I understand the full import of this Declaration, and I have emotional and mental capacity to make this declaration.

Dated: _____

_____ Signature

State of _____

County of _____

On this _____ day of _____, 200_____, before me, _____, a notary public in and for said county and state, residing herein, duly commissioned and sworn, personally appeared _____, personally known to me (or proved to me on the basis of satisfactory evidence) to be the person whose name is subscribed to the within instrument and acknowledged to me that he/she executed the same in his/her authorized capacity, and that by his/her signature on the instrument the person, or entity upon behalf of which the person acted, executed the instrument.

WITNESS my hand and official seal.

_____

Notary Public

FORM #3

DURABLE POWER OF ATTORNEY

WARNING TO PERSON EXECUTING THIS DOCUMENT:

THIS IS AN IMPORTANT LEGAL DOCUMENT. IT CREATES A DURABLE POWER OF ATTORNEY THAT BECOMES EFFECTIVE ON YOUR INCAPACITY AS HERE-AFTER SET FORTH. BEFORE EXECUTING THIS DOCUMENT, YOU SHOULD KNOW THESE IMPORTANT FACTS.

1. THIS DOCUMENT MAY PROVIDE THE PERSON YOU DESIGNATE AS YOUR ATTORNEY-IN-FACT WITH BROAD POWERS TO DISPOSE, SELL, CON-VEY, AND ENCUMBER YOUR REAL AND PERSONAL PROPERTY.

2. THESE POWERS WILL EXIST FOR AN INDEFINITE PERIOD OF TIME UNLESS YOU LIMIT THEIR DURATION IN THIS DOCUMENT. THESE POWERS WILL CONTINUE TO EXIST NOTWITHSTANDING YOUR SUBSEQUENT DIS-ABILITY OR INCAPACITY.

3. YOU HAVE THE RIGHT TO REVOKE OR TERMINATE THIS DURABLE POWER OF ATTORNEY AT ANY TIME.

POWER OF ATTORNEY TO BECOME EFFECTIVE
ONLY ON INCAPACITY OF PRINCIPAL

This durable power of attorney shall become effective only on the incapacity of the undersigned principal. The undersigned shall conclusively be deemed incapacitated for purposes of this instrument when the agent receives a written and signed opinion from a licensed physician that the principal is physically or mentally incapable of managing the principal's finances. Such written opinion, when received, shall be attached to this instrument. Third parties may rely on the agent's authority without further evidence of incapacity when this instrument is presented with such physician's statement attached. No licensed physician who executes a medical opinion of incapacity shall be subject to liability because of such execution. The principal hereby waives any privilege that may apply to release of information included in such medical opinion.

While the principal is not incapacitated, this durable power of attorney may be modified by the principal at any time by written notice given by the principal to the agent and may be terminated at any time by either the principal or the agent by written notice given by the terminating party to the other party.

This power of attorney shall continue after the principal's incapacity in accordance with its terms.

On the death of the principal, this power shall terminate and the assets of the principal shall be distributed to the duly appointed personal representative of the principal's estate; or, if no estate is being administered, to the persons who lawfully take the assets without the necessity of administration when they have supplied the agent with satisfactory documents as provided by law.

TO WHOM IT MAY CONCERN:

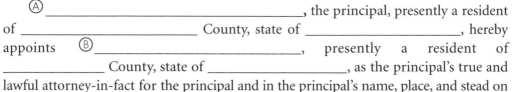

    Ⓐ _____, the principal, presently a resident of _____ County, state of _____, hereby appoints   Ⓑ_____, presently a resident of _____ County, state of _____, as the principal's true and lawful attorney-in-fact for the principal and in the principal's name, place, and stead on the principal's incapacity:

    1. To manage, control, lease, sublease, and otherwise act concerning any real property that the principal may own, collect and receive rents or income therefrom, pay taxes, charges, and assessments on the same, repair, maintain, protect, preserve, alter, and improve the same and do all things necessary or expedient to be done in the agent's judgment in connection with the property.

    2. To manage and control all partnership interests owned by the principal and to make all decisions the principal could make as a general partner, limited partner, or both, and to execute all documents required of the principal as such partner, all to the extent that the agent's designation for such purposes is allowed by law and is not in contravention of any partnership or other agreement.

    3. To purchase, sell, invest, reinvest, and generally deal with all stocks, bonds, debentures, warrants, partnership interests, rights, and securities owned by the principal.

    4. To collect and deposit for the benefit of the principal all debts, interest, dividends, or other assets that may be due or belong to the principal and to execute and deliver receipts and other discharges therefore; to demand, arbitrate, and pursue litigation on the principal's behalf concerning all rights and benefits to which the principal may be entitled; and to compromise, settle, and discharge all such matters as the agent considers appropriate under the circumstances.

    5. To pay any sums of money that may at any time is or become owing from the principal, to sell, and to adjust and compromise any claims which may be made against the principal as the agent considers appropriate under the circumstances.

    6. To grant, sell, transfer, mortgage, deed in trust, pledge and otherwise deal in all property, real and personal, that the principal may own, including but not limited to any real property described on any exhibit attached to this instrument including property acquired after execution of this instrument; to attach exhibits to this instrument that provide legal descriptions of all such property; and to execute such instruments as the agent deems proper in conjunction with all matters covered in this paragraph 6.

    7. To prepare and file all income and other federal and state tax returns that the principal is required to file; to sign the principal's name; hire preparers and advisors and pay for their services; and to do whatever is necessary to protect the principal's assets from assessments for income taxes and other taxes to receive confidential infor-

mation; to receive checks in payment of any refund of taxes, penalties, or interest; to execute waivers (including offers of waivers) of restrictions on assessment or collection of tax deficiencies and waivers of notice of disallowance of claims for credit or refund; to execute consents extending the statutory period for assessment or collection of taxes; to execute closing agreements under Internal Revenue Code section 7121 or any successor statute; and to delegate authority or substitute another representative with respect to all above matters.

8. To deposit in and draw on any checking, savings, agency, or other accounts that the principal may have in any banks, savings and loan associations, and any accounts with securities brokers or other commercial institutions, and to establish and terminate all such accounts.

9. To invest and reinvest the principal's funds in every kind of property, real, personal, or mixed, and every kind of investment, specifically including, but not limited to, corporate obligations of every kind, preferred or common stocks, shares of investment trusts, investment companies, and mutual funds, and mortgage participations that, under the circumstances then prevailing (specifically including but not limited to the general economic conditions and the principal's anticipated needs), persons of skill, prudence, and diligence acting in a similar capacity and familiar with those matters would use in the conduct of an enterprise of a similar character and with similar aims, to attain the principal's goals; and to consider individual investments as part of an overall plan.

10. To have access to all safe-deposit boxes in the principal's name or to which the principal is an authorized signatory; to contract with financial institutions for the maintenance and continuation of safe-deposit boxes in the principal's name; to add to and remove the contents of all such safe-deposit boxes; and to terminate contracts for all such safe-deposit boxes.

11. To make additions and transfer assets to any and all living revocable trusts of which the principal is a settlor.

12. To make direct payments to the provider for tuition and medical care for the principal's issue under Internal Revenue Code section 3503(e) or any successor statute, which excludes such payments from gift tax liability.

13. To use any credit cards in the principal's name to make purchases and to sign charge slips on behalf of the principal as may be required to use such credit cards; and to close the principal's charge accounts and terminate the principal's credit cards under circumstances where the agent considers such acts to be in the principal's best interest.

14. Generally to do, execute, and perform any other act, deed, matter, or thing, that in the opinion of the agent ought to be done, executed, or performed in conjunction with this power of attorney, of every kind and nature, as fully and effectively as the principal

could do if personally present. The enumeration of specific items, acts, rights, or powers does not limit or restrict, and is not to be construed or interpreted as limiting or restricting, the general powers granted to the agent except where powers are expressly restricted.

15. The agent is authorized and directed to commence enforcement proceedings, at the principal's expense, against any third party who fails to honor this durable power of attorney.

16. Notwithstanding any other possible language to the contrary in this document, the agent is specifically NOT granted the following powers:

(a) To use the principal's assets for the agent's own legal obligations, including but not limited to support of the agent's dependents;

(b) To exercise any trustee powers under an irrevocable trust of which the agent is a settlor and the principal is a trustee; and,

(c) To exercise incidents of ownership over any life insurance policies that the principal owns on the agent's life.

17. Any third party from whom the agent may request information, records, or other documents regarding the principal's personal affairs may release and deliver all such information, records, or documents to the agent. The principal hereby waives any privilege that may apply to release of such information, records, or other documents.

18. The agent's signature under the authority granted in this power of attorney may be accepted by any third party or organization with the same force and effect as if the principal were personally present and acting on the principal's own behalf. No person or organization who relies on the agent's authority under this instrument shall incur any liability to the principal, the principal's estate, heirs, successors, or assigns, because of reliance on this instrument.

19. The principal's estate, heirs, successors, and assigns shall be bound by the agent's acts under this power of attorney.

20. This power of attorney shall commence and take effect on the principal's subsequent disability or incapacity as set forth above.

21. The principal hereby ratifies and confirms all that the agent shall do, or cause to be done, by virtue of this power of attorney.

22. If the named attorney-in-fact is for any reason unwilling or unable so to serve, then the principal hereby nominates © _____, presently a resident of _____ County, state of _____, as the principal's true and lawful attorney-in-fact.

23. If a conservatorship of the principal's person or estate or both is deemed necessary, the principal hereby nominates Ⓓ
the principal's person and estate. If _____ is for any reason unwilling

or unable so to serve, the principal hereby nominates _____
as such conservator.

On the appointment of a conservator of the principal's estate, this power of attorney shall terminate and the agent shall deliver the assets of the principal under the agent's control as directed by the conservator of the principal's estate.

Ⓔ IN WITNESS WHEREOF, the principal has signed this springing durable power of attorney on _____.

_____

(Signature)

Ⓕ STATE OF _____
   COUNTY OF _____

On this _____ day of _____, 200____, before me, _____,
a notary public in and for said county and state, residing herein, duly commissioned and sworn, personally appeared _____ personally known to me (or proved to me on the basis of satisfactory evidence) to be the person whose name is subscribed to the within instrument and acknowledged to me that he/she executed the same in his/her authorized capacity, and that by his/her signature on the instrument the person, or entity upon behalf of which the person acted, executed the instrument.

WITNESS my hand and official seal.

_____

(Signature of Notary Public)

FORM #4

ACCOUNTS AND DEBTS ORGANIZER

List All Non-Tax-Deferred Accounts (Savings, Checking, Credit Union, Brokerage, CDs, Treasury Bills, Other)

Name	Value	Account #
_____	_____	_____
_____	_____	_____
_____	_____	_____
_____	_____	_____

List All Tax-Deferred Accounts (IRA, 401(k), Pension, Profit, Sharing, Keoghs, Tax-Deferred Annuities, Other)

Name	Value	Account #
_____	_____	_____
_____	_____	_____
_____	_____	_____
_____	_____	_____

List All Insurance Benefits (Military, Life, Home, Disability, Long-Term Care, Medical, Auto, Other)

Company	Policy #	Beneficiary
_____	_____	_____
_____	_____	_____
_____	_____	_____
_____	_____	_____

FREQUENT FLYER MILES

Many frequent flyer programs allow you to transfer miles in to your spouse and other family members. The airlines will require a copy of a death certificate and written documentation from you assigning the miles in your account. You can make written provision for the transfer in your Will or Trust.

Name of Airline Program	Account #	Customer Service #
_____	_____	_____
_____	_____	_____
_____	_____	_____
_____	_____	_____

List All Obligations (Home, Vacation Home, Time-Share, Automobile, Boat, Motorcycle, RV Loans, Bank Credit Cards, Department Stores, Other)

Name	Account #	Customer Service #
_____	_____	_____
_____	_____	_____
_____	_____	_____
_____	_____	_____
_____	_____	_____
_____	_____	_____
_____	_____	_____
_____	_____	_____

List All Checking Account Automatic Deductions (Internet, Cable, Satellite, Cell Phone, Newspapers, Insurance, Fitness Club, and Other Memberships)

Name	Account #	Customer Service #
_____	_____	_____
_____	_____	_____
_____	_____	_____

_____ _____ _____

_____ _____ _____

_____ _____ _____

_____ _____ _____

FORM #5

PERSONAL DATA AND RECORD LOCATOR

PERSONAL DATA

    Social Security Number _____ - _____ - _____

    Phone Number _____

    Email Address _____@_____

    Fax Number _____

    Driver's License Number _____

PROPOSED GUARDIAN OF MINOR CHILD/CHILDREN

    Name _____

    Address _____

    Phone Number _____

    Relationship to Child/Children _____

LEGAL AND FINANCIAL ADVISORS

    Name of Attorney _____

    Phone Number _____

    Name of Accountant _____

    Phone Number _____

    Name of Trustee/Executor _____

    Phone Number _____

    Name of Insurance Agent _____

    Phone Number _____

    Name of Financial Advisor/Stockbroker _____

    Phone Number _____

LOCATION OF DOCUMENTS

    Personal Address Book _____

    Estate Planning Documents (Will, Trust, Living Will, Powers of Attorney,

    Legacy Will) _____

    Organ Donor Cards _____

    Deeds/Titles to Real Estate and Personal Property _____

    Income Tax Records _____

Vital Statistics (Birth Certificate, Marriage License, Military Records)

_____

Funeral/Cemetery Contracts _____

Medical Records _____

Insurance Policies _____

Investment Certificates (Stocks, Bonds, 401K, IRA, Pension, Etc.)

_____

Vehicle (Auto/RV/Boat) Registration _____

Bank Statements _____

Credit Card Records _____

Insurance Policies _____

Extra Keys _____

Pet Records _____

Contracts _____

Home Repair/Warranties _____

Vehicle Maintenance _____

Frequent Flyer Miles _____

Passports/Social Security Cards _____

Unfinished Business (Leases, Contracts, Moneys Owed to You)

_____

Location of Home Safe _____

Ongoing Divorce or Other Court Proceedings/Judgments _____

_____

Trademarks, Copyrights, Patents, and Other Important Papers _____

_____

Safe-Deposit Records _____

Location of Key to Safe-Deposit Box _____

_____ **at** _____ **Bank**

PERSONAL COMPUTER ACCESSIBILITY

Screen Name _____

Password _____

EMPLOYMENT

Name of Employer _____

Phone Number _____

Immediate Supervisor _____

Benefits Dept. Phone Number _____

PERSONS TO NOTIFY UPON DEATH

Name _____ **Phone Number** _____

Name _____ **Phone Number** _____

Name _____ **Phone Number** _____

Name _____ **Phone Number** _____

ORGANIZATIONS TO BE NOTIFIED UPON DEATH

Name _____

Phone Number _____

Contact Person _____

Name _____

Phone Number _____

Contact Person _____

Name _____

Phone Number _____

Contact Person _____

APPENDIX G:
RESOURCES

Uniform Probate Code

www.cornell.edu/uniform/probate.html

This page, maintained by Cornell University Law School, identifies the several states that have adopted, at least in part, the Uniform Probate Code. Links are also provided to each state's version of the code.

Internal Revenue Service

www.irs.gov

The IRS website has information on the federal estate tax, including information on recent reforms to estate tax laws.

Help for Seniors

www.help4srs.org/articles/estateadmin.htm

The page maintained by the H.E.L.P. organization provides an overview of the executor's, personal representative's, and trustee's estate administration responsibilities.

Yahoo.com Estate and Probate Search Center

http://dir.yahoo.com/government/law/

The Yahoo.com estate and Probate Search Center provides links to probate and estate planning information websites.

American Bar Association

www.abanet.org

This American Bar Association resource provides general information on the probate process.

AARP

www.aarp.org

This AARP page provides practical information on the probate process.

INDEX

A

accountants, 9, 71, 116, 183, 188

acknowledgment of responsibilities, 12, 35, 111, 212

adoption, 40, 43, 71, 95, 129, 130, 134, 135, 140, 143, 193, 210

adult foster care, 29

advance directive to physician, 26

Affidavit of Death of Joint Tenant, 196

affidavits, 116, 150, 196

age of majority, 139

alternative housing options, 28

anatomical gifts. *See organ donations*

ancillary probate, 97, 98

annuities, 17, 76, 81, 168, 171, 172, 202

appointment, 6, 8, 10, 12, 14, 15, 29, 51, 53, 66, 75, 82, 92, 94, 101, 102, 105, 106, 111, 114, 115, 117, 119, 120, 157, 207, 216, 218

appraisal, 94, 120, 186

ashes, 34, 37, 38

asset management, 116, 119

asset map, 76

assets left to a group, 141

assignment of ownership, 195

assisted living facilities, 28

attorneys, 3, 6, 8, 9, 11, 12, 22, 25, 26, 43, 53, 56, 57, 58, 61, 66, 85, 96, 98, 99, 100, 105, 106, 109, 116, 134, 135, 138, 141, 158, 163, 164, 169, 172, 186, 189, 191, 196, 208, 209, 213, 214, 215, 216, 217, 218, 219

autopsies, 41, 42

B

balloon payment, 87

bank accounts, 17, 52, 65, 78, 86, 87, 96, 117, 119, 126, 143, 149, 150, 154, 156, 160, 176, 191, 193, 194, 204, 209

bank statements, 75, 76, 79, 80, 82

bankruptcy, 5, 55, 84, 85, 105, 106, 164

beneficiaries, 4, 9, 13, 14, 23, 51, 52, 53, 55, 57, 58, 66, 68, 91, 92, 100, 101, 102, 103, 116, 122, 123, 124, 125, 131, 139, 142, 143, 144, 145, 153, 154, 160, 167, 171, 172, 173, 175, 176, 177, 191, 192, 193, 194,

195, 200, 201, 203, 204, 205, 206, 207, 208, 209, 210, 211, 212, 214, 222

bequests, 53, 116, 124, 125

bereavement care, 31

bills, 4, 26, 59, 69, 75, 119, 156, 167

board and care facilities, 29

bonding companies, 114

bonds, 13, 17, 71, 76, 84, 114, 161, 162, 176, 177, 181, 193

breach of trust, 206, 207

brokerage accounts, 76, 78, 84, 150, 193

burial containers, 36, 37

burial plot, 35, 37, 38

business, 6, 10, 11, 12, 54, 84, 96, 114, 116, 119, 122, 133, 156, 159, 163, 164, 187, 188, 202, 216, 222

bypass trusts, 203

C

cancelled checks, 76, 77, 173

casket, 35, 36, 37

cemetery, 33, 34, 35, 36, 38, 39

certified copies, 68, 69, 111

change of address, 63, 81

charities, 5, 126

checkbooks, 76

children, 4, 5, 23, 33, 42, 43, 44, 45, 50, 56, 93, 95, 104, 110, 119, 123, 126, 130, 132, 134, 135, 136, 140, 141, 154, 158, 160, 161, 173, 186, 199, 213

claims, 11, 21, 22, 57, 85, 93, 94, 110, 116, 121, 122, 132, 154, 168, 192, 205

codicil, 109

coffin, 35

college, 54, 139, 146, 161, 213, 222

columbarium, 37

common-law marriage, 131, 132

communication, 9, 13, 14, 52, 53, 55, 63

compensation, 14, 70, 110, 120, 123, 161, 185, 186, 187, 188, 189, 207, 213, 214

conformed copy, 99

cotrustees, 206

counseling, 31, 49, 50, 200

court order, 8, 80, 98, 110, 111, 114, 117, 155, 186, 204

credit cards, 21, 66, 71, 101, 121, 166, 167, 187

credit life insurance, 166

credit union, 76, 164

creditor claims, 168

creditors, 11, 52, 66, 71, 81, 93, 94, 95, 96, 101, 110, 116, 120, 121, 122, 123, 153, 154, 164, 165, 167, 168, 179, 211

cremation, 20, 35, 37

criminal activity, 83

crypt, 35, 38

custody, 43, 44, 45

D

death benefits, 65, 70

death certificate, 35, 40, 63, 68, 69, 72, 78, 79, 83, 91, 117, 151, 171, 173, 176, 177, 196, 210

debts, 21, 24, 54, 116, 117, 119, 121, 122, 123, 164, 165, 166, 167, 168, 169, 179, 187, 211, 212

declaration of lost policy, 171

deeds, 17, 19, 20, 26, 87, 123, 153, 154, 196, 197, 198

Department of Motor Vehicles, 91

deposit, 17, 19, 20, 61, 64, 65, 76, 77, 78, 81, 82, 83, 84, 87, 88, 99, 117, 193

diminishing assets, 155

disability, 28, 32, 64, 65, 71, 93, 174

disbursements, 4, 52

distributions, 4, 52, 54, 55, 92, 93, 94, 96, 102, 116, 122, 123, 124, 125, 126, 129, 130, 137, 138, 140, 146, 154, 160, 176, 210, 211, 212, 213, 214, 216

divorce, 39, 43, 44, 131, 133, 144, 145, 172, 208

domicile, 97, 150, 152

Donate Life America, 27

driver's license, 27, 41, 97

drugs, 31, 56, 108

E

early termination, 166

earnings work credit, 174

education, 26, 54, 146, 222

embalming, 35, 36, 37

embarrassing assets, 83

emotional support, 49, 50, 200

emotions, 7, 10, 49, 50, 51, 221

employer, 65, 70, 117, 175

entitlement disease, 53

escheats to the state, 130

estate administration, 3, 13, 73, 95, 96, 109, 116, 161

estate identification number (EIN), 117, 182, 205

estate planning, 7, 17, 19, 20, 24, 25, 27, 45, 61, 129, 135, 150, 158, 191, 195, 196

eviction, 157, 158

evidentiary, 105

executor. *See representative*

extraordinary fees, 187, 188, 189

F

failure to thrive, 31

Federal Trade Commission (FTC), 34

fiduciary, 8, 205

filing fees, 27, 119, 185

final interment, 5, 18, 33, 34, 40

final order, 123

financial advisors, 161, 162

financial institution, 77, 79, 150

Financial Planners Association, 162

forgery, 108, 109

Form SS-4, 117

funding the trust, 203

funeral, 4, 5, 17, 18, 20, 24, 33, 34, 35, 36, 37, 38, 39, 40, 41, 57, 58, 59, 69, 70, 119, 142, 147, 181, 182, 185, 204, 221

Funeral Rule, 34, 37

G

gift tax, 183

gifts, 5, 23, 26, 41, 94, 122, 124–126, 137, 138, 139, 140, 143, 183, 195, 221, 222

conditional, 138

nonmonetary, 126

giving notice, 100

grantor, 201, 206

grave, 35, 36, 37, 38, 58, 141, 142, 222

greedy heirs, 49, 54

grieving process, 41, 49, 50, 59

grooming, 28

gross estate, 181, 182

group homes, 29

guardian, 4, 5, 15, 33, 42, 43, 44, 186, 199

H

handwritten wills, 103

health, 10, 25, 26, 27, 29, 31, 32, 41, 46, 66, 69, 70, 86, 196, 214

hearing, 9, 15, 44, 47, 53, 94, 100, 101, 102, 105, 106, 107, 114, 123, 153, 154, 169

heirs, 9, 10, 13, 17, 19, 23, 43, 49, 51, 52, 53, 54, 55, 56, 57, 63, 67, 68, 83, 91, 92, 93, 94, 95, 96, 100, 101, 102, 106, 107, 114, 116, 119, 120, 122, 126, 129, 130, 131, 133, 136, 149, 152, 153, 160, 166, 176, 179, 187, 188, 189, 195, 216, 218

estranged, 39, 49, 52, 56, 62, 104, 107, 156

heirs at law, 68, 102, 129, 131, 136

holographic will, 103

hospice, 18, 30, 31, 32, 50

housekeeping, 28, 29

I

if the decedent lived alone, 46

illegal provisions, 141

illogical provisions, 143

immediate burial, 36, 37

immediate family, 18, 33, 41

in rem jurisdiction, 97

in vitro fertilization, 135

incident of ownership, 195

independent living retirement communities, 28

inheritance, 5, 23, 54, 56, 89, 92, 93, 107, 116, 122, 131, 132, 133, 134, 135, 136, 139, 173, 191, 195

insurance, 11, 13, 17, 19, 20, 31, 52, 66, 67, 68, 69, 70, 71, 76, 78, 85, 87, 106, 114, 115, 144, 151, 152, 156, 157, 158, 161, 166, 168, 171, 172, 173, 181, 182, 185, 195, 202, 209, 210

inter vivos trust. See living trust

interested party, 96, 105

Internal Revenue Service (IRS), 52, 117, 164, 175, 179, 180, 181, 182, 183, 189, 195, 210

Internet, 65, 66, 78

interpretation of the will, 55, 137, 140, 158

intestate succession, 103, 104, 110, 129, 130, 131, 134, 136, 198

inure, 88

Inventory and Appraisal Report, 120

investments, 19, 71, 117, 159, 160, 161, 162, 209

issue, 51, 79, 94, 98, 106, 111, 134, 135, 140, 141, 153, 177, 187

itemizing the assets, 87

J

jewelry, 23, 55, 77, 78, 89, 124, 126

joint tax returns, 181

joint tenancy, 88, 154, 168, 191, 194, 196, 202

judge, 8, 9, 57, 107, 110, 187

L

landlords, 67

last wishes, 18, 221

lawsuits, 11, 21, 22, 53, 86, 96, 158

lawyer. *See attorneys*

legacy will, 19

legal notice, 101

letters of administration, 78, 111, 147, 155

liabilities, 9, 75, 76, 77, 79, 81, 83, 85, 87, 88, 89, 111, 155, 157, 159, 161, 163, 165, 167, 169, 182, 183, 210

life estate, 158

life insurance, 17, 20, 66, 68, 69, 70, 76, 144, 161, 166, 168, 171, 172, 173, 182, 195, 202, 209-210

liquidation, 160, 161

litigation, 11

living trusts, 4, 17, 19, 146, 191, 194, 202, 203, 204, 216

living will, 26, 41

loans, 70, 71, 87, 122, 165, 166, 173

M

mail, 63, 64, 68, 78, 81, 97, 166

maintenance, 69, 155, 158, 159, 162, 167

marriage, 39, 89, 131, 132, 133, 134, 136, 140, 192

mausoleum, 38

medical reimbursement, 166

Medicare, 31, 32
    hospice benefit, 32

medications, 28, 46, 108

memorial service, 17

mental incapacity, 108

minors, 139, 173

miscellaneous income, 86

misconduct, 8

monthly check, 64

mortgage, 69, 71, 87, 119, 156, 158, 164, 165, 166, 173, 211

murder, 62, 136

mutual funds, 17, 71

N

necessities of life, 4

negligence, 22, 85, 96, 144

noncustodial parent, 43, 44

notary public, 103, 150, 171, 196

notification, 61, 63, 65, 66, 67, 69, 71, 120

nurses, 30

nursing homes, 28, 30

O

organ donations, 18, 26, 27, 41
original will, 61, 93, 98, 99, 100, 109

P

pallbearers, 35
paperwork, 8, 9, 115, 219
parents, 5, 12, 23, 43, 44, 45, 50, 58, 69, 104, 130, 135, 136, 141, 199
partnership, 119, 131, 163
paternity, 136
payable on death accounts, 176, 191, 193
paycheck, 174
pension, 17, 70, 76
petition, 15, 27, 43, 44, 66, 68, 80, 93, 94, 95, 96, 97, 98, 99, 100, 101, 102, 106, 110, 111, 114, 149, 153, 154, 156, 188, 216, 217
petition for conservatorship, 27
pets, 33, 45, 140
physician, 26, 30, 40, 86
policy premium, 172
post office, 63, 81
pourover will, 5, 146
power of attorney, 6, 25, 26, 66, 196
    financial, 26
    health care, 25, 26
priority debt, 179
probate, 3, 4, 8, 9, 13, 15, 51, 61, 63, 68, 75, 79, 80, 88, 91, 92, 93, 94, 95, 96, 97, 98, 99, 100, 101, 102, 103, 104, 105, 106, 107, 109, 110, 111, 113, 114, 115, 116, 117, 119, 120, 121, 122, 123,

125, 127, 129, 130, 131, 132, 143, 144, 145, 146, 147, 149, 150, 151, 153, 154, 155, 157, 160, 164, 167, 168, 171, 172, 175, 185, 186, 188, 189, 191, 192, 193, 194, 195, 196, 198, 202, 203, 208, 209, 210, 211, 214, 215, 216, 218, 219
probate notes, 106, 123
probateable assets, 88, 144, 146
professionals, 9, 71, 85, 164, 186
promissory note, 122
proof of notice, 101, 102
proof of subscribing witness, 98
proper and moving party, 145
property, 4, 10, 18, 19, 23, 26, 54, 67, 68, 77, 78, 87, 88, 89, 91, 92, 93, 94, 97, 98, 107, 120, 123, 124, 126, 127, 130, 133, 138, 140, 143, 144, 145, 146, 151, 152, 153, 154, 156, 157, 158, 159, 163, 165, 168, 171, 173, 176, 181, 182, 192, 194, 195, 196, 197, 198, 205, 209, 216
    community, 92, 133, 153, 192, 198
    personal, 19, 23, 54, 68, 78, 87, 91, 120, 124, 126, 127, 138, 143, 151, 159
    unclaimed, 77, 78
protective service facility, 42
public guardian, 15

R

reading of the will, 62, 124
real estate, 10, 17, 67, 76, 77, 87, 97, 111, 116, 120, 122, 123, 126, 150, 153, 154, 156, 157, 161, 165, 166, 181, 182, 186, 187, 194, 196, 209, 210

reasonable expenses, 40, 205

receipts, 119, 123

records, 9, 17, 19, 20, 24, 27, 68, 75, 86, 87, 119, 123, 183, 188, 189, 197, 198, 205, 207

reimbursable expenses, 27, 45, 121, 186

religion, 31, 33, 42, 59, 222

rent, 29, 67, 157

representative, 3, 4, 5, 6, 7, 8, 9, 10, 11, 12, 13, 14, 15, 18, 20, 21, 22, 25, 28, 30, 33, 39, 40, 42, 45, 46, 47, 49, 50, 51, 52, 53, 54, 55, 56, 58, 59, 62, 63, 66, 67, 68, 75, 78, 80, 81, 82, 83, 85, 91, 92, 94, 95, 101, 102, 105, 106, 110, 111, 114, 115, 116, 119, 120, 122, 125, 126, 137, 138, 139, 143, 144, 145, 149, 155, 156, 159, 162, 165, 168, 171, 179, 181, 186, 187, 189, 196, 199, 200, 201, 215, 216, 218, 221, 222

residence, 40, 43, 44, 46, 61, 65, 77, 91, 97, 106, 150, 152, 156, 158, 187, 195, 209, 211

resignation of appointment, 15, 115, 207

restitution, 12

retirement account, 17, 19, 28, 64, 65, 70, 76, 144, 168, 174, 175, 176, 192, 210

revocable A/B trusts, 203

revocable trusts, 5, 145, 201-202, 203, 205, 207, 209, 211, 213

royalties, 86

S

safe-deposit box, 17, 19, 20, 61, 77, 81, 82, 83, 88, 99

same-sex relationships, 131, 195

savings bond, 176, 177

securities, 64, 71, 116, 154, 163, 193, 194

self-storage, 159

sentimental value, 23, 125

settlement, 22, 64, 109, 158

settlor, 201

siblings, 10, 49, 50, 51, 58
    rivalry, 10, 22, 49, 50, 51

small estate, 149

Social Security, 32, 64, 65, 69, 72, 76, 78, 79, 95, 117, 121, 174, 175, 182

Social Security Disability, 32, 64, 65, 174

social workers, 31

sound mind, 107, 110, 137

spouse, 10, 26, 27, 39, 65, 69, 88, 92, 93, 95, 102, 104, 129, 130, 131, 133, 136, 140, 144, 145, 171, 172, 174, 181, 192, 194, 195, 196, 198, 199, 200, 203
    former, 144, 172

statement of domicile, 150

stepchildren, 107, 134, 140

stocks, 17, 19, 71, 76, 84, 85, 116, 150, 162, 163, 181, 193

subscriptions, 66

successor trustee, 4, 5, 8, 11, 15, 146, 147, 176, 201, 202, 204, 206, 210

suicide, 41, 108

summary probate, 75, 91, 92, 101, 149, 153, 154

surety bond, 13, 105, 119

T

taxes, 11, 52, 54, 71, 75, 76, 82, 84, 86, 92, 94, 96, 97, 116, 117, 152, 156, 160, 161, 168, 172, 174, 175, 176, 179, 180, 181, 182, 183, 187, 189, 191, 194, 195, 203, 205, 210, 211, 214, 215, 216, 218

terminally ill, 30, 32, 204

testamentary trust, 145, 202

testator, 3, 8, 18, 19, 21, 22, 23, 24, 34, 42, 54, 62, 98, 102, 103, 104, 108, 124, 137, 138, 201

testimony, 57, 100, 105, 106, 131, 138, 169

therapists, 31

time commitment, 8, 11

title, 20, 67, 87, 91, 116, 123, 146, 153, 154, 158, 187, 194, 196, 198, 216

Totten trusts, 176

transfer by affidavit, 149, 150, 153, 154

Transfer by Surviving Joint Tenant, 196

travel, 8, 119, 177, 186

traveler's checks, 177

trustees, 4, 5, 8, 9, 11, 15, 66, 138, 145, 146, 147, 173, 176, 194, 201, 202, 204, 205, 206, 207, 208, 209, 210, 211, 212, 213

trustor, 4, 5, 173, 194, 201, 202, 204, 209, 210, 211, 213

trusts, 4, 5, 9, 15, 45, 145, 146, 147, 173, 176, 194, 201, 202, 203, 204, 205, 206, 207, 208, 209, 210, 211, 212, 213, 214

U

Uniform Anatomical Gift Act, 26, 41

Uniform Probate Code, 95, 130, 143, 210

Uniform Transfer to Minors Act (UTMA), 139

Uniform Transfer-on-Death Security Registration Act, 193

utilities, 29, 65, 119, 156, 167

V

vehicles, 70, 76, 91, 115, 137, 154, 155, 165, 166, 182, 193, 194, 209

veteran, 38, 39, 65

Veterans Affairs, 38, 65

W

wasting assets, 155

widow, 62, 158, 174, 175

will contests, 23, 92, 107, 109, 110

wills, 3, 4, 5, 13, 15, 19, 20, 23, 24, 25, 31, 34, 42, 43, 53, 54, 56, 57, 61, 62, 63, 91, 92, 93, 95, 96, 98, 99, 100, 101, 102, 103, 104, 106, 107, 108, 109, 110, 122, 124, 125, 129, 133, 134, 137, 138, 139, 140, 141, 142, 143, 144, 145, 146, 147, 158, 160, 187, 196, 199, 201, 218, 219

withdrawals, 150, 160, 161, 175, 176

witnesses, 98, 103, 104, 105

written notice, 67, 93, 172

wrongful death actions, 22, 85, 145

About the Author

Benjamin H. Berkley has practiced law for more than twenty-eight years, specializing in estate planning and estate administration. He earned his law degree from Western State University. In addition to being admitted to the State Bar of California and the United States Supreme Court, he is also licensed by the State of California and the Department of Justice as a private fiduciary for court appointments as a conservator and trustee of estates.

Mr. Berkley also serves as a panel referral attorney for the nation's largest prepaid legal programs, including ARAG Legal, Hyatt Legal, and GE Consumer Signature Legal. He is a network attorney for AARP members. He regularly conducts seminars on estate planning and has become an advocate for seniors' rights.

Ben lives with his wife and two children in southern California.